Hidden Patterns

A *Playbook* *for More Human* *Workplaces*

Clay Parker Jones

Matt Holt Books

An Imprint of BenBella Books, Inc.

Dallas, TX

Matt Holt is an imprint of BenBella Books, Inc.
8080 N. Central Expressway
Suite 1700
Dallas, TX 75206
benbellabooks.com
Send feedback to feedback@benbellabooks.com

BenBella and *Matt Holt* are federally registered trademarks.

Printed in the United States of America
10 9 8 7 6 5 4 3 2 1

Library of Congress Control Number: 2025042184
ISBN 9781637748589 (hardcover)
ISBN 9781637748596 (electronic)

Editing by Katie Dickman
Copyediting by Scott Calamar
Proofreading by Mary White and Lisa Story
Text design and composition by Jordan Koluch
Cover design by Brigid Pearson and Clay Parker Jones (author)
Emoji on page 13 courtesy of Neo – stock.adobe.com
Printed by Versa Press

For my mom and dad, who remind me that the points need to line up

And to Emily, whom I couldn't have done this without

Contents

FOUNDATIONS

STRUCTURING

DIRECTION

PRACTICE

LEARNING

SPACE

Why Is It Like This?
Why Does It Stay Like This?

2013

It was a glass-walled conference room at the sleek headquarters of a well-known hospitality brand. Everything in that space, from the modular tables to the bins full of multipurpose children's toys, felt too precisely calibrated for innovation, too aggressively designed to spark creativity and collaboration. Performative, maybe.

Some of the company's most senior executives were gathered around the table: the CMO, CTO, and chief innovation officer. Opposite them sat our small team: an embedded strategist and two developers from a digital innovation lab we'd carefully crafted and staffed within one of their flagship hotels, a strategic move to accelerate long-overdue breakthroughs. I was there as the strategy director and project lead for Undercurrent, a digital strategy firm where I worked from 2009 until its untimely demise in 2015.*

After weeks of immersive research and live prototyping with real hotel guests, we were finally presenting our insights. Midway through our presentation, the CMO abruptly grabbed a large, impressively bound document from a side table: a colossal portfolio of ideas previously generated by one of the world's leading innovation consultancies. He flipped to a specific page and pointed, grinning.

"You've just validated *their* concept," he said. And he was right. On that glossy page sat an impeccably detailed two-year-old prediction for a digital service

---

* It's still an influential thing, though! Undercurrenters continue to have a huge impact out there in the world, and I'm super proud of that. IYKYK.

strikingly similar to what we had just presented, complete with slick illustrations, clear implementation strategies, and thorough risk assessments. It was beautiful work, exhaustively researched, and had cost around a million to produce. Yet here it sat, untouched, gathering dust in the strategy room.

None of those brilliant ideas had ever made it out of that hefty book, let alone been tested with real customers or put into practice.

I left that room struck by a single question: Why is it like this?

It wasn't a lack of talent or creativity. I'd seen abundant ingenuity within their teams.

It certainly wasn't a lack of resources. After all, the company had clearly invested significantly in innovation (they were paying us, and all those consultants implicated in the making of the book, millions of dollars).

It wasn't really a structural issue. We'd purposefully constructed the ideal conditions for innovation, from scratch.

It was something else. Something invisible yet powerful. Something hidden deep down. Something within the *patterns* of how their organization worked was blocking their path.

LATER THAT YEAR

My colleague Alex and I had been banging our heads against the same wall for weeks. A Fortune 50 CMO wanted to know why his team's carefully crafted content never seemed to land, while single tweets exploded and BuzzFeed churned out hit after hit. We kept searching for the big insight that would unlock everything—which had more or less boiled down to the true-but-unsatisfying "they understand the internet, and you don't"—until we cracked open Christopher Alexander's *Notes on the Synthesis of Form* (1964). In *Notes*, Alexander argues that any design challenge is really a knot of variables, some that fit with each other and some that don't. You don't solve the knot with one genius stroke; you map the context, surface the pressure points, and let clusters of reinforcing patterns guide you toward a form that fits better with its context.

That might feel a little abstract, so let's try an example from the real world, right outside my door: the Pacific Street × Nevins Street intersection adjacent to Brooklyn's PS 38.

Morning drop-off is chaos. Kids dart between double-parked cars; trash trucks and school buses duel for space in the single driving lane; delivery vans idle in crosswalks; drivers blast down Pacific to skip Atlantic Avenue traffic; and massive trucks turn down Nevins despite the clearly marked "No Trucks" sign. Let's map this corner's ecosystem in three columns: clusters, misfits, and patterns. Clusters capture what's happening, misfits spotlight what's broken, and patterns are the small changes that together form the grammar of a solution.

Cluster	Misfits	Patterns
Sight & Safety	Blind corners, hidden kids	DAYLIGHTING: ban parking 20 ft. from corners; paint bump-outs with flex posts with enough room for delivery trucks to park
Speed Control	30 mph cut-throughs	VERTICAL DEFLECTION: raise the entire intersection, making it easier and safer for mini scooters to cross and forcing cars to slow
Curb Management	Double-parking, honking standoffs	TIME-BOXED LOADING ZONES for buses and trash trucks; visible/tactile NO-STANDING STRIP
Ped Flow	Crowded sidewalks, diagonal crossings	CURB EXTENSIONS widen waiting space and shorten crossing distance
Route Choice	Commuters racing the light	Really dreaming here: automatic RETRACTABLE BOLLARDS at Pacific and 3rd that prioritize school buses at key times

None of these tweaks solve the entire problem, but together they reinforce one another: Daylighted corners improve the raised-table crossing's visibility; shorter crossings mean fewer cars trapped in the box; dedicated loading space clears the travel lane so drivers have no reason to swerve. Suddenly the intersection "fits" its most important purpose—moving six- to eleven-year-olds safely—instead of providing rush-hour commuters convenient passage.

Using that mindset, Alex and I mapped the CMO's media ecosystem the same way we just diagnosed the intersection. We drew a network of patterns that showed *how creators and platforms win on the internet* on one side of the whiteboard, and we drew the Big-Co equivalent on the other, and then we looked for gaps and contradictions:

- **Speed & Volume.** The internet thrives on low CYCLE TIME and high OUTPUT VOLUME; the major gap for Big-Co here was CONTENT APPROVAL LENGTH. In talking to editors and creators at key platforms, we found this pattern was the biggest gap between necessity and reality.
- **Audience Intimacy.** Content lives and dies on its TASTE PROFILE and COMMUNITY SPECIALIZATION; Big-Co led with PEDIGREE, broadcasting brand polish instead of relevance to the culture.
- **Distribution & Dependency.** Platforms own their CONTENT DISTRIBUTION METHOD and are literally built around their USER DEPENDENCY; Big-Co rented reach on expensive, indifferent channels.
- **Autonomy & Trust.** Winners tended to give frontline editors wide berth (CREATIVE FREEDOM, MISSION OVER MEANS, AT ARM'S LENGTH); Big-Co buried creators under layered reviews.
- **Credibility Loop.** STREET CRED and DATA TRANSPARENCY compounded goodwill; Big-Co collected METRICS THAT MATTER but never surfaced them, so trust couldn't accrue.

This way of looking at the problem changes everything for us. Instead of seeing the problem as one big thing that requires one big answer, we can start to see the interconnectedness of the problems and the solutions. We have new ways to intervene that make more sense for us and for our clients.

2015

We were the kind of consultants who stayed late arguing about the definition of "authority" while the rest of the floor went dark. Strategy work paid the bills, but the real puzzle—the one that kept us glued to whiteboards—was structure. Why did good ideas stall after the kickoff? Why did "high-potential" teams drift back to business as usual? By 2013 the hunch inside Undercurrent was clear: The operating system, not the PowerPoint, held the bottleneck. (Although PowerPoint continues to cause its own related problems.)

So we ran an experiment on ourselves. Via a blog post by Medium, we discovered Holacracy, an operating system that promised distributed authority, peer-defined roles that can be created or dissolved as needed, and clear decision rules. We installed it wholesale, and after a few weeks, our Monday all-hands meetings looked nothing like the agency stand-ups we'd grown up with. The language felt strange ("tensions," "objections," "integrative decision-making"), but the effect was magnetic. Projects moved faster, small teams formed and dissolved without drama, and client work picked up momentum we could see directly in our P&L.

We tried to tell our clients what was happening. Most of them looked at us the way you look at a friend who's joined a particularly earnest cult. Like most people around that time—see *Harvard Business Review*'s "Beyond the Holacracy Hype"— they heard the enthusiasm and the jargon and tuned out. That reaction bothered me, because buried inside the legalistic way of describing "the new work" was a practical insight: Specific moves, used at specific moments, unlock better outcomes at essentially no cost. I needed a way to show that without asking an entire company to swap out its DNA.

The breakthrough came at 7:24 PM on March 25, 2014. Aaron Dignan—my boss at the time and the eventual founder of organizational design consultancy The Ready and AI agent software company Plumb, as well as the author of *Game Frame* and *Brave New Work*—and I were huddled in a hallway,* red and green markers squeaking across our signature glass whiteboards. I wrote "OUTPUT LANGUAGE" in block letters, nodding to Holacracy's tidy categories: roles, policies, projects. Those labels proved that even a rudimentary network of patterns can have a massive impact on how a company operates: Define a role with a few fixed properties, phrase every accountability the same way, and anyone can help shape the work. Without guardrails like these, self-governing systems drift toward representation and away from direct participation: A random citizen can't just stroll into Congress and table a bill, so you need trained experts to bring your interests forward. By limiting proposals to just three clearly defined types—roles, policies, and projects— Holacracy lets any teammate bring an idea forward, no special training required. A beat later I slashed a line through "OUTPUT" and replaced it with "PATTERN," and the rest of the whiteboard snapped into focus.

---

* Eventually, turn to WHITEBOARDS AT INTERSECTIONS (74).

INFO PROCESSING CAPABILITY

PATTERN
~~OUTPUT~~
LANGUAGE

PROJECT	RATIONAL	CONSTANT
MANAGEMENT	AUTHORITY	PARTICIPATORY
MEETINGS		ORGANIZATION
DEVOID OF B.S.		

PATTERN LANGUAGE: ONE PART OF

GROWING INFO PROCESSING CAPABILITY (2015)

In that moment, Christopher Alexander's *A Pattern Language* (1977) became the blueprint behind this book and the foundation for a decade-long search for a way to help more people connect their intention to their output. In *APL*, Alexander, alongside architects Sara Ishikawa and Murray Silverstein, distilled decades of fieldwork into 253 remixable "patterns," each numbered and described so that everyone—from architects to people picking a short-term rental—could bring unselfconscious but purposeful quality to their built environment. Their patterns are roughly arranged from gigantic and hard to change to quite small and shiftable. At the top end, think of AGRICULTURAL VALLEYS (4), which describes how settlements thrive when they sit between fertile lowlands and protective slopes. A few hundred pages later, SIX-FOOT BALCONY (167) shows that a balcony meant for conversation will need to be at least six feet deep, while DIFFERENT CHAIRS (251) nudges us to vary seating if we want real gathering.*

Thinking about systems this way was incredibly clarifying for me: I needed to figure out how to take a coherent system for organizing work, shrink the various component pieces until they could fit on a miniature 2.75x1.1-inch Moo card, let people try one at a time, and let the big picture take care of itself. For example: We tried a super-obvious facilitation method that we started calling "Rounds"—participants speak in turn in response to a prompt, no interruptions. A simple Retrospective script built off of three questions that we encountered in a meeting with InsideOut Development: What worked? Where did you get stuck? What might we do differently next time? A Kanban board visible to the team and the client, each

---

* The numbers you'll see in parentheses throughout *Hidden Patterns* work the same way. They're identifiers and a bit of shorthand that can make connections easier to process and easier to spot.

card with a title, a "why it matters" blurb, and the minimum rules for running it well. Simple stuff. Not always *easy* stuff.

Undercurrent's story ended elsewhere (a story for another book, another day), but the pattern idea refused to die. When a few of us founded August, an organization design and team coaching consultancy, in 2015, the idea came with us and shaped everything from hiring to profit sharing. We kept adding things that seemed to work as we, and others in the broader community, came across them: the Colleague Letter of Understanding from a tomato-processing company in California; Harrison Owen's Open Space Technology for large-group problem-solving; Amy Edmondson's research on psychological safety, which reminded us that safety can be structural *and* cultural. Every project surfaced fresh variants. We wrote them down, tested them, kept what worked, tossed what didn't.

A decade later August is still running with lean teams, clear scopes, and explicit working agreements, and the pattern language is, if I may, baked into the walls. The patterns have multiplied, and I've moved on to Airbnb, but it's still true for me that no concept survives if it can't fit on one side of cardstock and be explained in under a minute.

This book is the next logical step: a permanent record of the patterns, organized so you can pick what you need, leave the rest, and move forward. A pattern, in these pages, is a proven response to a recurrent problem in modern work. It is not a silver bullet, a full operating system, or a promise of enlightenment. Think of it more like a chess opening or a mirepoix:* humble, repeatable, waiting for you to adapt it to local taste.

2016

A gray, drizzly afternoon in a small, forgettable conference room outside London. The space was cramped, greige, and a little damp, a stark contrast to the sleek innovation labs and vibrant open-plan offices where I typically found myself. But something special was happening here.

---

* One of my favorite things about learning to cook is *all the different kinds of holy trinities out there.* Once you learn them, you can cook just about anything, and it's literally just three vegetables (more or less) that make a dish taste like a region.

Around a cluttered table sat four junior employees from a global consumer goods company, each buried in their laptops. Their intensity was very real, eyes locked onto a shared Google Sheet.* For days, they had been quietly hacking away at a critical problem: reviving a product line that had been languishing for months.

Suddenly, one of them said, "We did it."

Their faces lit up, mixing excitement with disbelief. These four had cracked the code by designing a pricing and packaging strategy that would soon reverse months of declining sales.

Just one week earlier, these same four employees had been stuck. Not in a room with their peers but silently at their desks. Not due to a lack of skills or ambition, but because their attention had been divided across endless meetings, reports, and interruptions that left no room for deep, focused thinking.

We had intervened, convincing their bosses (15 senior managers, consultants, and various administrators) to take a leap of faith: Clear these four people's calendars completely, for just two weeks. Allow them to focus. Let them work without distraction.

The experiment was *rudimentary*, but it was one of the most valuable engagements in my company's history. One team member later described the experience to me as transformative: "Honestly, this has been life-changing. I finally feel like I'm doing something with my life. I'd been thinking about that problem for about a year, but never had any real time to work on it. Having solved that riddle, that way . . . I'll never go back to the old way of doing things."

In the weeks and months that followed, the impact of their two-week sprint radiated outward, reshaping the way teams across the organization approached work. The product line flourished, and so did the careers and lives of those involved.

Reflecting on this moment, I'm still struck nearly a decade on by how simple it was. No new technology required. No extra expense was *really* necessary. The team didn't have to work harder. They didn't need new skills or a new head count. They just needed a clear team purpose and plenty of time to focus.

---

* Quick note: Google Sheets were specifically not allowed at this company, but there was no way they were going to be able to collaborate in real time on this financial model on Excel in 2016. No matter how much you like Excel—and you'd be right to like it—it's still so difficult to work in real time with others on the same .xls document.

2021

Flash forward to a work session I hosted with a midsized consumer packaged goods (CPG) company while working at marketing-org change consultancy Black Glass— our client was well known enough to fill supermarket shelves nationwide, but not so large as to be a truly global family of brands. This was early 2021, so we were deep into remote working, all Zooming in from bedrooms and kitchen tables and, yes, closets.

The team assembled here was bright and accomplished—a project manager, a strategist, an art director, and a media planner—all eager, thoughtful, and exhausted. Each carried impressive credentials and deep expertise, but their energy had been drained by mundane tasks and uninspiring strategies. It wasn't just the pandemic. The work itself was crushing their souls.

Originally, the brief from leadership had been modest: "Reduce campaign creation timelines from nine months to six weeks." This was the kind of goal that rarely inspires passion or sparks ingenuity. Important, probably hard, but not especially interesting.

But we challenged this team to think differently, pushing them beyond incremental improvements to something genuinely transformative. "If you could redefine marketing entirely," we asked, "what would you do?"

Their answer was bold, clear, and inspiring.

Instead of just speeding up timelines, they wanted to throw out the plan and work in direct connection to consumers, tastemakers, and the owners of the platforms where their audience spent their time, like Reddit and Twitch. Instead of routing ideas through senior leadership panels, they'd ship anything that wasn't expressly disallowed by the brand guidelines. Cycle times dropped to *minutes* (from months), and the team's work got smarter, and smarter, and smarter. It was no longer necessary to bring in research companies like Forrester (or similar) to share a generalized view of how to target and talk to Gen Z audiences. These millennial and Gen X marketers became fluent in the language of their people.

And yes, they even tried things with NFTs *when that was relevant.* While that moment has passed, for a company mostly considered to be behind the times, this was a coup.*

---

* Are we saying "coup" in 2025?

It's worth noting that after laying out their ambition, they hesitated a bit: Bold ambitions like these rarely traveled smoothly through their company's more traditional approval chains. Nevertheless, they took matters into their own hands, quietly building momentum without waiting for explicit permission. The work itself attracted more talent from across the company, turning a once-quite-chilled project into a vibrant, purposeful mission.

Six months later, their radical new way of working turned into a comprehensive marketing playbook for the organization. At its unveiling, the reaction wasn't just positive, it was *electric*. Leaders actually applauded the team. The company found itself suddenly at the heart of industry conversations, admired by peers, envied by competitors.

And they ended up growing their share of wallet by four percentage points, each worth $100 million.

Reflecting later, it became clear what had made the difference. This is going to sound familiar at this point: The budget hadn't changed, and neither had the people. We just recognized and then fixed the invisible roadblocks holding teams back from taking bold, meaningful action.

THE HUMAN COST

These success stories are painfully rare. But what if we could repeat these wins (limited as they are) within every project, for every team, at every company?

You know that dysfunction is the norm rather than the exception. It comes at a staggering human cost, quietly draining potential and leaving behind a legacy of missed opportunities. It comes with a hit to the bottom line, as companies pour millions into strategic initiatives, leadership training, and process improvements.

And nothing fundamentally changes.

And as I write this at the end of 2024 and into the start of 2025, I'm worried that what we know about life at work—bad as it already is—is only going to get much worse.

Gallup's surveys show that in the United States, barely a third of employees are actively engaged in their work. Another half are just going through the motions, disengaged and disconnected from any real sense of purpose. And most troublingly, a full 17% of employees are actively disengaged, essentially working against their employers and colleagues, contributing negatively to the very workplaces they're paid to sustain.*

These numbers represent real lives, real dreams, and real potential wasted. Imagine the countless good ideas that vanish, unheard, every single day; the creativity stifled under layers of administrative tasks and approval processes; and the groundbreaking solutions that remain locked away, never brought to life simply because their creators are buried under routine, uninspiring responsibilities.

The ripple effects of this dysfunction reach far beyond office walls, touching society as a whole. Disengagement drives slower economic growth, higher healthcare costs from stress-related illness, and thinner civic participation. Meanwhile, according to Deloitte, purpose-driven organizations vastly outperform their purposeless counterparts in virtually every meaningful metric, from employee and consumer trust to genuine innovation and even true adoption of diversity and inclusion initiatives.[1] But most teams cannot even articulate their mission clearly, let alone pursue it effectively.

Again, there are lives at stake. Studies have consistently linked workplace dissatisfaction and chronic stress to severe mental health outcomes, including anxiety, depression, and burnout. A report by BambooHR noted that employee satisfaction scores fell precipitously between 2022 and 2023. *Fifteen times faster than the prior two years combined.*[2] Workers today are more exhausted, more overwhelmed, and less fulfilled than at any time in recent memory.

And while innovation stagnates, productivity somehow continues to rise: Between 1973 and 2014, worker productivity increased by 72%. But wages climbed a mere 9%.[3] Workers today are nearly twice as productive as their counterparts decades ago, yet they see little of this reward. This divergence between productivity and pay is a reflection of how deeply our organizations have distorted, favoring short-term efficiency over sustainable human flourishing. And even though it is true that productivity is rising, "number go up" is hardly satisfying in the face of our felt reality: that most hours, most days, for most people, are spent on

---

* Jim Harter, "U.S. Employee Engagement Sinks to 10-Year Low," *Gallup*, January 13, 2025, https://www.gallup.com/workplace/654911/employee-engagement-sinks-year-low.aspx. Gallup's latest panel survey finds 31% of US employees engaged, 52% not engaged, and 17% actively disengaged, confirming that barely a third feel connected to their work while a sizable minority work against their employers.

unnecessary administrative tasks, endless meetings, and cumbersome bureaucratic procedures.

Imagine instead a world where those billions of lost hours spent were redirected toward meaningful work. Work that fulfills, inspires, and genuinely innovates. Work that pays exceptionally well because it's performed in a context that prioritizes equity and performance in equal measure. Evidence from four-day-workweek studies suggests it's possible to achieve the same productivity in less time, potentially returning hundreds of hours annually back to employees to invest in family, community, and personal growth.

The opportunity cost of our current dysfunction is enormous. It's measured in dollars and in lives wasted and possibilities unrealized. It's a managerial issue. It's a deeply human problem.

WHY CHANGE FAILS

Across decades, organizations have cycled through waves of management trends, each promising transformative change. Yet most leaders quietly acknowledge that despite good intentions, lasting improvement remains elusive. Why?

For one, top-down change is fun for executives who are bored with their work.

These ambitious, sweeping initiatives, often championed by charismatic execs, typically follow a predictable rhythm. They start with bold announcements, big training programs, and meticulous rollout plans. A year or two later, these grand strategies often dissolve quietly, leaving behind only glossy brochures and frustrated employees. The reason is simple: Real change cannot be imposed solely from above. Transformation demands more than executive decrees or cascading key performance indicators (KPIs): It requires deep engagement and ownership from those who actually do the daily work.

Then there's the ultimately misleading notion of "best practices."

Execs, eager for success, frequently look outward, searching for neatly packaged solutions validated by external benchmarks. But what worked beautifully at a Silicon Valley tech giant or an iconic manufacturing brand seldom translates directly to your own unique context. Context matters. Leaders visit renowned innovators and become enamored with visible artifacts, like open-plan offices, agile rituals, elaborate brainstorming sessions, or the latest book by a hand-wavy consultant.

(How meta!) Believing that success is found in copying what others have done, companies invest heavily, only to discover later that they've replicated the "what" without grasping the "why." *Those things that worked elsewhere only worked because they came to existence in a web of supportive tissue.*

And beneath all of this is the human element. Change initiatives overlook the lived experiences, hopes, fears, and frustrations of the people they aim to influence, relying heavily on logic, data, and structural adjustments. In my experience, employees don't resist because they're stubborn or averse to change, but because they sense intuitively when changes will be bad for them. Without recognizing and honoring this human reality, even the best-designed change programs inevitably fall short.

Two things are clear about these common routes to failure: (a) They suck the life and energy out of an organization; (b) They're signals pointing toward deeper systemic issues. To create genuine, lasting change, we must shift our approach entirely.

What if there were a fundamentally different way? What if there was a method of change rooted not in grand plans, external solutions, or charismatic leadership but in something subtler and far more powerful?

HELLO, AND WELCOME TO PATTERN THINKING AND DOING

Pattern thinking and doing acknowledges that meaningful change can and does begin anywhere, at any level. It doesn't require formal authority or a big budget; instead, it relies on small actions and decisions made in daily routines. Consider the junior team from our earlier story, quietly transforming an entire product line simply by creating space for focused attention; all it took was recognizing and adjusting one small but significant problem: distraction.

This capacity to make change without positional power *is* the extraordinary potential of small moves. *Especially if everyone makes moves.* Tiny adjustments in daily behaviors, meeting formats, or decision-making routines can and do ripple outward, reshaping entire organizations over time. Each little shift changes the underlying patterns of interaction, communication, and decision-making, creating impact far beyond the initial scope. Authentic transformation happens through persistent, thoughtful adjustments made over time.

Pattern thinking and doing empowers individuals at all levels of an organization to see differently: to observe their environment through a lens of interconnected patterns rather than isolated problems. Rather than becoming overwhelmed by complexity, people begin recognizing recurring issues, hidden opportunities, and subtle leverage points for change. The simple act of seeing these patterns clearly changes how teams engage with their work, their colleagues, and the larger organizational mission.

Building better organizations is something for all of us, where every person feels equipped to make meaningful improvements from wherever they stand. It's never been the case that leaders bear sole responsibility for change, but in working this way, we're recognizing that the role of "leader" shifts to *nurturing* conditions where pattern recognition and thoughtful experimentation flourish. By applying patterns associated with small-scale trials, transparent sharing of insights, and safe spaces for reflection, leaders help cultivate a culture of continuous, authentic learning.

Pattern thinking and doing offers, and relies on, a hopeful vision of the future. It reminds us that the keys to transformation are already present, embedded in everyday routines and interactions, waiting only to be recognized and reshaped. In this book, you'll learn how to spot these hidden opportunities, understand their dynamics, and intervene to create lasting positive change. Welcome to a new way of seeing, and doing, organizational design.

How This Book Works

If you picked up this book, I assume that you are one of the great many impatient folks out there who know that we need a gigantic change in the way that we work. (I also assume that you do not need to be convinced that there is something better out there.) You've seen the slide decks and TED Talks that promise agility, customer obsession, cloud-native reinvention, AI transformation ... and then watched as nothing substantial changed about how work got done for those around you. We've established that one of the big challenges facing *the impatient* is that we ask or hope for big-bang changes. Five stories in a single bound. This book contains the risers, the treads, and the framing that build the stairs to where you want to go. It contains 75 individually named patterns:

> Each pattern describes a problem that occurs over and over again in our environment, and then describes the core of the solution to that problem, in such a way that you can use this solution a million times over, without ever doing it the same way twice.
>
> —Christopher Alexander[4]

They are organized from the deepest and most philosophical patterns I've found along the way—TRUE PURPOSE (1), RULE OF LAW (2), and STRUCTURAL & PSYCHOLOGICAL SAFETY (3)—to the most tangible and tactile: MOVABLE EVERYTHING (75), WHITEBOARDS AT INTERSECTIONS (74), HIDING PLACES (73).* As a result, there are at least four ways to read, and use, this book:

---

* Worth noting that HIDING PLACES (73) is at least partly inspired by Alexander's ALCOVES (179).

Read it front to back

Begin with purpose, safety, and governance, then layer on structure, rhythm, and space. If you love root-cause analysis or you're redesigning an organization from scratch, this is your jam.

Read it back to front

Start with the surface stuff that you can change *tomorrow* and work backward through to bedrock constraints. Great for teams that need relief now and can't wait for the enterprise to catch up—or for local offices of large companies that are outside the all-seeing eye of corporate.

Pick a starting point your stakeholders actually care about

Flip to the Goal Index in the back of this book. Find the Stakeholder Goal that's burning a hole in your leadership agenda. Under that goal, locate the patterns with the highest numbers on the list. It will be something concrete you can pilot next week. Run it. Log what you learn. Then climb down the list toward the deeper patterns that underpin your goal.

- For *agility*, this will mean starting with something like PROCESS ON THE WALL (68) or ADAPTIVE AGENDA (49), rather than EXPANDED AVAILABLE POWER (4). One of my clients that adopted similar patterns saw a 40x improvement in project completion pace on like-for-like work. Another particularly *stuck* team saw a 200x improvement.
- For *engaged culture*, maybe try NO LEADERSHIP OFFICES (70) or ROUNDS (48). One client put these patterns to work and saw a 40-point jump in autonomy, customer connection, iteration, and decision-making; a 17-point gain in inclusion of diverse views; and an 87-point Net Promoter Score (NPS) for the patterns themselves.
- For *innovation*, try FAIL WALL (69) or RETROSPECTIVES (66). Patterns like these underpinned ideas that delivered $750 million in new revenue in a single category and (I've already mentioned this case, above) drove $400 million in share gains with zero extra spend.
- For *quality execution* (this is the biggest goal-oriented section by far, which highlights, at least for me, how this movement is about going *toward*

accountability rather than away from it), try SPACE FOR WORK (72) or one of my favorites, CADENCE (65). Results: My client teams cut escalations to leadership by 64% and reversed a profit slide, ending up at 2x their previous growth rate.

- For *strategic clarity*, try TEAM CHARTER (43) or FUTURE BACKWARD (42). Media teams I've helped use these patterns outperformed industry peers by 2x, while a category president told us, "Without this, we couldn't compete against clever, fast-moving outliers." Oh, and teams also spent 70% less time on non-value-added busywork.

Pick a starting point you care about

Let's say you're a CEO or president or equivalent, and you've fallen in love with the Haier RenDanHeYi case study, where hundreds of thousands of employees have reorganized into thousands of entrepreneurial teams. *Exciting.* You want to announce, "From next quarter we'll operate as microenterprises!" Skip the temporary excitement, confusion, and eventual reorg that looks suspiciously like the old org chart and start with NETWORK OF TEAMS (13), which describes autonomous squads and tight customer feedback loops, and promises cycle times that shrink from months to weeks. These are very real outcomes that you should expect if you can implement that pattern. But its implementation presumes (at least):

- DISSOLVABILITY (9) where teams, roles, and even whole processes are presumed temporary, ready to vanish when their job is done. Without this higher-order assumption of impermanence, networks harden instead of flex.
- DISTRIBUTED MANAGEMENT (14) where everyday leadership chores are shared within a team, not exclusively above them.
- TALENT MARKETPLACE (20) where people can slide across teams quickly, so capacity matches shifting bets.
- DOMAINS, ASSETS & STANDARDS (23) so everyone knows what they own and what they must not break.
- BOUNDARY MANAGEMENT (67) making handoffs explicit, so speed doesn't bleed into chaos.

Skip these layers and your network will likely collapse under staffing bottle-necks, decision wrangles, and Service Level Agreement (SLA) debates. Work the chain from small to big: Prototype BOUNDARY MANAGEMENT inside one product group; adopt DOMAINS & STANDARDS to make those boundaries real; launch a lightweight TALENT MARKETPLACE so squads can restaff in days; prac-tice DISTRIBUTED MANAGEMENT so authority sits with the work. Keep DIS-SOLVABILITY visible and top of mind: Teams should expect to end themselves once the mission is met. Only when those muscles are built should you talk about the network everywhere.

WHAT'S IN A PATTERN?

- **Problem.** A concrete gripe you've probably voiced aloud.
- **Pattern.** The recurring solution, distilled into a two-sentence "therefore…"
- **Why it works.** A quick sketch of the social, economic, and/or cognitive mechanics.
- **Connected patterns.** Your map to the next experiment.
- **Things to try.** An action you can run this month with one squad.
- **(In many cases) Common traps.** Because someone, somewhere, has al-ready tried a bad version so you don't have to.

These patterns are organized into thematic categories:

Foundations

Bedrock principles upon which effective organizations are built, covering essential aspects like shared purpose, transparency, and trust. You'll find patterns here that create clarity about why teams come together, how purpose shapes boundaries, and why trust and openness are necessary for long-term success.

1	True Purpose	The enduring reason that drives meaningful action and connects individuals, teams, and organizations to shared goals.
2	Rule of Law	Nobody in the organization is above the rules that the org sets for itself.
3	Structural & Psychological Safety	Psychological safety allows for innovation and learning, while structural safety ensures that decision rights and organizational status are protected.
4	Expanded Available Power	When leaders give away some of their decision-making authority and resources to other levels, innovations and adjustments in course are possible without the say-so of the boss.
5	Curiosity	Lead with wonder, and allow rapid experiments and shared insights to outpace tidy certainty.
6	Do No Harm	Actively prevent unnecessary harm, whether to employees, communities, or the environment.
7	Wholeness	Allow employees to bring their full selves to work.
8	Role-Soul Distinction	Decouple your personal identity from your professional roles.
9	Dissolvability	Teams, roles, and processes should be assumed to be temporary and regularly reassessed.
10	Consent & Consensus	Distinguish between consent (acceptable) and consensus (actively supported).
11	Pace Layers	Different aspects of an organization evolve at different speeds; structure decision-making to respect these layers.
12	Cooperation	Cooperation thrives in environments where discord is acknowledged and structured into productive negotiation.

Structuring

These patterns illuminate how to thoughtfully shape teams, departments, and even entire organizations. From deliberately small, autonomous groups designed for agility to interconnected yet independent units that support resilience, these patterns help you understand how structure impacts innovation, collaboration, and efficiency.

13	Network of Teams	Networks of teams balance autonomy with structured coordination through explicit interfaces and protocols.
14	Distributed Management	Management responsibilities are shared within a team, rather than centralized in an individual human.
15	Elections	Leaders are chosen through structured elections rather than appointments.
16	Purpose, Customer, Platform	Structure the organization around purpose-driven customer needs, with platforms enabling customer-focused work.
17	Platform Teams	Internal support teams (HR, finance, IT) function like product teams, offering scalable self-service tools.
18	Self-Managed Teams	Teams operate autonomously within clear boundaries, making decisions independently.
19	Lean Teams	Small, focused teams outperform large teams by reducing complexity and improving execution.
20	Talent Marketplace	A digitally enabled marketplace for talent and work within the organization.
21	Guilds	Cross-team communities that voluntarily share knowledge and learning.
22	Chapters	Role-based communities set standards and share best practices, allowing teams to remain independent.
23	Domains, Assets & Standards	Clear ownership of domains and assets reduces friction; each team knows its decisions and resources.
24	Upward Representation	Teams select representatives to participate in higher-level decisions, ensuring decisions reflect teams' input.
25	Team Incentives	Incentives structured at the team level promote collaboration instead of competition.

Direction

Clear, compelling visions and making decisions inclusively and effectively. Patterns around transparent goal-setting, decision-making frameworks that favor clarity and consent over slow-moving consensus, and strategies for clear, purpose-driven communication are outlined.

26	Do the Right Thing	Clarify long-term purpose before optimizing execution.
27	Active Steering	Empower teams to make frequent, smaller adjustments rather than relying on rigid plans.
28	Objectives & Key Results	Define ambitious objectives with measurable results to track and adjust progress.
29	Strategy Heuristic	Simplify strategy into memorable rules that clarify decision-making.
30	Structured Decision-Making	Use explicit, transparent processes for making major decisions.
31	Advice	Separate input from decision-making authority to increase valuable feedback.
32	Transparency	Default to open information sharing, balanced with privacy when necessary.
33	Relative Targets	Use relative performance benchmarks rather than rigid annual budgets or goals.
34	Pull Updates	Leaders directly access updates rather than relying on reports.
35	Demos	Replace status reports with demonstrations of actual work.
36	Metrics Review	Regularly integrate performance metrics into discussions.
37	Backlog Management	Maintain a clear backlog to keep priorities explicit and transparent.
38	Conflict as a Resource	Treat constructive conflict as essential and beneficial for progress.
39	Conflict Resolution	Implement clear, structured methods to resolve conflict effectively.
40	Colleague Letter of Understanding	Explicitly document working agreements among colleagues.
41	Open Space Technology	Run self-organizing, participant-driven workshops.
42	Future Backward	Envision ideal outcomes first, then identify steps needed to achieve them.
43	Team Charter	Explicitly define team purpose, roles, decisions, and processes in writing.

Practice

The routines, habits, and processes that support great work. These patterns aren't mere procedures but deep practices: frequent retrospectives that promote continuous improvement, simple communication habits that build trust, and lightweight documentation approaches that enable rapid learning and adaptation.

44	Check In & Out	Brief check-ins at meeting start and end create space for presence and connection.
45	Only Important Notes	Limit notes to decisions, key changes, and actions to reduce information overload.
46	Iterative Shipping	Frequently share work in progress for early input rather than polishing in isolation.
47	Action Meeting	Structure meetings explicitly around actions rather than passive discussion.
48	Rounds	Structure turns in conversation to be sure everyone has a voice without interruption.
49	Adaptive Agenda	Keep meeting agendas flexible and dynamically prioritized.
50	Work in Public	Make work visible through shared documents and dashboards instead of private updates.
51	Meeting Roles	Clearly assigned facilitator, notetaker, and timekeeper roles keep meetings structured (but that's only the start).
52	Triage	Assess and categorize issues by urgency and importance before tackling them.
53	Have One Conversation	Meetings should have a single conversation at a time for discipline and clear focus.
54	Pairing	Pair work enhances learning, quality, and shared problem-solving.
55	Kanban	Use visual task boards to clarify workflows and priorities.
56	Facilitation	Skilled facilitation structures conversations and supports decision-making.

Learning

Patterns to cultivate learning at every level. Patterns in this section emphasize the importance of continuous feedback, safe-to-fail experimentation, and proactive knowledge sharing across boundaries. You'll learn how to build cultures that naturally evolve, grow, and thrive through ongoing, collective learning.

57	Logbook	Record key decisions and insights in a team logbook to track progress and history.
58	Emergent Leadership	Leadership emerges from expertise and context.
59	Health Check	Regularly assess team and process health to proactively identify issues.
60	Hack Day	Periodically dedicate time to explore new ideas freely outside regular routines.
61	Flow State Work	Design environments that support focused, uninterrupted periods of deep work.
62	Experimentation	Regularly test new ideas through small experiments to continuously improve.
63	Team/Process as Product	Apply product management thinking to continually refine how teams operate.
64	Length Limit	Impose explicit length constraints on assignments and policies.
65	Cadence	Establish consistent cycles for work and reflection to sustain steady progress.
66	Retrospectives	Regular team reflection sessions identify improvement opportunities.
67	Boundary Management	Clearly define role and team boundaries to prevent confusion and enhance accountability.

Space

The physical and virtual environments that shape daily interactions and productivity. These patterns consider how environments can either nurture creativity or (oops!) hinder it. You'll get insights into creating spaces that actively encourage the behaviors, interactions, and cultures your organization seeks.

68	Process on the Wall	Make workflows visible and accessible by putting processes on display.
69	Fail Wall	Publicly document failures and learnings to normalize experimentation.
70	No Leadership Offices	Leaders sit with teams to reinforce transparency and approachability.
71	No Assigned Desks	Flexible seating encourages collaboration.
72	Space for Work	Design physical spaces intentionally around the types of work performed.
73	Hiding Places	Provide quiet, private spaces for focused, uninterrupted work.
74	Whiteboards at Intersections	Place whiteboards in common areas to encourage spontaneous collaboration.
75	Movable Everything	Furnish the workspace with flexible, movable elements to adapt quickly.

PATTERN CONNECTIONS

Let's start somewhere simple, like HIDING PLACES (73): spaces explicitly designed for quiet, focused work. Many corporate offices thoughtfully and expensively provide these spaces. I toured an *amazing* new telecom HQ some years ago and found that every single one was unused. But all the open-plan desks and meeting rooms were full. Asking around, it turned out that this was the norm.

Why?

Tracing backward from HIDING PLACES (73) reveals a web of reasons why these spaces went unused. People don't use hiding places that are designed for deep work in public because there isn't a cultural acceptance or expectation for FLOW STATE WORK (61). It just doesn't happen during the workday, so the main zones for this mode of working are *my couch at home on the weekend* and *talking to myself on my commute*. Deep work isn't actively encouraged, and employees worry about being seen as unproductive or unavailable.

Some part of this could be solved with a CADENCE (65) that allows for deep work, rather than an unpredictable slurry of back-to-back 1:1s and status meetings from 8 AM to 6 PM.

But why even worry about changing the schedule? After all, the job of a manager (and it would appear that most people in an office building are some kind of manager—or have that word in their official title) is *to manage*, which means *you need to be in a lot of meetings.* That's because DISTRIBUTED MANAGEMENT (14) doesn't exist: All of the management tasks are trapped in one person, rather than being broken out and given to the people who can do those tasks best.

And why haven't they tried to spread the wealth? No STRUCTURAL & PSYCHOLOGICAL SAFETY (3). Because there are no TEAM INCENTIVES (25) baked into the structure. But also because most meetings are leader led, without FACILITATION (56), to say nothing for hearing every voice in the room via ROUNDS (48).

An insights leader at one of the large CPG organizations that I worked with in the past mentioned to me that one of their recent billion-dollar new brand launches would have ended up on the cutting room floor if not for a multiyear new-way-of-working program that was built on top of these patterns. And it sounds unreasonable to say that the best way to invent a new, market-making brand is to take turns in conversation to be sure everyone in a meeting gets to speak.

But that's the truth.

WHAT'S NOT IN THIS BOOK?

You might wonder why certain common buzzwords, like "feedback," don't appear as patterns here. It's intentional.

In my experience, feedback itself isn't a pattern; it's a behavior embedded within patterns like ADVICE (31), LEAN TEAMS (19), and EXPERIMENTATION (62). Patterns offer structural conditions that *support* effective feedback, rather than trying to prescribe giving and taking feedback. You also won't find feedback directly mentioned here because the quality and utility of feedback depend entirely on the safety, context, and connection between people and their work. Without STRUCTURAL SAFETY (3), without a clear linkage to the meaningful work of a team, feedback is empty (regardless of whether it's critical or positive).

Similarly, this book doesn't present technology-first solutions. Technology isn't the point. Apps and platforms help only when they serve a solid pattern; chase them for their own sake and you just collect shiny distractions. The real leverage lives in how we interact, decide, and share power—all of which can run perfectly well with nothing more than a whiteboard.

Accountability also isn't a single idea you can bolt on; it's the sum of several other patterns working in concert. When roles are clear (TEAM CHARTER 43), information is visible (LOGBOOK 57), decisions follow agreed rules (RULE OF LAW 2), and work rhythms automatically surface indicators of progress (CADENCE 65), accountability shows up automatically. Strip away any of those conditions and what leaders call "accountability" is really just code for "I don't think that person over there is doing their job very well." Because it emerges from a lattice of patterns rather than existing as a freestanding idea, I've kept it off the list.

Also absent here are "values": those abstract, often aspirational words listed on office walls but rarely embodied in everyday actions. Values statements can be inspiring, but they aren't a pattern. Patterns like TRUE PURPOSE (1) and RULE OF LAW (2) will do most of the work leaders hope their values statements might—but rarely do.

Finally, you might wonder why diversity isn't explicitly outlined as a stand-alone pattern. Authentic, sustainable diversity, meaningful equity, and true inclusion emerge from a combination of deeper, underlying patterns. True diversity arises as a direct consequence of consistently applied policies and behaviors that actively dismantle barriers and expand opportunities. As an example, when an organization commits to STRUCTURAL SAFETY (3), EMERGENT LEADERSHIP (58), DISTRIBUTED MANAGEMENT (14), UPWARD REPRESENTATION (24), and genuine WHOLENESS (7), diversity is supported on a permanent, thorough basis. Diversity thus becomes an organic and inevitable outcome, rooted deeply in the structures and practices of the organization itself.

In this book, you'll find patterns that lay groundwork for healthier, more humane workplaces rather than prescriptive tactics masquerading as guaranteed quick fixes. The omissions you find here are deliberate.* They reflect my belief in the power of underlying structural and behavioral conditions to produce lasting, genuine change.

---

* Someday I might be persuaded that "accountability," "feedback," or some other crowd favorite deserves its own pattern. Just because I don't see it that way today doesn't mean you, or your team, have to agree. This collection reflects one practitioner's take at one moment in time; treat it as a starting point.

A DIFFERENT KIND OF PLAYBOOK

"Best practices" break. They're alluring because they're easy to adopt: clearly defined, seemingly reliable solutions borrowed from other successful organizations. But they inevitably fall apart, because what makes something work in one place rarely matches exactly what's needed somewhere else. Best practices fail precisely because they lack context.

Patterns have an edge because they explicitly provide these connections. *The patterns are the context!* Every pattern in this book connects logically and practically to others, forming chains of change that reflect genuine organizational realities.

This book prioritizes principles over procedures. Each pattern is a tested, fundamental idea, not a formula. If the examples or templates don't seem immediately relevant, that's fine. The core principle is what matters. Take the idea, apply it flexibly, and test it out. Make it your own.

Finally, emphasize adaptation over adoption. Please don't treat patterns like rules; I hope you see them and use them as ideas that take shape within your own environment. They're meant to be bent, experimented with, and improved upon until they fit. So encourage real problem-solving over following rules, and empower your teams to act decisively, pragmatically, and effectively.

THE POWER OF SCALE

Starting small isn't the same thing as thinking small. Imagine this: 100 teams, each with about 10 people, decide to thoughtfully rework their team charters. This is relatively easy work that will not take any of these teams much time or effort. Looking at each individually, you might miss the size of the impact they're creating. Seen collectively, it's 1,000 people realigning their roles, clarifying decision rights, sharpening their focus, and reclaiming valuable hours for meaningful work. Small moves, replicated at scale, have immense transformative potential.

When you shift a single small practice—like reducing unnecessary meetings or restructuring daily decision-making—you create room for the work that matters most. Removing just two unnecessary meetings per week gives each team member back hours of deep, productive time. *Multiply that across your entire organization, and suddenly thousands of hours are available again for focused, creative, and genuinely fulfilling work.* Every 2,000 hours we get back is the same as adding an entire person to the team. And it costs nothing.

Momentum builds quickly once patterns take hold. Say your team experiments with something simple, like CHECK IN & OUT (44) or ADAPTIVE AGENDA (49). Suddenly, meetings become sharper, quicker, and easier. Conversations feel safer, which means teams become comfortable handling more difficult issues head-on. Now, something like CONFLICT AS A RESOURCE (38) is both feasible *and* welcomed. Before you know it, teams interact more fluidly, naturally evolving toward a NETWORK OF TEAMS (13). Each small pattern reinforces others, creating a powerful cycle of positive change.

Connecting local improvements to global change comes down to visibility and replication. When one team finds success with a new pattern, openly sharing that success inspires and encourages others. I've seen firsthand how local experiments become global movements when their impacts are shared and celebrated.

That team I described from the London conference room ended up trying and implementing more patterns—notably ROUNDS (48), ITERATIVE SHIPPING (46), and TEAM/PROCESS AS PRODUCT (63)—that spread across the entire organization. If you handed the whole organization this book and said, "Here, do all 75 of these patterns," none of it would ever stick. The point is starting somewhere and communicating a small set of memorable things that can spread socially, peer to peer.

Okay. Let's dive in.

FOUNDATIONS

1 True Purpose

Purpose is a guiding "why" that informs every "what" and "how"

Purpose is the "why" that drives meaningful action and connects individuals, teams, and organizations to shared goals. It serves as a compass for work, giving clarity, resilience, and alignment, even in uncertain times.

At an organizational level, **purpose drives . . . everything,** focusing on big, transformative goals that improve talent density, accelerate decision-making, and provide stable long-term direction.

For teams, purpose gives focus to **shorter-term, bounded goals.** It supports better, faster decisions. It clarifies their unique role within the organization. It provides cohesion and direction.

At an individual/personal level, **purpose can work as an internal compass,** connecting personal motivations (and day-to-day tasks) with broader goals and ideally the purpose of the team and the broader organization. When we take the time to craft and internalize a personal purpose, it affords resilience, focus, and a sense of fulfillment. It also helps us know when to move on from a team or organization to a new one.

Without a clear purpose, we lose direction and motivation. For individuals, a lack of purpose can lead to disengagement and burnout. Teams risk becoming transactional, and organizations risk losing relevance, becoming reactive instead of proactive.

Research on visionary companies has shown that authentic purpose drives success.*

---

* Jim Collins and Jerry I. Porras, *Built to Last: Successful Habits of Visionary Companies* (Harper Business, 1994). Turns out these companies weren't 100% great indicators of long-term visionary success, but I don't think that means we throw out the idea.

Organizations with **purpose** attract talent, accelerate decision-making, and adapt better to change. But superficial, vague purpose statements can erode trust and effectiveness. So authenticity is nonnegotiable.[1] People can sense when purpose is real versus contrived.*

THEREFORE...

A well-defined purpose statement encapsulates what an organization, team, or individual is deeply passionate about, what it/you can excel at, and what drives your economic engine. Organizationally, a good purpose is not a one-size-fits-all slogan; it's a specific statement that summarizes the impact the organization wants to have on the world. So it's hard to get right. It's easy to veer into vague generalities or metrics that don't capture the true "why" behind the work. Team purpose enables agility and cohesion by translating organizational intent into short-term goals. Personal purpose, when aligned with team and organizational aims, connects day-to-day work to broader meaning, promoting resilience and engagement.

Consider these three ideas as guidance:

Make It Durable
It withstands change, guiding decisions through uncertainty.

Make It Fractal
It works at every level, with alignment from company-wide goals to personal career paths.

Make It Clear
It provides an actionable North Star for decisions, avoiding ambiguity.

A brief note on language: Consistency matters. While terms like "mission" or "vision" are common, using "purpose" uniformly is clear and coherent across levels. It reinforces the idea that every layer of the organization, from individuals to teams to leadership, shares a unified driving force.

---

* Scott Galloway calls this trend toward vague, aspirational, bullshitty company mission statements "yogababble," and it's a term that helps me stay grounded when doing this kind of work.

Google	GoFundMe	Morning Star
Org Level	**Org Level**	**Org Level**
Organize the world's information and make it universally accessible and useful	Help people help each other	Produce tomato products that consistently achieve the highest quality standards
Team Level	**Team Level**	**Team Level**
Search Quality	*Trust & Safety*	*Harvest Logistics*
Ensure search results are relevant, reliable, and serve user needs	Protect donors and recipients while maximizing legitimate fundraising success	Optimize field-to-factory flow, ensuring peak ripeness processing
Personal Level	**Personal Level**	**Personal Level**
ML Engineer	*Data Analyst*	*Logistics Coordinator*
Build software that helps underserved language-speakers find the information they need	Identify patterns that distinguish genuine needs from potential fraud	Maintain real-time communication between growers and processing facilities that minimizes waste and maximizes quality

These examples demonstrate how authentic expressions of organizational intent genuinely guide action and decision-making across all levels:* Teams can make faster, more aligned decisions; leaders can focus less on directives and more on enabling autonomy; individuals can find deeper engagement and meaning. This coherence helps an organization adapt with intention, grounded in identity rather than external trends.[2]

At the organizational level, it requires clear RULE OF LAW (2) to ensure consistent application and STRUCTURAL & PSYCHOLOGICAL SAFETY (3) to enable authentic expression. The purpose must flow through an effective NETWORK OF TEAMS (13), supported by DISTRIBUTED MANAGEMENT (14) that empowers

---

* I'll note here that the examples are sketches of what might be true within these organizations. They do not reflect actual team descriptions or jobs and are for illustration only.

decision-making at all levels. SELF-MANAGED TEAMS (18) operating with CURI-OSITY (5) translate purpose into action: The organization is able to DO THE RIGHT THING (26), while embracing EXPERIMENTATION (62). Meanwhile, BOUND-ARY MANAGEMENT (67) keeps teams and individuals focused. This distributed activation of purpose depends on robust TRANSPARENCY (32) and mechanisms like COLLEAGUE LETTER OF UNDERSTANDING (40), TEAM CHARTER (43), and LOGBOOK (57) to maintain alignment.

2 *Rule of Law*

Hold everyone to a handful of important standards

It's tempting to bypass established protocols in favor of achieving a quick win. It probably always will be. It's also true that history shows that sustainable organizations—like successful societies—thrive when governed by principles rather than personalities.

Of course it's true that all organizations (even the smallest, youngest ones) have policies. Some of those policies are driven by local regulation; breaking some of those policies can result in losing your standing with the organization, regardless of your position. But when it comes to the really important stuff, like who gets to make which important decision, organizations: (a) don't have policies to follow, and (b) wouldn't necessarily follow them even if they existed. They lack a fundamental commitment to predictable, equitable rulemaking and rule following . . .

> . . . that creates the structural and psychological safety necessary to take big leaps
> . . . that allows an organization to collaborate, innovate, and grow.

Just as citizens invest and build lives in nations with stable legal systems,* employees **fully engage** only when they trust in the fairness of their organizational environment.[3] Given the rarity of this pattern in the world of work, this means that **most people working today haven't experienced full engagement at work.**

---

* Although let's be real: It feels like this is a *little* bit in question as I write this at the start of 2025. Hopefully things have improved by the time this book is in print.

When rules are unclear, inconsistently applied, or circumvented by leaders, organizations become unstable. Decisions feel unfair or capricious, and trust erodes.[4] This leads to confusion, resentment, and a lack of engagement. Teams may begin to fragment, focusing on protecting their own interests rather than contributing to collective goals.[5] At the individual level, the absence of clear rules creates ambiguity and disempowerment. People waste energy navigating unclear expectations or advocating for their own fairness in an environment that seems inherently inequitable.

The benefits of the rule of law (at very least in the workplace) are obvious, and nearly every other pattern in this book relies on this pattern being in place.

THEREFORE...

Establish the rule of law within your organization—an agreed-upon system of principles and practices that governs behavior, decision-making, and conflict resolution. For this to be true, these rules need to apply universally, regardless of position or status, and must (obviously?) reflect shared values and goals.

The rule of law in organizations requires at least three elements:

A **Constitutional Framework**, defining irrevocable (or at very least hard-to-change):	Fundamental rights and responsibilities of all members
	Decision-making frameworks and authorities
	Mechanisms for change and adaptation
	Core values and their practical applications
A **Governance System**, including transparent processes for:	Policy creation and modification
	Conflict resolution and appeals
	Performance evaluation and rewards
	Resource allocation and prioritization
Cultural Reinforcement through supporting mechanisms:	Regular training and communication about organizational principles
	Recognition systems that reward adherence to proper processes
	Leadership development focused on principled decision-making
	Open feedback channels for suggesting improvements

These elements must work together to create what management scholar Edgar Schein calls a "learning culture" where rules evolve through conscious, collaborative processes rather than executive fiat.*

This point—that there may be "local," individual, and organization-wide rules—is essential, and . . . challenging. Rules surrounding the most consequential elements of the organization and each stakeholder's relationship with it should change slowest and apply most universally; we should not allow individual fiefdoms to form around managers with their own special rules of engagement that contravene the rules of the org as a whole. Individual or team rules should be substantially easier to change, but again, they shouldn't contradict the whole.

CONSIDERATIONS

- Ensure that rules are co-created with input from those who will be governed by them, or at the very least, that those who are governed by the rules have consented to them.
- The rules should be easily accessible and communicated to all members.
- Establish clear mechanisms for enforcing rules fairly and consistently. It should be obvious to all which rules can be bent and which rules, if broken, lead to removal from the organization.
- Rules should allow for evolution in response to changing needs or contexts while maintaining their core principles; edits to the rules should follow the first consideration on this list.

ORGANIZATIONS

At the organizational level, rules govern broad systems like decision-making processes, resource allocation, and governance structures. Who gets to decide? How are conflicts resolved? How is performance evaluated? What determines membership (and loss of membership)?

---

* Edgar H. Schein, *Organizational Culture and Leadership*, 5th ed. (Jossey-Bass, 2017), chapter 17. This chapter is particularly interesting in the context of this book overall; Schein notes a few pattern-like observations about learning cultures, like: "Positive assumptions about human nature" and "Commitment to full and open task-relevant communication."

Example: An organization might adopt a constitution that outlines a clear decision-rights framework with a deep emphasis on the boundaries of power for the highest-ranking positions in the organization so that teams know exactly how empowered they are to make change.

TEAMS

Teams operate best when they have clear agreements about how work is divided, how decisions are made, and how success is measured. These agreements—TEAM CHARTERS (43), ground rules, or working agreements—ensure alignment and reduce conflict.

Example: A team charter might outline roles, decision-making processes, and rules for conflict resolution to ensure every member knows how the team works.

INDIVIDUALS

At an individual level, the rule of law is about integrity and accountability. Clear expectations, performance metrics, and behavioral guidelines help individuals know how their work contributes to the larger whole and that they are held to the same standards as their peers.

Example: A personal code of conduct might include adhering to shared values, such as respecting others or committing to data-driven decision-making.

So, the rule of law builds a foundation of fairness and trust. Members know what's expected, how decisions get made, and how they will be treated. This structural and psychological safety allows people to focus on their work even when faced with internal politics or uncertainty. Returning to the point about skipping steps from the beginning of this chapter, the rule of law is a pattern that would push us to follow agreed-upon guidelines that would keep the organization safe; it's the pre-flight checklist followed with precision. Safety when we need it, with innovation as a happy side effect.

When everyone from the CEO to the newest hire operates under the same shared rules, the organization gets more resilient, adaptable, and aligned. Consistency fosters a strong culture where fairness and integrity are ideals and lived realities that deepen with time.

The rule of law does not necessarily mean that "everyone must communicate in legalese" or that "a policy governs everything we do."

Google's "Ten Things We Know to Be True" is a set of principles that produce decisions across the organization.[6] Amazon's leadership principles create consistent decision-making criteria across diverse business units—and they stick to them as rigorously as any culture I've observed.[7] Procter & Gamble's "Moment of Truth" framework standardizes customer experience evaluation so that all marketers within the business (and even those who move on to other organizations, pollinating P&G's culture across the business world) have a common language for discussing insights and action.[8] Starbucks's *Green Apron Book* provides clear behavioral guidelines for all employees.[9] At Ritz-Carlton, any employee may spend up to $2,000 on the spot to fix a guest problem or create delight—no manager sign-off required.[10] And so on.

DEALING WITH PUSHBACK

"Isn't this slower?"
Clear rules speed things up by removing hidden friction—ad hoc exceptions make every decision a fresh negotiation, and negotiation is slow.

"What if breaking a rule works out?"
Treat it as a signal that the rule was wrong. Capture the lesson, update the rule if warranted, and hold the process accountable.

"Our CEO plays by different rules."
OK, but make carve outs explicit, narrowly scoped, and transparent. Otherwise call it what it is—arbitrary power—and drop the rule of law label. Try another pattern instead!

At the organizational level, STRUCTURAL & PSYCHOLOGICAL SAFETY (3) creates the baseline trust needed for rules to function. Clear rules require TRANSPARENCY (32) in how they're created and enforced, with CONSENT & CONSENSUS

(10) guiding their evolution. When conflicts arise around rules, CONFLICT RES-OLUTION (39) provides a structured path forward. Rules must be documented clearly through ONLY IMPORTANT NOTES (45), and their effectiveness could be regularly examined through HEALTH CHECK (59) and RETROSPECTIVES (66). For day-to-day operations, rules are reinforced through COLLEAGUE LETTER OF UNDERSTANDING (40) and TEAM CHARTER (43), which translate organizational principles into human-scale agreements.

3 *Structural & Psychological Safety*

What happens if I speak up?
What happens if I screw up?
Maybe I'll just do nothing instead.

The ability to innovate, learn, and adapt depends on people feeling safe to take risks, share ideas (especially when those ideas are countercultural), and admit mistakes. Safety is a feeling or cultural attribute *and* it requires concrete structures and practices that protect and enable vulnerable behavior. Without both psychological and structural safety, even the best-intentioned organizations, teams, and individuals will struggle to unlock their full potential.

Psychological safety, as defined by Amy Edmondson, is "a shared belief that the team is safe for interpersonal risk-taking." But this belief must be anchored in real organizational structures that make such risk-taking possible.

Structural safety manifests as codified organizational mechanisms that protect member status, resource access, and decision rights regardless of role or circumstance. While psychological safety operates at the behavioral level, structural safety embeds these protections into the organization's operating system through explicit process, policy, and protocol. When these protections are firmly in place, they create the foundation that makes psychological safety sustainable rather than situational. Members can take meaningful risks knowing their organizational status is secured by process rather than personality.

This is not easy work, but it is essential.

When this pattern isn't in place, people default to self-protective behaviors that privilege individual survival over collective flourishing. They withhold critical information, avoid smart risks and good spending, deflect accountability, and optimize for appearance rather than impact. These defensive routines become deeply embedded in organizational culture, creating what Chris Argyris termed "skilled incompetence"—the art of avoiding threat while appearing highly capable.[11]

The gap between aspiration and reality manifests some rather interesting contradictions. Organizations promote psychological safety through cultural initiatives while maintaining systems that undermine it. Performance management is meant to improve performance but ends up simply punishing failure. It raises the bar and lowers the ceiling. Hierarchies are meant to transmit information rapidly up and down the org but make speaking up dangerous. So they only transmit good news—and slowly. Resource management processes are intended to put the organization's limited material to work for its highest and best purpose but foster competition, hoarding, and opacity. Information systems are intended to help team members maximize their potential impact every day but are hard to use, enable centralized surveillance, and frequently break. Decision rights are intended to make it clear who gets to make what call, but naturally trend toward a byzantine level of complexity that means they never get created; when teams *do* write down who makes what call (actually), they notice a concentration of power that increases fear of authority.

Organizations claim to value learning but maintain zero-tolerance policies, while leaders ask for trust while maintaining systems of control and compliance.

THEREFORE...

Create integrated systems of psychological and structural safety, with three key mechanisms working in harmony.

First, organizations must establish protected spaces through clear boundaries and agreements that make vulnerability possible. This includes explicit social contracts about how people will treat each other, physical and digital spaces designed for psychological safety, and clear protocols for handling sensitive discussions. These spaces need strong consequences for violating safety agreements and regular renewal of safety commitments.

Second, enabling structures must be built into organizational systems that actively enable and protect safe behavior. This means implementing decision rights that distribute power and reduce fear of authority, information systems that support transparency while protecting privacy, and resource-allocation processes that reward collaboration over competition. Performance systems must separate learning from evaluation, with clear paths for surfacing and addressing concerns.

Third, leadership practices must model and maintain safety. This includes demonstrating personal vulnerability that shows safety in action, responding quickly to violations, regularly assessing both psychological and structural safety, actively soliciting feedback about barriers, and making visible changes based on safety-related input.

When organizations successfully integrate psychological and structural safety, they unlock extraordinary capabilities. The immediate impact is more-honest communication, faster problem-solving, increased innovation, better decision-making, and stronger collaboration. It feels like magic when times are good, and when conditions change, the organization is ready and the people dig in to help.

Structural and psychological safety manifest in diverse ways, but perhaps the simplest way to bring these to life is through **careful session design.**

Pixar's "Braintrust" sessions explicitly separate notes from decisions, removing power dynamics from creative dialogue.[12] Directors maintain ultimate creative control, creating psychological safety to receive feedback as advice, and without the usual corporate "defensive routines." The physical space itself—a dedicated room with specific seating arrangements—reinforces equal participation regardless of role.

The UK's National Health Service (NHS) demonstrates how safety systems can scale across complex organizations. Their "Learning from Excellence" program combines structural elements (protected time for positive incident review, standardized documentation processes) with psychological enablers (celebration of success, peer-to-peer recognition).[13] Most notably, they've created "Safety Huddles"—brief daily meetings with explicit psychological safety protocols that have measurably reduced adverse incidents.[14]

●▼✦■✿✿

Safety, in general, begins with DO NO HARM (6), which establishes protective boundaries, and EXPANDED AVAILABLE POWER (4) and DISTRIBUTED

MANAGEMENT (14), which structurally reduce fear through shared authority. The governance layer requires CONSENT & CONSENSUS (10) and STRUCTURED DECISION-MAKING (30) for collective choice making, strengthened by ELECTIONS (15) and UPWARD REPRESENTATION (24) to ensure multidirectional power flows. COOPERATION (12) and ADVICE (31) help competitive modes of working become more collaborative and learning focused. When times get tough, CONFLICT AS A RESOURCE (38) and CONFLICT RESOLUTION (39) provide clear pathways forward, supported by TRANSPARENCY (32) and LOGBOOK (57) to maintain trust and organizational memory. Regular HEALTH CHECK (59) and RETROSPECTIVES (66) ensure the system evolves intentionally through collective wisdom.

4 Expanded Available Power

Power isn't zero sum

Hierarchies are a powerful servant to an organizational need to streamline decision-making for a predictable world. The entrepreneurial vision—deciding markets, products, and strategies—was concentrated at the top, while the middle managed operations, and the bottom carried out tactical directives with little decision-making power. This separation made sense when organizations valued control and efficiency above all else, and was appropriate given the broader economic context of the early twentieth century, when industrial giants were making new markets from scratch.[15]

But in today's fast-moving, complex environment, this rigid distribution of power limits innovation and adaptability. Test-and-learn approaches, for instance, often fail because the power to experiment is centralized; teams tasked with learning have neither the authority nor the resources to act.

In almost every case, centralization creates a bottleneck.* Decisions at the top often take too long to trickle down to the people closest to the work, and by the time they arrive, they may already be outdated. This lack of distributed authority creates inertia, stifles innovation, and demoralizes employees who feel their contributions are undervalued or ignored.

---

* This may be valuable in cases where one individual, or one team, holds a sense of taste that cannot easily be distributed across the whole of an enterprise. Those cases are exceedingly rare, and I'd suggest that a more interesting idea than centralization is *education*: "How might a leader, or a team, educate the organization on their taste level?" That feels like real differentiation, to me.

Simply redistributing decision-making power isn't enough, because in most cases, teams at the edges of the organization lack the support, resources, or confidence to act entrepreneurially. Without expanding the total amount of power available, decentralization can create confusion, inconsistent priorities, and chaos.*

THEREFORE ...

Expand available power by coaching teams at all levels to take on both entrepreneurial and operational decisions. This pattern can work well even in hierarchical systems, where leaders use their positional power to allow and encourage more people to participate in decision-making and give them the necessary resources, authority, and support they need to bring those decisions to life. This creates a system where more people have access to both entrepreneurial (what we do) and operational (how we do it) decision-making authority.†

Expanded Available Power involves three key shifts:

1. **More people making more decisions:** Encourage employees at every level to take ownership of decisions within their scope. This might mean frontline workers experimenting with customer-facing processes or middle managers piloting new operational models.

2. **Entrepreneurial energy at the edges:** Equip teams closest to customers and markets with the authority to test ideas, learn from results, and iterate quickly—without waiting for approval from the top.

3. **Support through coaching and guardrails:** Provide the tools, training, and boundaries needed to ensure decentralized decisions align with organizational goals. Leaders shift their role from decision-makers to enablers, creating an environment where teams feel empowered to act.

---

* This happens far more frequently than I think we're all prepared to admit, and we've probably all seen it! A leader will express the desire to decentralize and empower but won't actually give up some of their authority to the teams around them.

† Another concept that I love from Chandler, and one I often refer back to when thinking about "What is strategy? And what is tactics?" Strategy is when we haven't decided where to spend our resources. Tactics is after.

Expanding available power begins with a clear articulation of who has authority to make which types of decisions. This requires a shift in mindset, moving from a command-and-control model to one that prioritizes autonomy and experimentation. Consider Haier's RenDanHeYi model, where the organization has been transformed into over 4,000 microenterprises, each with entrepreneurial authority to innovate, set goals, and make decisions in service of customers.[16] This radical decentralization has driven remarkable results, helping transform it from a small, near-bankrupt refrigerator factory in 1984 to a global powerhouse.

It's also essential that an organization meaningfully commits its resources to back up the expansion of power. Google's "20% Time" practice is a perfect example of this, empowering employees to spend a portion of their time on projects they believe are valuable.[17] This drives entrepreneurial activity across all levels of the company while maintaining alignment through clear data visibility and shared metrics.

The implementation of expanded power also depends heavily on cultural transformation. At Starbucks, local store managers are encouraged to personalize offerings based on community preferences, balancing corporate strategy with local innovation.[18] This demonstrates how expanding power requires a culture of accountability and learning, where teams feel safe to take risks and learn from mistakes without fear of punishment. Leaders can model this behavior by celebrating experiments—whether successful or not—and emphasizing the value of iteration over perfection.

●▼◢■✳●

TRUE PURPOSE (1) provides the essential context for distributed decision-making, and RULE OF LAW (2) establishes the guardrails within which power can be safely expanded. STRUCTURAL & PSYCHOLOGICAL SAFETY (3) creates the baseline trust needed for people to exercise expanded power effectively. DISTRIBUTED MANAGEMENT (14) and NETWORK OF TEAMS (13) provide the structural framework for distributed authority. SELF-MANAGED TEAMS (18) and TEAM INCENTIVES (25) create the local conditions for expanded power to flourish, while DOMAINS, ASSETS & STANDARDS (23) clearly defines the boundaries of that authority. TRANSPARENCY (32) and STRUCTURED DECISION-MAKING (30) ensure that expanded power is exercised wisely. ADVICE (31) and CONSENT &

CONSENSUS (10) provide mechanisms for coordinating decisions across the organization. When challenges arise, CONFLICT AS A RESOURCE (38) and CONFLICT RESOLUTION (39) help navigate the tensions that naturally emerge from distributed authority. Regular HEALTH CHECK (59) and RETROSPECTIVES (66) allow teams to reflect on and adjust their use of expanded power. EXPERIMENTATION (62) and ITERATIVE SHIPPING (46) enable teams to learn and adapt as they exercise their authority.

5 Curiosity

Learning is more important than being right

First, a quick game. I call it **Builders**—credit to the mystery facilitator who showed it to August years ago. You split a group of workshop participants into two teams with identical supplies: Post-its, scissors, glue sticks, scrap paper, a few Sharpies. The brief is simple: "Design and build as many paper houses as you can in fifteen minutes."

Call team one "Perfect Corp" and give them four rules: We never make mistakes; we're obsessed with quality; we speak in statements, never questions; and we respect the line manager's authority at all times. (Ask them to pick a line manager.) Call team two, "Appreciative Homes," with four nearly opposing rules: Quality emerges from collaboration; we care about each other; we give no directions, only questions; and every builder has full autonomy.

What happens next is predictable. Perfect Corp huddles, debates, polishes a blueprint, re-polishes the blueprint, and—if the timekeeper is kind—manages to erect a single immaculate bungalow. Appreciative Homes, meanwhile, spends the same 15 minutes firing questions back and forth ("How small can a door be and still feel like a door?" "What if we fold one sheet into two units?" "Who sees an easier way?"). They improvise, test, and iterate. When the buzzer sounds, their table is covered with a village—fifteen homes, give or take, each one good enough and getting better with every pass.

There is power, and a paradox, in curiosity. Questions move work forward faster than polished directives. Certainty feels efficient, but it's brittle. Advantage

belongs to people and organizations who keep asking "What else might be true?"
(And in a crisis, they ask "How does this happen?" versus "Who do I blame?")

THEREFORE...

Design work so that curiosity is both a celebrated (and cultivated) personality trait
and a repeatable move anyone can make.

Cultivate Curiosity in Yourself

Shift from expert to explorer. Keep a small notebook at hand and treat it as a running scrapbook of oddities, half-formed hunches, and mind maps. Each day, pick
something mundane—the way a report is formatted, the route you commute—
and ask "Why?" until the next answer would require evidence. Use it to inform
or inspire bite-sized tests, drawing on the mindset of EXPERIMENTATION (62).
When a hunch flops, pin the lesson to the office FAIL WALL (69) or share it in chat.
Publicly celebrating the miss tells your brain—and your peers—that the real prize
is learning.

Spark Curiosity in the Team

Ritual practice is better than a leadership mandate. Kick off the weekly stand-up
with a quick round of "What are we noticing?"—a move borrowed from MEETING
ROLES (51) that forces everyone to surface one fresh observation before solutions
creep in. Ask one teammate to embody the role of explorer each sprint—a nod to
the feedback muscles in ADVICE (31), and with ROLE-SOUL DISTINCTION (8)
in mind—so someone is always shadowing customers or sniffing around adjacent
teams for surprises. Wrap work blocks with a two-question debrief ("What surprised us?" and "What will we try next?"), turning RETROSPECTIVES (66) into a
rhythmic curiosity pump.

Protect Curiosity Across the Organization

A curious culture needs scaffolding. Leaders model STRUCTURAL & PSYCHO-
LOGICAL SAFETY (3) when they admit what they don't know and reward people who surface awkward questions. Default-open dashboards, decision logs, and
experiment results—combining PULL UPDATES (34) and TRANSPARENCY

(32)—turn idle interest into informed inquiry. Keep a small, always-available budget for tests so ITERATIVE SHIPPING (46) can scale quickly when the data say it should.

Curiosity amplifies CADENCE (65), where regular time-boxed cycles of work and reflection slot every "What did we learn?" into the next calendar block and keep wonder from dying in the backlog; it powers DEMOS (35), because showing unfinished work invites "How might we . . . ?" questions that turn observation into live feedback; it thrives in WORK IN PUBLIC (50), where visible dashboards and open docs let anyone spot oddities and ask fresh questions, multiplying the surface area for discovery; it underwrites every HACK DAY (60), channeling the "I've always wondered if . . ." backlog into rapid prototypes; it fuels TEAM/PROCESS AS PRODUCT (63), where treating the workflow itself as a product makes each upgrade begin with one essential prompt: "What would make the next version better?"

6 Do No Harm

Externalities eventually become internalities

Organizations wield significant power—over employees' lives, communities, ecosystems, and societal outcomes. Traditionally, this power has been exercised with primary focus on financial returns, often creating "externalities" that represent real harm: burnout and stress, community disruption, environmental damage, or societal inequities. These harms were seen as unfortunate but necessary costs of doing business.

Yet in an interconnected world, harm eventually cycles back to affect organizational success. Employee burnout leads to turnover and lost knowledge. Community damage creates recruitment challenges and regulatory backlash. Environmental degradation threatens supply chains. What once seemed like external costs become very real internal problems.

Without an explicit commitment to avoiding harm, organizations face several critical challenges:

Short-term optimization creates long-term damage. Pushing teams to unsustainable performance levels might hit quarterly targets but destroys the human capacity needed for long-term success. Cost-cutting measures that ignore community impact might improve margins but erode the social license to operate. Environmental shortcuts that boost current profits create future liabilities.

Moreover, when organizations lack clear principles about harm prevention, decision-makers face impossible trade-offs. Without guidance on how to weigh different types of impact, they typically default to what's easily measurable (usually financial metrics) while ignoring harder-to-quantify harms to people, communities, and ecosystems.

THEREFORE...

Embed "do no harm" as a fundamental operating principle that guides decisions at all levels by actively identifying and preventing unnecessary harm where possible.

Apply this principle across three areas of influence:

- Human: Protecting the physical and psychological well-being of employees and stakeholders
- Social: Preventing damage to communities and societal fabric
- Environmental: Avoiding unnecessary harm to natural systems

This pattern asks leaders to think about harm prevention as a sophisticated organizational capability that goes far beyond typical corporate responsibility theater. Patagonia demonstrates this brilliantly: They've transformed impact analysis from a constraint into a catalyst for innovation, rewiring everything from materials science to supply-chain architecture.[19] The Body Shop's early stance against animal testing shows how principled harm prevention drives innovation. While their industry was constructing elaborate justifications for "necessary" testing, The Body Shop's categorical rejection of this premise forced the development of entirely new validation methodologies, reimagining how beauty products could be developed and validated.[20] When REI chose to close on Black Friday, they were explicitly rejecting industry practices that created demonstrable harm to employee well-being and family structures.[21]

Implementation requires three interconnected mechanisms:

1. Clear, courageous policies that establish nonnegotiable harm-prevention boundaries
2. Sophisticated decision frameworks that capture full-spectrum impact
3. Early warning systems capable of surfacing potential negative consequences before they manifest

●▼◢■✳◆

Do No Harm builds on TRUE PURPOSE (1) and RULE OF LAW (2) to establish ethical operating parameters. It works through EXPANDED AVAILABLE POWER (4) and DISTRIBUTED MANAGEMENT (14) to ensure that decentralized authority enhances rather than compromises system integrity. TRANSPARENCY (32) and STRUCTURED DECISION-MAKING (30) provide the mechanisms for identifying and preventing negative impacts, while HEALTH CHECK (59) and RETROSPECTIVES (66) ensure these capabilities evolve as the organization learns. EXPERIMENTATION (62) enables innovation within ethical boundaries, while LOGBOOK (57) captures and institutionalizes crucial learnings about effective harm prevention.

7 *Wholeness*

Your whole self is your best self

Modern organizations often create an artificial divide between "professional" and "personal," expecting people to compartmentalize themselves and bring only their "work self" to the office. This fragmentation emerged from industrial-era thinking that viewed humans as interchangeable parts in a machine, where personal feelings, creativity, and individual expression were seen as distractions from efficiency.

Yet humans are inherently whole beings, with our experiences, emotions, and identities inextricably linked. When organizations force people to fragment themselves, they create psychological strain and lose access to the full range of human capabilities that drive innovation, creativity, and meaningful connection.

When people feel they must leave significant parts of themselves "at the door," they expend enormous energy maintaining a professional facade.[22] This constant self-monitoring depletes the cognitive and emotional resources needed for complex problem-solving and creative thinking.[23] Teams lose access to diverse perspectives and experiences that could inform better solutions.

Moreover, the pressure to conform to narrow definitions of "professional behavior" stifles psychological safety and authentic connection.[24] People hesitate to share concerns, admit uncertainty, or bring forward unconventional ideas. The organization gets rigid and risk averse, missing opportunities for innovation that emerge from genuine human interaction and expression.

THEREFORE ...

Actively create environments where people can practically show up as their full selves. This means rethinking what professionalism looks like, creating space for emotion and individuality, and aligning work with deeper values.

1. Support what matters to people, not just their productivity.
If there's something your company cares about, and your employees care about it, too, actively support them in taking action in support of that cause. Identify what activities they might undertake to show their support, and work with finance and/ or workforce planning teams to budget an allowance for using company time and money in those spaces.

2. Treat well-being as an operational investment, not a perk.
SAS Institute has spent decades refining a simple but radical idea: People do their best work when they have a full, stable, and healthy life outside of work. They provide on-site childcare, unlimited sick days, and even subsidized housecleaning services to remove unnecessary stressors that prevent employees from focusing, creating, and thriving.[25]

3. Make space for reflection and presence.
Before diving into agendas and decisions, take a moment to pause, breathe, and fully arrive. This small ritual acknowledges that work doesn't happen in isolation from everything else. People bring their full internal worlds—their stresses, their distractions, their energy levels—into meetings.

4. Celebrate individuality.
IDEO is legendary for a creative culture that goes beyond good design by appreciating people as individuals,[26] valuing their quirks over a "professional mask." Employees build personalized workspaces that reflect their personalities. Meetings often involve offbeat rituals and unexpected moments of play. Creativity thrives in environments where people feel free to be themselves.

5. Lead like people matter.
Barry-Wehmiller, a manufacturing firm, has a guiding philosophy they call "truly human leadership."[27] It's the radical notion that employees should be treated with

the same care and respect as family. As a result, the company has a history of refus-
ing to lay people off, even in financial downturns, finding creative ways to cut costs
while preserving jobs. This kind of leadership signals that people's whole selves are
valued.

Wholeness depends on STRUCTURAL & PSYCHOLOGICAL SAFETY (3) to ensure that people feel secure in showing up fully. It is reinforced by EXPANDED
AVAILABLE POWER (4), which allows people to bring their full capacities to work
without fear of repression. To be sustained, wholeness requires DISTRIBUTED
MANAGEMENT (14) and SELF-MANAGED TEAMS (18), where autonomy and individuality are respected. TRANSPARENCY (32) and PROCESS ON THE WALL
(68) create environments where people's contributions are visible and valued. CON-
SENT & CONSENSUS (10) ensures that participation is genuine.

8 Role-Soul Distinction

You are not your job

Occasionally, but more often than we'd like to admit, we conflate our identity with our role. This conflation is risky: Roles are fluid, evolving as the organization's needs change, whereas our intrinsic human worth (the "soul") endures.* When people define themselves solely by their job title or position:

- They cling too tightly to particular responsibilities and resist necessary changes.
- They take feedback on their work as a personal attack, creating friction and needless emotional labor.[28]
- They treat their role as static rather than something that adapts over time.

For the organization, this often leads to rigid structures that resist change, silos driven by personal agendas rather than collective goals, and a stunted ability to pivot in response to market shifts or user feedback.[29]

A clear separation between these ideas is therefore vital for building a more adaptive, resilient organization. By decoupling who we are from what we do at any given moment, we free ourselves to focus on meaningful outcomes and shift roles

---

* I first came across this idea and related practices through applying Brian Robertson's Holacracy to Undercurrent, where I worked from 2009 to 2015. I can tell you that it's very strange at first, but it's one of those things that has a bit of a life- and career-altering impact. All the critiques of this management system are very real and worth studying, but the basic ideas are worth applying. Reader, if we ever meet in person, I'd be happy to discuss this at length over a coffee or a beer.

as needed. Instead of protecting hierarchies or clinging to static job descriptions, the organization (and its people) can stay aligned with the actual work that needs doing.[30]

THEREFORE ...

Emphasize the distinction between roles and souls, allowing for flexibility, adaptability, and focus on delivering outcomes that matter.[31] Roles exist to serve the organization's goals and customers; they can (and should) be dissolved, reshaped, or renamed as needed. The soul remains intact throughout these changes. By recognizing the difference, organizations encourage people to evolve their responsibilities while preserving their intrinsic worth and dignity.

To bring this to life:

1. **Define some roles as multi-filled.** Multiple individuals may share a single role, ensuring that whenever the scope or responsibilities of that role change, those changes apply to all who fill it.
2. **Have people fill more than one role.** If individuals hold multiple roles at once, there's less territoriality over a single title—and more openness to collaboration and growth.
3. **Fill roles at multiple levels.** For instance, someone filling the "CEO" role might also have discrete roles such as "public speaker" or "copy editor," which speak to their capabilities *and* can be filled by more junior people at the same time (see the first item in this list). This creates more parity in more situations and helps chart longer career paths for folks earlier in their careers.

KEY PRINCIPLES

- Roles are not fixed identities. They must evolve alongside the organization's needs.
- Feedback is about the role, not the person. Critiques should serve the work, never undermine personal worth.
- Souls bring unique value. Individuals are more than the sum of their

current responsibilities, and a strong Role-Soul Distinction preserves creativity, values, and motivations.

AT THE ORGANIZATIONAL LEVEL

This pattern allows leaders to design flexible structures where roles can be multi-filled and reconfigured without being hitched to a single person's identity. Over time, this reduces the reliance on rigid hierarchies and focuses everyone on the evolving needs of the work. Distributed, multilevel roles also disperse authority, helping to minimize fear and encourage broader ownership.

AT THE TEAM LEVEL

Separating roles from souls encourages collaboration and trust. Teams become less territorial about who "owns" a responsibility; they can shift or divide tasks with minimal drama and no existential angst. The focus moves from job titles and personal prestige to collective success and shared learning.

FOR INDIVIDUALS

Once you stop equating your role with your identity, you become more open to new responsibilities or shifts in scope. Feedback is easier to digest because it's no longer an indictment of your self-worth. This mindset also fosters resilience—when a role changes, you can adapt without losing your sense of self.

Role-Soul Distinction thrives in an environment rooted in DO NO HARM (6), where safety and respect are foundational. It aligns with EXPANDED AVAILABLE POWER (4) and DISTRIBUTED MANAGEMENT (14) to prevent any single role from becoming too closely tied to personal authority. The governance structures of CONSENT & CONSENSUS (10) and STRUCTURED DECISION-MAKING (30) make it easier to create, modify, or dissolve roles collaboratively, while ELECTIONS (15) and UPWARD REPRESENTATION (24) ensure that role changes reflect the voices of all levels. Emphasizing COOPERATION (12) and using ADVICE (31)

instead of hoarding decision-making fosters a healthy boundary between what a person does and who they are. When disagreements arise, CONFLICT AS A RE-SOURCE (38) and CONFLICT RESOLUTION (39) keep tensions constructive and separate from personal identity, aided by TRANSPARENCY (32) and LOGBOOK (57) so changes and conversations are openly documented.

9 Dissolvability

Permanence is a trap

Once a team, role, or process is established, it's normally treated as a permanent fixture—even if its purpose disappears. This rigidity stifles innovation, clogs up resources, and leaves people defending structures long past their relevance. By contrast, this pattern assumes all organizational constructs are temporary. They exist to solve a problem or seize an opportunity and should be reconfigured or dismantled as soon as they stop creating real value.

Some of today's most adaptive companies put this principle into action:

Basecamp structures product work in six-week cycles. Small, dedicated teams form around a specific project, then disband (or re-form around new goals) once that cycle ends. This prevents outliving a project's usefulness or tying people indefinitely to a single initiative.[32]

IDEO fields project-specific teams for each client challenge. Once a design problem is solved, the teams naturally dissolve and members shift to new engagements, preserving agility and preventing inertia.[33]

Netflix practices rapid prototyping and decommissioning of internal systems. Once a service no longer meets the needs of users, it is retired quickly, preventing bloat and unnecessary maintenance.[34]

By building "sunset clauses" into teams and roles from the start, you remove the emotional baggage around reassignments and dissolutions. People can freely commit themselves to a project or team, knowing that when it's time to move on, they won't be leaving anyone "high and dry"—it was designed that way.

THEREFORE...

Design everything with an expiration date. Make dissolving a team or role feel as natural as creating it, backed by clear policies for redeployment and upskilling. Balance this pattern with STRUCTURAL & PSYCHOLOGICAL SAFETY (3) so people understand they are secure even when a specific structure ceases to exist.

This pattern aligns with ROLE-SOUL DISTINCTION (8), recognizing that people aren't defined by any single position. When used alongside EXPANDED AVAILABLE POWER (4) and DISTRIBUTED MANAGEMENT (14), dissolvability helps prevent organizational calcification by keeping authority fluid. Finally, COOPERATION (12), ADVICE (31), and TRANSPARENCY (32) keep the process of dissolving structures open and collaborative, minimizing friction and maximizing learning for whatever comes next.

10 *Consent & Consensus*

Optimize for collective wisdom

Many organizations swing between two extremes in decision-making: imposing decisions from the top or insisting on unanimous agreement. Both approaches can undermine momentum and morale. Yet there is a more effective middle way. By treating consent ("I can live with this") and consensus ("I actively support this") as distinct but complementary standards, groups can learn to move swiftly on day-to-day issues while reserving deeper deliberation for strategic or mission-critical choices.[35]

When every decision requires consensus, teams risk getting stuck in endless debate. Minor operational matters become drawn-out controversies, leading to fatigue and watered-down compromises.[36] Conversely, if an organization defaults to mere consent for everything—even high-stakes initiatives—it won't build the strong collective ownership essential for successful implementation. Big moves that shape identity or values often require more robust alignment than "fine, whatever."

THEREFORE...

Use consent for operational decisions that are "safe enough to try," where the cost of a mistake is relatively low and learning by doing is valuable.[37] Consensus is best reserved for high-impact decisions that demand wholehearted endorsement—those that define culture, chart new strategic territory, or affect core principles that can't be easily reversed. Clear communication about which standard applies to each decision type is essential; it spares teams from guesswork and burnout, and it gives people confidence that their efforts will be supported.

Open-source projects tend to apply this pattern as a matter of course. At Wikipedia, policy changes affecting the entire encyclopedia typically go through extensive consensus building, while everyday content edits operate on a lightweight, consent-based model. The teams developing the Linux kernel have a similar pattern. Though known for having a "benevolent dictator" in Linus Torvalds,* major architectural shifts are generally agreed upon via consensus. Day-to-day patches, however, are accepted by trusted maintainers under a consent-like approach.

How to Apply

1. **Define the terms.** Make sure everyone understands that consent doesn't mean apathy and consensus doesn't mean unanimity at all costs. They each serve different purposes.
2. **Map the decisions.** Identify which topics generally need consent (e.g., routine budget allocations, day-to-day process tweaks) versus consensus (e.g., major strategic pivots, cultural values).
3. **Set clear criteria.** In consent-based decisions, you move forward unless someone has a substantive, reasoned objection. In consensus decisions, all participants must actively support the outcome.
4. **Encourage** TRANSPARENCY (32). If a decision is defined as needing consent, be explicit about why. If it's labeled a consensus issue, explain its significance. Clear, open communication prevents misunderstandings.

Consent and Consensus lays the foundation for healthy governance, enabling broader patterns like STRUCTURED DECISION-MAKING (30) to function smoothly. It works in tandem with DISTRIBUTED MANAGEMENT (14) and

---

* Allegedly, Torvalds still maintains the highest/ultimate authority for deciding what changes get committed to the kernel, but this is fairly hard to corroborate with public sources.

EXPANDED AVAILABLE POWER (4) by inviting multiple perspectives and clarifying when deeper agreement is needed. By distinguishing consent from consensus, teams enhance COOPERATION (12), employ ADVICE (31) more effectively, and defuse tension before it becomes conflict, feeding into CONFLICT AS A RESOURCE (38). It enables more (and higher-quality) CURIOSITY (5) when clear decision rules reassure people that asking disruptive questions won't stall momentum.

11 *Pace Layers*

Organizations contain multiple simultaneous realities

Insisting that tomorrow's urgent tasks and ten-year strategic bets march in lock-step is the fastest way to create organizational whiplash. This approach flies in the face of reality: Different kinds of work naturally move at different speeds. Some initiatives demand quick iteration and "fail fast" experimentation; others require long-term patience and deep reflection. By layering these time horizons instead of flattening them, organizations become both more stable and more innovative.

Building on Elliott Jaques's stratified systems theory and Stephen Drotter's leadership pipeline,[38] we can identify at least six layers operating in parallel, each with its own typical timeframe and value to the organization. Jaques's says work falls into six strata, each defined by the longest time span a person can responsibly own—from 90-day tasks to 20-year stewardship. Drotter mapped six matching passages of value creation, moving from delivering your own output to steering the whole enterprise. Stewart Brand, riffing on Frank Duffy and Brian Eno, framed six "pace layers" where the fast ones innovate and the slow ones stabilize. Stack those three lenses and a clear six-horizon model emerges, captured in the table on the next page.

1. 90 Days

Production & Execution. Deliver tangible results within short sprints or quarters.	Meeting defined specs, hitting near-term metrics, satisfying immediate customer needs.

2. 3–12 Months

People Management & Training. Coaching, monitoring performance, and setting day-to-day standards.	Translating top-level direction into concrete actions for teams, ensuring alignment and skill development.

3. 1–2 Years

Annual Operating Plans. Solving open-ended problems, exploring user challenges, and moving key metrics.	Connecting the tactical world to broader capability building and bridging short-term tasks with medium-range goals.

4. 2–5 Years

Functions & Capabilities as Sources of Advantage. Creating cross-functional solutions and designing robust systems.	Enhancing structural capacity (e.g., better processes, tools, or platforms) that support long-term differentiation.

5. 5–10 Years

Business Unit Strategy & Operating Model. Shape market positioning, run strategic experiments, and define new sources of revenue or impact.	Aligning structural capabilities with broader enterprise direction and laying the groundwork for future expansions.

6. 10–20 Years

Corporate Mission & Values. Setting purpose, culture, and entrepreneurial bets that can outlast current market trends.	Establishing the organization's identity, vision, and guiding principles.

Each layer depends on the others. Fast layers (e.g., daily production) feed learning upward, while slower layers (mission, culture) provide coherence and resilience.[39] Problems arise when an organization forces all layers into the same cadence or tries to govern them using a one-size-fits-all model.

THEREFORE...

Design each organizational layer to operate at its natural pace and link them in ways that preserve both agility and stability. For instance:

- Toyota marries stable long-term production methods with frequent continuous-improvement cycles, ensuring that process innovation doesn't undermine core manufacturing principles.[40]
- Amazon encourages rapid frontline experiments in product teams while maintaining steadfast cultural "Leadership Principles" that shape the company's identity over decades.[41]
- Academic institutions honor centuries of tradition but also invest in new research, letting core values and purpose endure while short-term initiatives push the boundaries of knowledge.*

By explicitly acknowledging these pace layers, organizations can tailor governance, decision-making, and incentives to each time horizon. Fast layers (e.g., 90-day sprints) support agile tactics and continuous learning, while slow layers (mission and culture) provide coherence and resilience. This layered understanding of power ensures no single approach stifles creativity or erodes what's essential for long-term success.[†]

Pace Layers is a useful design tool for DOMAINS, ASSETS & STANDARDS (23) and PURPOSE, CUSTOMER, PLATFORM (16) by clarifying which layers steward which resources over various timescales, while STRUCTURED DECISION-MAKING (30) ensures each layer addresses decisions most suited to its horizon. In the faster layers, EXPERIMENTATION (62) thrives on rapid learning cycles. All layers benefit from CADENCE (65) and RETROSPECTIVES (66) to maintain long-term alignment and cultural stability. This multispeed design also echoes TEAM/PROCESS AS PRODUCT (63), enabling teams to iterate at the right pace for their domain without losing sight of deeper organizational goals and identity.

---

* Hello there, academic! You probably disagree with this point, and you're probably right. But it should be this way, shouldn't it?

† I've combined all of this thinking with a much more specific application here: https://www.cpj
.fyi/pace-layers-for-organization.

12 *Cooperation*

Cooperation is contrasted with discord; but is also distinguished from harmony. Cooperation, as compared to harmony, requires active attempts to adjust policies to meet the demands of others. That is, not only does it depend on shared interests, but it emerges from a pattern of discord or potential discord. Without discord, there would be no cooperation, only harmony.

—Robert O. Keohane, *After Hegemony*

Tension precedes alignment

Stop confusing cooperation with docile agreement. In modern organizations, interdependence is everywhere—teams share resources, overlap priorities, and rub against each other's goals. That friction is exactly where cooperation is born.[42] The moment we try to erase all discord, we also erase the creative spark and deeper alignment that real cooperation demands.

At Bridgewater Associates, this dynamic is explicit: "Thoughtful disagreement" is a mandatory part of maintaining good standing with the organization. By insisting that people voice competing viewpoints, the firm uses friction for insights instead of burying it in polite silence.[43] Similarly, at Valve, where teams self-organize around new game projects, daily negotiation is the norm; each employee's interests don't vanish, they just meet in the open for honest debate.[44]

THEREFORE ...

Build dynamic cooperation with three key moves:

1. **Acknowledge discord.** Safely and openly reveal diverging perspectives; don't wish them away. Productive friction creates better decisions and surfaces blind spots.
2. **Establish mechanisms for alignment.** Create forums and frameworks to guide debates toward actionable policy adjustments. This means structured negotiations, not hand-waving.
3. **Train for "cooperative tension."** Equip leaders and teams to live in the tension between self-interest and shared goals, forging solutions stronger than either side's initial stance.

Cooperation thrives when STRUCTURAL & PSYCHOLOGICAL SAFETY (3) and DO NO HARM (6) give people room to voice tough truths, while CURIOSITY (5), CONFLICT AS A RESOURCE (38), and CONFLICT RESOLUTION (39) provide a road map for turning friction into alignment. When combined with TRANSPARENCY (32) and LOGBOOK (57), teams can trace how tensions get resolved and learn from each conflict, ultimately fueling the ongoing, adaptive cycles highlighted by RETROSPECTIVES (66).

STRUCTURING

13 *Network of Teams*

Hierarchies are dead, but networks need structure

In 2010, a catastrophic explosion ripped through BP's *Deepwater Horizon* oil rig, killing 11 workers and triggering what is widely regarded as the largest accidental marine oil spill in history.[1] Subsequent investigations revealed a confluence of technical failures—including problems with the blowout preventer and cement work.[2] Multiple reports also highlighted critical safety warnings that did not receive sufficient attention at senior levels; organizational silos and communication breakdowns contributed to a failure to act on these warnings.[3]

This tragedy illustrates the flaw in traditional organizational hierarchies. Designed for stable, predictable environments, these structures can fragment information as it moves up the chain, distorting reality with each layer it passes through.[4] By the time insights reach decision-makers, they may be sanitized, delayed, or lost entirely. Meanwhile, frontline workers—those closest to customers and operations—spend more energy satisfying bosses than solving real problems.[5]

Yet organizations that simply declare "we're flat now" or remove management layers without creating alternative structures often find themselves in equally dangerous territory.* Decisions stall as no one knows who can make the call. Information scatters across disconnected teams. Hidden power dynamics grow more toxic than formal hierarchies.

---

* Flattening one level of an organization actually increases the concentration of power at the next level up, rather than distributing authority as advertised.

THEREFORE...

Design the organization as a network of teams that connects autonomous but interdependent units around actual value creation. Unlike a traditional hierarchy organized by function or division, a network organizes teams end to end around customer journeys, products, or services—with explicit protocols for how they interact.

As a general example, imagine a large, traditional bank reorganizing its operations using this approach. Rather than structuring around traditional banking products or functions (loans, deposits, know your customer), they could organize into customer journey teams—"onboarding," "everyday banking," "lending"—each with all the skills needed to deliver their part of the customer experience. These teams could connect through explicit interfaces rather than managerial layers. In other similar situations, teams organizing in this way have reduced product development cycles from 18–24 months to less than five weeks.

A well-designed Network of Teams delivers immediate benefits in speed, innovation, and engagement. Teams can respond to customer needs without waiting for multiple approvals. Information flows directly to where it's needed rather than through distorting hierarchical filters. People feel greater ownership and purpose when they see how their work directly contributes to outcomes.

The long-term benefit is resilience: Networks reconfigure easily and readily as conditions change. Teams can form, merge, split, or dissolve based on emerging needs rather than through disruptive reorganizations.

You can apply this pattern in three phases: network design, network infrastructure, and network implementation. Consider testing this in a discrete area of the organization before expanding it to the broader whole.

1. NETWORK DESIGN

Network design goes beyond the sticks and boxes of an org chart. Effective teams in a network structure require thoughtful boundaries and interfaces that enable autonomy and coordination across the organization. Teams should be designed with clear ownership, direct connections to other teams, and transparent work processes.

Network Design Principle

- **Purposeful:** Design the teams around complete chunks of value delivery, following the PURPOSE, CUSTOMER, PLATFORM (16) pattern. Each team should own a discrete DOMAIN (23) with clear customer-facing outcomes.
  - At Spotify, each *squad* owns a specific aspect of the user experience (e.g., search functionality, playlist management, artist pages), with all the skills needed to deliver that feature from concept to production.[6]
- **Connected:** Enable teams to interact laterally without managerial intermediaries. Establish clear protocols for cross-team collaboration using CONSENT & CONSENSUS (10) and STRUCTURED DECISION-MAKING (30).
  - Morning Star creates explicit COLLEAGUE LETTERS OF UNDERSTANDING (40) documenting how teams will interact, enabling coordination without traditional management.[7]
- **Legible:** Make work and dependencies transparent across team boundaries using WORK IN PUBLIC (50) and visualizing workflows through KANBAN (55).
  - Are.na has a public road map for its product, hosted on its website, for customers and backers to see and review.[8]

2. NETWORK INFRASTRUCTURE

Beyond individual teams, a network requires supporting infrastructure that enables coordinated action without hierarchical control. This infrastructure creates the conditions for autonomous teams to align their efforts toward common goals while sharing knowledge across boundaries.

Infrastructure Element

- **Shared Purpose & Principles:** Teams' purposes will be informed and constrained by TRUE PURPOSE (1) and RULE OF LAW (2) holding the network together, providing alignment without control.
  - W.L. Gore & Associates unites its network with four simple principles that guide all decisions: freedom, fairness, commitment, and waterline (don't sink the ship).[9]

- **Good Boundaries:** Create explicit agreements about where one team's responsibility ends and another's begins using DOMAINS, ASSETS & STANDARDS (23) and BOUNDARY MANAGEMENT (67).
  - Amazon uses APIs between teams that clearly specify what each team provides to others and what they can expect in return.[10]
- **Cross-Network Learning:** Establish forums for knowledge sharing across the network through GUILDS (21), CHAPTERS (22), and regular RETROSPECTIVES (66).
  - Valve Corporation uses temporary interest groups to share learning and solve crosscutting problems without creating permanent hierarchical structures.[11]

3. NETWORK IMPLEMENTATION

Moving from concept to reality requires a deliberate, step-by-step approach that works through both structural and cultural change. To transform your organization into a Network of Teams:

Network Implementation Phase

1. Map value flows: Start by tracking how work actually moves through your organization to deliver customer value. Ignore official org charts and focus on real activity flows.

- Map the end-to-end journey of your products or services from conception to customer.
- Identify key handoffs, bottlenecks, and broken connections.
- Note where current reporting lines help or hinder this flow.

A large hospitality company mapped its guest experience journey from booking to checkout, discovering that 32 separate systems and nine departments touched a single reservation. Despite having an official five-step process, frontline staff used 17 unofficial workarounds to meet guest needs promptly. Room maintenance requests averaged 26 hours for resolution due to handoffs between departments, though guests expected fixes within four hours.

2. Design team boundaries: Create teams with end-to-end responsibility for discrete value streams, perhaps guided by the PURPOSE, CUSTOMER, PLATFORM (16) model.

- Purpose teams: Organized around specific customer needs or journeys
- Customer teams: Focused on distinct market segments or user types
- Platform teams: Providing services and capabilities that support multiple teams

For each team, clearly define:

- The specific outcomes they own
- Their scope of authority (what decisions they can make autonomously)
- The resources and capabilities they need to deliver their outcomes

The company reorganized from traditional departments (housekeeping, front desk, food service) into journey-based teams responsible for complete guest experiences. They created arrival & welcome teams, stay-experience teams, and departure & return teams, each with staff from multiple disciplines empowered to resolve issues without escalation. Each property also established a small special-requests team with expertise in handling unusual situations.

3. Design interfaces: Make the connections between teams explicit and efficient.

- Create service agreements that clearly state what each team provides to others.
- Establish communication protocols (when teams sync, how they share updates).
- Define escalation paths for conflicts or dependencies.
- Build shared visibility systems so teams can see each other's work.

They developed service agreements between teams that clearly specified hand-offs and responsibilities. For example, the stay-experience and departure teams created explicit protocols for how guest checkout information would transition, including timing, data sharing, and exception handling. They implemented a digital guest journey board visible to all teams showing real-time status of all guests, enabling teams to coordinate without constant meetings.

4. Build network capabilities: Invest in developing the skills needed to operate in a network.

- Train teams in conflict resolution and negotiation.
- Develop EMERGENT LEADERSHIP (58) across the organization.
- Teach effective meeting facilitation using FACILITATION (56).
- Build capability in giving and receiving ADVICE (31).

Before fully implementing the network structure, the company ran decision simulations where teams practiced handling guest scenarios that crossed traditional boundaries. They created a network playbook with common terminology and protocols for cross-team collaboration. Every employee completed a workshop on collaborative problem-solving focusing on how to navigate situations without escalating to managers. They started with low-season pilot properties to refine their approach before rolling out company-wide.

5. Create feedback mechanisms: Establish ways to continuously evolve the network.

- Regular HEALTH CHECK (59) processes to assess network effectiveness
- Cross-team RETROSPECTIVES (66) to identify improvement opportunities
- Periodic network mapping to spot emerging bottlenecks or gaps
- DISSOLVABILITY (9) protocols to reconfigure teams as needs change

The hospitality company implemented experience retrospectives where representatives from all teams reviewed the complete guest journey data weekly, identifying improvement opportunities across team boundaries. They created shared metrics focused on guest outcomes rather than departmental KPIs. Then, they established a quarterly network evolution process whereby teams could propose boundary adjustments based on guest feedback and operational data.

DEALING WITH PUSHBACK

Resistance to this approach comes in a few forms:

"This will create chaos without clear reporting lines."
Network structures actually reduce chaos by making coordination explicit rather than dependent on hierarchical authority. Traditional reporting lines often mask underlying confusion about who decides what. Establish clear decision protocols through STRUCTURED DECISION-MAKING (30) and build capability in CONFLICT RESOLUTION (39).

"We'll lose economies of scale without Centers of Excellence."
Shared services and capabilities can still exist as PLATFORM TEAMS (17) that support multiple value streams. These teams maintain specialized expertise while connecting directly to customer-facing teams instead of operating as isolated silos.

"Leaders won't give up control."
Control isn't going away. It's being redistributed to where it's most effective, and we are gaining more ways to adjust as we learn. Use EXPANDED AVAILABLE POWER (4) principles and begin with pilot teams to demonstrate success before scaling.

14 *Distributed Management*

Control is an illusion

Modern management has become an impossible job. A single person is expected to simultaneously be a visionary, technical expert, coach, conflict mediator, resource allocator, bureaucrat, and politician.[12] The span of control for the average manager has expanded from seven direct reports in the 1980s to over eleven today,* while the complexity of work has increased exponentially. The result of that flattening is a management bottleneck that slows organizations to a crawl, burns out managers, reduces decision quality, and disengages teams while they watch their work and careers stall.

The data tell the story. In Microsoft's global Work Trend Index, 64% of workers say they struggle with the time and energy to do their jobs, and 68% say they lack uninterrupted focus time during the workday.[13] A McKinsey survey of 1,200 managers found fewer than half say decisions are timely, and 61% say at least half of the time spent making decisions is ineffective; they estimate this wastes ~530,000 manager-days/year—about $250M in wages—at a typical Fortune 500 company.[14] Burnout is widespread: 53% of managers reported being burned out in Microsoft's 2022 Work Trend Index pulse.[15] The financial stakes are huge: Gallup estimates low engagement costs the global economy ~$8.9 trillion annually (≈9% of global GDP).[16]

---

* In 1980, the U.S. Government Accountability Office (then called the *General Accounting* Office) reported supervisor-to-nonsupervisor ratios of about 1:7.4 in the US federal government and 1:5.9 in comparable private-sector industries—i.e., roughly six to seven direct reports per supervisor. A generation later, Deloitte's *Global Human Capital Trends* 2016 found managers average ~9.7 direct reports, rising to ~11.4 at large companies. The measures aren't identical (ratio vs. counted direct reports; different sectors and levels), but together they draw a clear picture of the situation.

This isn't the individual manager's fault, though. I'd invite you to see this as a structural problem: The traditional hub-and-spoke management model where all authority, information, and decisions flow through a single person simply cannot scale to meet modern organizational complexity. Even more flattening will only make the problem worse.

THEREFORE...

Distribute management tasks by breaking the manager role into the *actual work* that we're referring to when we think of what great managers do. Duties like getting things done, negotiation, assignments, vision setting, coaching, and development. One person *might* be able to do it all equally well, but this is vanishingly rare. Then, working with the team—perhaps after a FUTURE BACKWARD (42) session—capture the tasks that the team *needs* to achieve its ambition. Write those down in your TEAM CHARTER (43), LOGBOOK (57), or COLLEAGUE LETTER OF UNDER-STANDING (40). Assign them to the right person, perhaps using ELECTIONS (15).

"MANAGEMENT" TASKS[17]

Getting Things Done	Negotiation	Assignments	Vision Setting	Coaching	Development
Process design	Balancing work between teams	Assigning	Goal setting	Guiding	Teaching
Logistics	Connecting across teams	Supervising	Motivating	Mentoring	Championing
Organizing	Shielding teams	Driving	Strategizing	Role modeling	Sponsoring people
Monitoring	Convincing other leaders	Assessing		Coaching	Advancing careers
Facilitating		Approving			Advocating for causes

Now all the important work that a single manager *may or may not do especially well* is in the hands of the right person.

Standard agile roles in software development are a time-tested example of how this works in practice. Agile frameworks distribute management roles like "scrum master" (that is, a *lowercase-f* facilitator) and "product owner" (that is, a *lowercase-p* prioritizer), ensuring that leadership is not concentrated in a single manager but shared based on responsibilities.

Netflix goes further, with a Freedom and Responsibility model that enshrines a *limited* set of responsibilities for managers. While managers at Netflix set direction, team members have significant autonomy to make decisions and allocate resources within that framework—giving Netflix managers more time to be truly great at setting direction.[18]

Organizations that embrace Distributed Management become more adaptable and resilient. By spreading management tasks across the team, they avoid bottlenecks, reduce burnout, and ensure critical decisions are made closer to the action. Team members feel more engaged, as they have a direct role in shaping their work and their team's success. At the same time, this model builds a deeper bench of EMERGENT LEADERSHIP (58), as more people gain experience in management roles.

15 *Elections*

Power should flow from choice, not chance or charm

The executive team sat around the conference table, debating who should lead the new digital transformation initiative.

"I think Sarah would be great," said the CEO. "She's got the technical background."

"But her team is already stretched thin," countered the COO. "Marcus? He's been pushing for this for months."

"Marcus doesn't have the relationships with the regional offices," the CFO pointed out. "Maybe Ava?"

"Ava's too junior," someone muttered.

Meanwhile, down the hall, the people who would actually implement the initiative—engineers, designers, data analysts—continued their work, completely unaware that their fate was being decided behind closed doors. When the announcement eventually came, surprise would give way to confusion, then to resignation: another top-down decision they'd have to make work, somehow.

This scenario plays out constantly. Critical leadership roles are filled through backroom discussions, "gut feelings," or worst of all, the path of least resistance. This anti-pattern is the source of *so many problems*, not least of which is the maintenance of bias and homogeneity—to say nothing of employee disengagement and squandered skills.

Why not try something new?

THEREFORE ...

Try a form of STRUCTURED DECISION-MAKING (30) tuned specifically for assigning people to roles. The most radical option would be to allow everyone in the company to *vote with their feet* by assigning themselves to projects, as Valve (makers of *Half-Life* and Steam) does.[19] Or you could do as W.L. Gore & Associates (makers of Gore-Tex) has done for decades: peer selection of leaders. Their "sponsor" roles—internal mentors who guide associates' development—are filled not through HR assignments but by associates nominating colleagues they trust to support their growth.[20]

If applied to every role described in every TEAM CHARTER (43)—that is, not just *some* roles—this pattern would build ACTIVE STEERING (27) and EMERGENT LEADERSHIP (58) into the core of the organization.[21]

The process described below comes from sociocracy, and it works.[22]

PROCESS

This process provides a structured facilitation method for gathering collective wisdom with *minimal* preparation. The process has six key steps, and *none of the steps involve traditional, majority-rule ballot-style voting.* Feel free to adjust the process after you become familiar, but the first time you try it, try to stick to the plan.

For all of the below, consider using ROUNDS (48) to surface the most wisdom possible.

Step 1: Present and Nominate

- Share a clear role description focusing on outcomes rather than tasks.
- Collect nominations silently and anonymously to prevent anchoring.
- Display all nominations where everyone can see them.
- Ensure each nomination is tagged with the nominator's name.

Step 2: Illuminate

- Guide each participant to share only positive reasons for their nomination.
- Prevent interruptions or questions during this phase.

- Allow passes but return to those who initially pass.
- Take light notes to aid in final synthesis.

Step 3: Share ADVICE (31)

- Open space for additional context about nominees.
- Welcome constructive concerns about nominations.
- Maintain a round-robin format without interruption.
- Keep focus on business impact rather than personal preference.

Step 4: Enable Changes

- Ask each participant if they want to change their nomination based on new information.
- Capture changes in real time and record reasons.
- Allow natural convergence but watch for social pressure.
- Celebrate the learning that leads to changed perspectives.

Step 5: Synthesize and Select

- The facilitator summarizes key arguments and patterns.
- Make a clear recommendation based on the strongest arguments presented.
- Deliver the decision with confidence and clear rationale.
- Connect the selection explicitly to the role requirements.

Step 6: Seek CONSENT (10) (Optional)

- Ask for objections to the selection.
- Create space for concerns to surface.
- Look for nonverbal cues of disagreement.
- Address objections through timeboxing or counterproposals.

TIME MANAGEMENT

Per role, budget baseline 15 minutes plus 5 minutes per participant: For a team of seven, plan for approximately 50 minutes. Add 10–15 minutes of extra time if the group has never done this *specific* process before.

LOGISTICS

Select appropriate tools for gathering nominations (email/private messaging for remote teams, paper/Post-its for in-person). Ensure videoconferencing capability for remote participants. Prepare a shared display method for nominations (digital document or physical board).

CONSIDERATIONS FOR REMOTE TEAMS

Use collaborative documents (like Google Docs or Miro) for real-time nomination tracking. Ensure all participants have video capability when possible to catch non-verbal cues. Consider gathering nominations through a survey before synchronous discussion.

CONSIDERATIONS FOR LARGE GROUPS

While this is an ideal process for LEAN TEAMS (19), it can scale to teams of teams and even whole organizations with some modifications. Gather nominations and rationales via survey before live discussion. Circulate a compilation of nominations and rationales in advance. Focus live session on information gathering and change rounds.

CONSIDERATIONS FOR NEW TEAMS

Have a positional leader facilitate initial elections until the process is familiar. Spend extra time explaining each step and rationale. Document process and outcomes carefully in a LOGBOOK (57). Plan for shorter election cycles, with a LENGTH LIMIT (64) of around three to six months to build confidence in the process.

DEALING WITH PUSHBACK

Resistance to this way of filling roles comes in a few forms:

"This is too time-consuming."
It only feels time-consuming because it is especially focused. If you were to add up all the hours most organizations spend on assignments, I'd bet that ~50 minutes is *much shorter* than "normal," and it comes with many benefits that "normal" doesn't offer.

"What if we elect the wrong person?"
Use a shorter LENGTH LIMIT (64) and reelect with new data. More broadly, this kind of pushback opens up a line of introspection for the organization around the question: "What conditions do we have in place that would lead us to elect the wrong person?" Perhaps a top-level RETROSPECTIVE (66) could help resolve the issue. Or, if you want to *go big*, use OPEN SPACE TECHNOLOGY (41) with an invitation focused on this topic.

Elections relies on the safety net provided by STRUCTURAL & PSYCHOLOGICAL SAFETY (3); otherwise, the pattern is likely to preserve existing power structures rather than opening new doors. For example, a NETWORK OF TEAMS (13) creates an easier flow of talent to opportunity.

16 *Purpose, Customer, Platform*

Why we exist,
Who we serve,
How we scale

The quarterly review meeting was tense. Marketing blamed engineering for not implementing features fast enough. Engineering blamed product development for changing priorities too often. Product blamed sales for making unrealistic promises. Meanwhile, HR, finance, and legal sat on the sidelines, throwing up occasional roadblocks when initiatives threatened their policies or budgets.

Lost in the drama was any mention of the customer, to say nothing for shared purpose. The company's functional design*—each with its own goals, metrics, and incentives—optimized for individual departmental capability rather than customer outcomes.

This situation is so common, so normalized, that it's *boring*. Traditional structures arranged by function (marketing, sales, engineering), geography, or division create artificial barriers between people who should be collaborating. Teams focus on pleasing their bosses rather than serving a true business outcome. Support functions become gatekeepers rather than enablers.

---

* This happens in divisional orgs, too, but at a smaller, easier-to-manage scale.

THEREFORE…

Structure your organization in three distinct layers, designed in a specific sequence from purpose outward, creating a hierarchy of service rather than control.*

PURPOSE LAYER: WHY WE EXIST

The foundation begins with dedicated teams organized directly around fulfilling your TRUE PURPOSE (1). These purpose-aligned teams focus on the fundamental reason your organization exists beyond profit. They translate your *reason for being* into concrete initiatives, maintain alignment as conditions change, and ensure the voice of purpose remains present in key decisions.

Large Pharmaceutical Company *Purpose: Advance human health through accessible, innovative medicine*	Midsize Consumer Technology Company *Purpose: Create intuitive technology that enhances everyday life*	Regional Restaurant Chain *Purpose: Cultivate community through memorable dining experiences and local flavors*
Patient Outcomes: Drive treatment solutions that measurably improve quality of life	**Digital Well-Being:** Design technology that promotes healthy relationships with devices	**Food Heritage:** Preserve regional culinary traditions while creating contemporary experiences
Healthcare Access: Expand medicine availability to underserved populations worldwide	**Inclusive Design:** Build products that work for people of all abilities and backgrounds	**Community Connection:** Transform restaurants into meaningful gathering spaces for locals
Medical Innovation: Accelerate the translation of scientific discoveries into treatments	**Sustainable Tech:** Develop products with minimal environmental impact throughout life cycle	**Food Sustainability:** Pioneer practices that reduce waste and support local agriculture

---

* A version of this pattern is expressed in Niels Pflaeging and Silke Hermann's "Cell Structure Design," where they design organizations from the sphere of activity (the customer), to the periphery (customer-serving teams), to the center (teams serving the periphery): https://www.redforty2.com/cellstructuredesign.

A note here: The org has its own, unifying purpose. Each team will have a purpose. There will be some teams that are part of this purpose layer. Applying all these patterns at once will mean you're saying "purpose" a lot. This is a feature, not a bug.

CUSTOMER LAYER: WHO WE SERVE

Once purpose is established, organize primary teams around distinct customer segments, journeys, or needs. These teams should have end-to-end responsibility for their designated customers, with the authority and resources to deliver complete solutions.

Large Pharmaceutical Company	Midsize Consumer Technology Company	Regional Restaurant Chain
Chronic Care: Develop integrated solutions for patients managing lifelong conditions	**Family Tech:** Create products that strengthen connections between family members	**Weeknight Diners:** Provide quick, satisfying meals for busy professionals seeking convenience
Pediatric Health: Address unique medication needs of children and adolescents	**Creative Professionals:** Build tools that expand creative capabilities for designers and artists	**Celebration Groups:** Craft memorable dining experiences for special occasions and gatherings
Senior Wellness: Deliver age-appropriate health solutions for older adults	**Small Business:** Develop accessible technology solutions for entrepreneurs and startups	**Health-Conscious Eaters:** Create nutritious menu options without sacrificing flavor
Emergency Medicine: Supply critical treatments for acute care settings	**Remote Workers:** Solve productivity and connection challenges for distributed teams	**Weekend Brunchers:** Provide relaxed, social dining experiences for weekend leisure

PLATFORM LAYER: HOW WE SCALE

Position enabling functions (HR, finance, IT, etc.) as service platforms that support the customer-facing teams. These platform teams should measure their success by how well they enable other teams to serve customers and fulfill the organization's purpose. Read more on this in PLATFORM TEAMS (17).

Large Pharmaceutical Company	Midsize Consumer Technology Company	Regional Restaurant Chain
Clinical Data: Build systems that transform medical data into actionable insights	**Developer Experience:** Create frameworks that enable rapid, reliable product development	**Kitchen Operations:** Design efficient systems that deliver consistent quality at scale
Regulatory Navigation: Streamline compliance processes while maintaining safety standards	**Customer Insights:** Transform user feedback into continuous product improvements	**Staff Development:** Build training programs that create exceptional culinary and service teams
Manufacturing Excellence: Ensure reliable, high-quality medicine production at scale	**Infrastructure Reliability:** Maintain systems that customers can depend on 24/7	**Supply Chain:** Source ingredients that meet quality standards while supporting local producers
Research Accelerator: Provide tools and processes that accelerate scientific discovery	**Security & Privacy:** Protect user data while enabling valuable personalized experiences	**Digital Experience:** Create ordering and loyalty systems that enhance the dining experience

DESIGN IN SEQUENCE

Always start by establishing purpose teams, then organize customer teams around specific segments, and finally create platform teams to support the other layers. This sequence ensures that supporting functions serve customer needs rather than imposing constraints.

Purpose, Customer, Platform supports and is supported by NETWORK OF TEAMS (13), unlocks DISTRIBUTED MANAGEMENT (14) by organizing around value creation rather than control, and makes DOMAINS, ASSETS & STANDARDS (23) clearer by aligning them with customer needs.

This pattern creates the conditions for SELF-MANAGED TEAMS (18) to thrive within clear boundaries. It reinforces TRUE PURPOSE (1) by making it the explicit foundation of organizational design. It allows PLATFORM TEAMS (17) to grow out of their roots as control functions.

17 Platform Teams

Essential, but unloved

Corporate Functions—such as HR, finance, legal, and marketing—tend to operate as back offices designed to support the core business. As a result, they're treated as *cost centers*, which leads them to focus on compliance and efficiency (e.g., "Please follow our centrally mandated rules") rather than innovation or impact (e.g., "How can we make you more effective?").[23]

As a result, these teams tend to be bottlenecks in the flow of business. Teams seeking support face cumbersome processes, slow response times, and rigid, one-size-fits-all solutions.

This disconnect between service providers and their internal customers gets in the way of progress. It's frustrating. It's disengaging. And it creates a downward spiral: poor service → pressure to cut costs → limited investment in innovation → even less effective and less valuable services. In the end, an organization is left with a grab bag of hollowed-out compliance teams.

While this model obviously works to a certain extent,* it's possible for these units to evolve into more dynamic, responsive, and scalable support systems.[24]

---

* Look, who's kidding who here? I'd imagine that this anti-pattern has existed as long as companies have existed—and companies are still around. It just doesn't have to be this way.

THEREFORE ...

Reframe these services as platform teams. These teams can deliver their value as if they were independent businesses, offering products and services to other teams across the organization. To reduce the transaction costs to a minimum, these services should operate similarly to an application programming interface (API): They should be modular, accessible, and designed to scale. Inside the teams, the mindset should be similar to that of a startup, with a focus on continuous improvement of their offerings and a radical focus on internal customers. Digital theorist David Weinberger calls this logic "library as platform": Open every service and dataset so others can build on top, and the platform's value compounds with every use.[25]

If a central service cannot or will not operate in this way, the organization should seriously consider divesting that function to an external partner that specializes in delivering such services. The result is a leaner, more focused organization where every function directly creates value.

CHANGE PEOPLE OR CHANGE PEOPLE

Platform Teams are a fundamental redesign of *how* central functions operate. This begins with reframing their role within the organization—from *passive supporters* or rulebook thumpers to active enablers of growth, of innovation, of employee engagement.

Let's try on some examples.

HR leaders might stop managing compliance and payroll in isolation and instead offer their services through a suite of platforms that allow managers to hire, onboard, and develop employees autonomously. Finance might build tools that enable teams to track budgets and forecast spending in real time, eliminating the need for endless back-and-forth approvals. Legal and risk departments might offer standardized templates or contract-building tools that empower teams to manage low-risk agreements independently.

This shift requires investing in technologies that make services more discoverable and easier to use. It also requires building a customer-focused culture within central services. Teams should be empowered (and pushed!) to gather feedback, measure satisfaction with a METRICS REVIEW (36), and practice ITERATIVE SHIPPING (46) to improve their offerings.

NOT JUST INTERNAL CUSTOMERS

This approach also creates opportunities for central services to eventually become profit centers by offering their expertise and tools to external customers. Once the internal work is running well, these teams might package their capabilities and sell them as standalone products or services. By doing so, they not only diversify revenue streams but also cultivate a spirit of innovation within the team that drives EXPERIMENTATION (62).* The more these Platform Teams prove their value externally, the more likely they are to be seen internally as essential partners rather than overhead costs. *We've reversed the downward spiral.*

A few organizations have already followed such paths. For instance, Amazon Web Services (AWS) was originally an internal infrastructure group, designed to scale and improve continually. Over time, it became a standalone business unit, offering services externally and revolutionizing the cloud services landscape. It's now a multibillion-dollar business. Outside of AWS, you might think of Stripe as a set of Platform Teams turned into a business.

---

* Once upon a time, I toyed with a "simple rule" for organizing that went something like this: "Every team has to have a customer." I still feel like that might be the most interesting single idea in this book. When you have a real, paying customer, *everything* changes. You've got to be economical. Your budget becomes a P&L. You do more with less.

	Center of Excellence	Platform Team
Shared Ideas	Thought leadership; skill-building home for critical capabilities	
Unique Attributes	• Best practices and measurement • Consultants and execution partners to operating units—accelerate delivery of critical practices • Work toward being the best in their subject matter expertise	• Building tools that internal teams need to do their jobs • Driving usage of, onboarding to, and ensuring teams' success with tools • Improving and iterating on tools with feedback from users • Building a backlog based on user needs
Rationale	• Expertise that is difficult or expensive to replicate • Execute core programs and processes • Assure focus on the most critical capabilities • Help build one culture through best practice	• Build shared practice through shared tools • Put execution closer to commercial objective and reporting lines • Use technology, instead of hours or effort, as a point of leverage • Self-serve model that supports many cultures

Platform Teams are possible when many of the preceding patterns are in place. And they make many of the other challenging patterns for internal teams possible: DO-MAINS, ASSETS & STANDARDS (23), DO THE RIGHT THING (26), and DEMOS (35) can feel like management theater without a clear sense of a customer. Platform Teams will also enjoy more FLOW STATE WORK (61) and will find it easier to WORK IN PUBLIC (50).

18 *Self-Managed Teams*

Liberating structure

Traditional management hierarchies emerged in an era when information flowed slowly and decision-making needed to be centralized for efficiency.* Today's world demands something different: Organizations face rapidly shifting markets, distributed knowledge, and unprecedented complexity. The old model of managers directing work and making all key decisions creates bottlenecks and fails to tap into the full potential and intelligence of teams.

You'll feel the need for this pattern when teams become passive and risk averse, waiting for permission instead of taking initiative. When innovation stalls as good ideas get stuck in approval chains. When engagement drops as capable people feel infantilized by excessive oversight. When resources are wasted on coordination and control instead of value creation.

It's not just that the old way is worse.

We also deserve something better. A new generation of workers seeks TRUE PURPOSE (1) and autonomy in their work, not just direction from above. They bring skills, insights, and capabilities that often exceed those of their managers in specialized areas. So how can organizations use this distributed expertise while maintaining coherence and alignment?

---

* If you look at some of the earliest org charts, you'll notice that they look eerily similar to the ones we use today. The main difference is that it would have been implausible to assume that teams would be able to self-direct their activities, using data they gather from their customers, without suboptimizing for the rest of the business. But that's just not the case today. We have the internet.

Deleting *management* isn't the answer. DISTRIBUTED MANAGEMENT (14) solves for more participation in management tasks, and EMERGENT LEADERSHIP (58) recognizes that everyone must have a chance to lead. We can go a step further by embedding these ideas in our structure.

THEREFORE...

Use the related patterns in this book to move teams from A to B on Richard Hackman's "authority matrix." Hackman, a Harvard organizational psychologist, introduced this framework in *Leading Teams* to map how responsibility shifts from managers to teams across four key capabilities.[26]

	Manager-Led Teams	Self-Managing Teams	Self-Designing Teams	Self-Governing Teams
Setting Overall Direction				D
Designing the Team and Its Organizational Context			C	
Monitoring and Managing Work Process & Progress		B		
Executing Team Tasks	A			

This is a straightforward shift that can be done with or without the other structural patterns we've described; your organization doesn't need to become a NETWORK OF TEAMS (13) or use GUILDS (21) and CHAPTERS (22), though these will make life easier.

MOVING FROM A (MANAGER-LED) TO B (SELF-MANAGING)

To shift your team from manager-led to genuinely self-managing, start by clarifying the team's TRUE PURPOSE (1) and connect this to a shared understanding of how their work will be assessed, using OBJECTIVES & KEY RESULTS (28). EXPAND AVAILABLE POWER (4) by delegating authority on key decisions to individual roles on the team—and don't backtrack when things get challenging. Codify what you've delegated in a LOGBOOK (57) or TEAM CHARTER (43). This will be easier for everyone involved if the team commits to WORK IN PUBLIC (50); leaders will feel more confident giving away authority if the work is visible.

MOVING FROM B (SELF-MANAGING) TO C (SELF-DESIGNING)

When your team consistently manages its own daily processes effectively, you might consider helping them transition toward becoming self-designing. This means handing over the power to adjust their internal structure, roles, and membership. Begin by adopting COLLEAGUE LETTERS OF UNDERSTANDING (40) to establish clear expectations and boundaries between roles. Encourage DISTRIBUTED MANAGEMENT (14) so managerial responsibilities naturally shift to team members. Employ ELECTIONS (15) to place individuals into roles. Provide training in CONFLICT RESOLUTION (39) and STRUCTURED DECISION-MAKING (30) to ensure that the team can productively handle structural decisions without intervention from above.

MOVING FROM C (SELF-DESIGNING)
TO D (SELF-GOVERNING)

Finally, moving from self-designing to truly self-governing involves giving the team control over their direction and external coordination. Support this shift by building the team's capability in STRATEGY HEURISTIC (29) and expanding their understanding of PLATFORM TEAMS (17) to better integrate with the broader organization. Encourage the use of DOMAINS, ASSETS & STANDARDS (23) to ensure the team responsibly handles strategic decisions. Rely on RELATIVE TARGETS (33) and METRICS REVIEW (36) to maintain clarity and accountability for performance without direct oversight. Allow EMERGENT LEADERSHIP (58) so that strategic responsibility is fluid, naturally shifting to those best positioned to lead.

19 *Lean Teams*

Constraints work

Organizations often default to expanding the size of the team as complexity increases. The impulse is natural: More work seems to demand more hands. But this instinct, while understandable, contradicts a fundamental truth about human collaboration: that beyond a certain threshold, adding more people to a team decreases rather than increases its effectiveness.[27]

Lean Teams embraces the counterintuitive wisdom that smaller teams, typically no more than 8–10 people, are more effective than larger ones. This pattern draws inspiration from various sources, including Amazon's "Two-Pizza Teams" (teams small enough to be fed by two pizzas) and countless studies showing that communication overhead grows exponentially with team size. (You don't even need to look at a study to understand this. You just need to be able to count. In a team of five, there are 10 possible one-on-one connections. If the team doubles its size to 10, this jumps to 45 connections.)

Large teams will also struggle to apply other patterns in this book. ELECTIONS (15), UPWARD REPRESENTATION (24), and TEAM INCENTIVES (25) are more challenging with more people to consider. STRUCTURAL & PSYCHOLOGICAL SAFETY (3) and DISSOLVABILITY (9) are harder to come by and pull off. It's harder to DO THE RIGHT THING (26) because there are too many definitions of "right."

The challenge here is in our mindsets: Leaders dismiss small teams as risky ("How could they possibly get all of that done?")[28] or inefficient ("If we have 1,000 teams of eight people, how will we manage the complexity?"); team members resist them because larger teams feel safer ("More people to share the load and blame!") or because they confer more wealth and status.[29] We can break these bad habits and create new mindsets with patterns like STRATEGY HEURISTIC (29), UPWARD REPRESENTATION (24), and TEAM INCENTIVES (25).

This pattern, though, is exceptionally simple: Keep teams small and focused. When more capacity is needed, do not expand the existing team. Instead, create new ones that can coordinate through light-touch interfaces. *That's it.*

APPLICATION

Implementing Lean Teams requires both structural changes and cultural shifts:

Org Level	• Create clear guidelines for team formation and splitting. • Build lightweight coordination mechanisms between teams: as simple as WORK IN PUBLIC (50) and as rigorous as public/group-level BACKLOG MANAGEMENT (37). • Measure team effectiveness, not just size or output.
Team Level	• Establish clear boundaries of ownership and authority with a TEAM CHARTER (43). • Develop efficient interfaces with other teams. • Maintain rigorous focus on core priorities by aligning work to OBJECTIVES & KEY RESULTS (28).
For Leaders	• Resist the urge to grow teams as a solution to problems. • Coach teams to work effectively within size constraints by leaning on TRUE PURPOSE (1). • Focus on outcomes rather than team structure.

An organization that structures around Lean Teams will have several advantages. In the immediate term, organizations see faster execution and clearer accountability, as small teams naturally cut through the coordination overhead that typically bogs down larger groups.[30] Decision-making becomes crisper and more decisive, while team members report higher engagement and satisfaction, finding it easier to see their direct impact on outcomes.[31]

In the longer term, the *structure itself* gets more adaptable, as small teams can form and re-form more readily than large ones. The organization will enjoy faster and more widespread leadership development, with more opportunities for people to lead small teams. Innovation is more likely *and more successful* as small teams feel more comfortable taking calculated risks without the burden of building consensus across a large group.[32]

20 *Talent Marketplace*

The portfolio is the new career path

Organizations waste talent when people are locked into rigid roles and teams. Hidden capabilities remain undiscovered, while emerging needs go unmet. People's careers stagnate in silos, and the organization's potential for dynamic adaptation diminishes.

Most organizations believe they know who can do what, but this knowledge is trapped in managers' minds, outdated performance reviews, or systems so cumbersome that finding the right person for a specific need feels like archaeology. The system privileges stability over adaptability, resulting in widespread disengagement as people's unique strengths remain underutilized.[33]

Traditional models assume career progression means moving linearly up a ladder, but modern work is complex. People are multifaceted, and our complexity is what makes us special! A software engineer might also excel at facilitation; a finance analyst might have untapped design skills; a marketer might solve complex operational problems.[34] These capacities remain invisible when we force people into narrow role definitions and dedicated assignments.

In the absence of internal mobility, talent leaves. If it weren't so tragic, it'd be funny: Organizations spend enormous resources recruiting externally while neglecting to discover and deploy the wealth of capabilities already present internally. This is worse than inefficient, as it drives profound disengagement through a nearly explicit acknowledgment that folks' full potential will go unseen and undervalued.[35]

The gap between aspiration and reality drives contradictory organizational behaviors. Executives say they value growth and agility while they maintain rigid job descriptions and approval processes that discourage internal movement. HR leaders track skills in systems that quickly become outdated and aren't connected to real-time needs. Resource allocation committees carefully guard and steward talent that isn't anywhere close to fully utilized. Managers hoard their best performers while simultaneously failing to develop them.

The corporate rhetoric champions "career growth and empowerment," while the working reality is that there are limited pathways for authentic contribution beyond prescribed roles.

THEREFORE ...

Create a dynamic internal talent marketplace where skills and opportunities flow freely across organizational boundaries.

A well-designed Talent Marketplace makes both talent supply and demand transparent, allowing people to build their careers through a portfolio of contributions rather than a linear path through fixed positions.

Organizations must build unified visibility platforms that make skills, experiences, and interests discoverable. These systems should go beyond traditional credentials to surface the full spectrum of capabilities people possess—including those not reflected in current roles. Everyone should be able to easily maintain their "talent profile" with minimal friction, updating skills, sharing work samples, and expressing aspirations. The goal is to make these talent profiles rich, dynamic, and connected to the actual work happening across the organization.

Organizations need clear processes for flexible allocation that balance individual agency with organizational priorities. This includes standardized ways to post opportunities, transparent selection criteria, simple approval workflows, and appropriate guardrails that prevent burnout or neglect of core responsibilities. The system should enable various engagement models, from full-time role changes to micro contributions, part-time allocations, and internal sabbaticals.

Compensation and recognition systems must evolve to reward portfolio contributions rather than rigid role fulfillment. This means developing models that acknowledge work across multiple teams, fairly attribute value created in collaborative contexts, and recognize both depth and breadth of contribution. Managers must be evaluated not just on team performance but on talent development and sharing—incentivizing them to help people grow beyond their current roles.

When Talent Marketplaces function effectively, they create virtuous cycles of development and contribution. People build more diverse skills and networks through varied experiences, increasing both their value to the organization and their sense of engagement. Teams access capabilities they couldn't otherwise afford or justify hiring permanently. The organization becomes more responsive to changing conditions, deploying talent dynamically to emerging needs rather than remaining constrained by historical structures.

●▼✱■✳◆

Talent Marketplace connects naturally with EXPANDED AVAILABLE POWER (4), distributing authority over career paths to individuals rather than managers alone. It depends on STRUCTURAL & PSYCHOLOGICAL SAFETY (3) to make vulnerability and exploration possible, and CURIOSITY (5) to truly understand people's intentions. The pattern strengthens when combined with ROLE-SOUL DISTINCTION (8), as people can explore various roles without tying identity to any single position. DISSOLVABILITY (9) is required by this approach, as is TRANSPARENCY (32), by enabling the marketplace to function effectively. TEAM INCENTIVES (25) address the compensation challenges of multi-team contributions. EXPERIMENTATION (62) benefits from talent fluidity by allowing teams to quickly form around new ideas, and EMERGENT LEADERSHIP (58) flourishes when people can contribute where their capabilities are most needed.

21 *Guilds*

Knowledge, networked

Organizations regularly fragment expertise through well-intentioned structural decisions. Product teams, customer segments, and geographical divisions all create boundaries that contain knowledge that should flow freely. Meanwhile, people crave genuine connection with others who share their craft, facing similar challenges across different contexts.

The gap between formal structure and information architecture (IA)—aside from pulling many IA professionals into the world of organizational design—gets in the way of progress. Novices struggle without access to expert guidance beyond their immediate team. Experts lack mechanisms to influence DOMAINS, ASSETS & STANDARDS (23) beyond their direct sphere. Great ideas emerge and die in isolation rather than spreading. The organization optimizes for functional or customer alignment while neglecting an *essential architecture of expertise.*

THEREFORE...

Create *voluntary* communities of practice organized around specific areas of professional interest, cutting across formal organizational boundaries, called guilds.*

---

* Henrik Kniberg and Anders Ivarsson, "Scaling Agile @ Spotify with Tribes, Squads, Chapters & Guilds," Crisp, accessed February 2025, https://blog.crisp.se/wp-content/uploads/2012/11 /SpotifyScaling.pdf. This name is a bit wonkish, but was spread by Henrik Kniberg's writing on Agile at Spotify. The concept of a guild appears to go back to at least 2000 BCE. *Management innovation, folks!*

These communities are focused on sharing knowledge, supporting practitioners, and spreading expertise across an organization. Unlike CHAPTERS (22), which are more formal and focus on aligning practices and setting standards, guilds are informal groups driven by enthusiasm. Think of guilds as the lightweight cousin to chapters—they prioritize emergent knowledge exchange and flexible collaboration over formal governance.

To set up effective guilds, first identify areas where practitioners naturally want to share ideas or solve common problems together. These DOMAINS (23) could be technical (such as data engineering or front-end development), methodological (like design thinking or user research), or skill based—such as FACILITATION (56), project management, or CONFLICT RESOLUTION (39). Look especially for topics where inconsistent approaches create inefficiency, or where people working alone could benefit from the support of a community.

Midsize Technology

Purpose: Harness technology to expand human potential and shape a smarter, fairer world.

Data Science

Empower ethical innovation through shared expertise and open knowledge exchange.

Offer monthly meetups where data scientists present and discuss practical techniques, evaluate new tools collaboratively, and openly work through ethical dilemmas in machine learning. The guild maintains a simple, accessible code repository of reusable algorithms and common data analysis patterns.

Front-End Development

Improve User Experience with creativity, skill sharing, and practical collaboration.

Offer weekly informal office hours giving developers a place to solve challenging UI problems together. Host quarterly "state of front-end" workshops to collectively apply emerging practices, enabling alignment and continuous growth without mandated standards.

Technical Writing

Consume complexity by building a supportive community dedicated to quality documentation.

Hold biweekly peer review sessions where documentation specialists review each other's work in a friendly, supportive environment. The guild maintains an evolving, lightweight style guide and reusable documentation examples to streamline writing across teams without rigid rules.

Midsize Manufacturing

Purpose: Build the foundations of progress by constantly reinventing what's possible in industry.

Materials Innovation

Spark breakthroughs by discovering unexpected connections across disciplines and industries.

Present an informal community where engineers, designers, and production specialists spontaneously share insights about novel materials and innovative applications. Regularly host "unexpected materials" workshops designed to inspire fresh ideas by exploring surprising use cases from diverse industries.

Factory Floor Hacks

Amplify frontline ingenuity by openly sharing practical innovations.

Provide an informal group where shop-floor operators and technicians freely exchange grassroots productivity improvements and creative workarounds. Maintain a simple, searchable database of "tacit knowledge," capturing valuable insights that might otherwise stay hidden within individual teams or locations.

Automation Enthusiasts

Fuel curiosity and innovation through hands-on exploration of automation technologies.

Assemble a voluntary group of robotics enthusiasts from multiple divisions experimenting informally with new automation concepts during off-hours. Create a relaxed "robot playground" space where members test and share ideas without the immediate pressure of production targets or formal evaluation.

Midsize Entertainment

Purpose: Uplift lives by creating unforgettable experiences that captivate hearts and minds.

Storytelling Craft

Improve every story we tell by blending creative wisdom from all corners of our organization.

Host informal gatherings of writers, designers, and producers from film, gaming, and theme park teams who use narrative techniques across different mediums. Regular "story jams" allow cross-divisional teams to collaboratively tackle storytelling challenges, borrowing ideas and inspiration from unexpected sources.

Creative Technology

Inspire groundbreaking entertainment experiences by fearlessly exploring emerging technologies.

Assemble an experimental group of technology enthusiasts showcasing new possibilities in AR/VR, projection mapping, and interactive systems through informal demonstrations and playful experimentation. Maintain a shared "tech toy box," inviting guild members to test out innovative tools and concepts without formal project constraints.

Audience Psychology

Deepen our connection to audiences by uncovering insights that cross traditional boundaries.

Provide a forum for a voluntary community of professionals exploring audience engagement patterns across films, games, theme parks, and digital platforms. Members share insights and ideas informally, allowing findings from one entertainment medium to inspire innovations in another, outside of official research structures.

Create minimal structures that help guild members stay connected without adding bureaucracy. Use regular gatherings—whether in-person or virtual—alongside dedicated communication channels, forums, or knowledge-sharing spaces designed for TRANSPARENCY (32) and WORK IN PUBLIC (50). Assign minimal facilitation roles to maintain momentum, relying on EMERGENT LEADERSHIP (58) rather than formal authority.

Remember that guild participation is voluntary, driven by personal motivation;

guilds thrive because members genuinely want to participate and see clear value in doing so. So if they DISSOLVE (9), it's not a big deal. Leadership within guilds emerges organically, based on contributions and recognized expertise rather than job titles or hierarchy, according to EXPANDED AVAILABLE POWER (4) and mediated, perhaps, by ELECTIONS (15).

Guilds strengthen an organization by quickly spreading knowledge across teams, leading to more and better EXPERIMENTATION (62). They can reduce redundant problem-solving and provide support networks for specialists who might feel isolated within cross-functional groups, in support of STRUCTURAL & PSYCHOLOGICAL SAFETY (3). Guilds also offer pathways for emerging leaders to influence the organization beyond their formal roles and create a sense of professional pride and community, boosting intrinsic motivation and shared identity WHOLENESS (7).

22 *Chapters*

Autonomy & alignment

Matrix structures represent a paradox: the simultaneous pursuit of *specialized depth* and *integrated breadth*. This is a worthy pursuit! But what we experience in a matrixed organization is a bureaucratic labyrinth where authority diffuses, accountability blurs, and execution stalls. We complain about these outcomes while forgetting that the purpose of a system is what it does:[36]

> *It is a system which tends to diminish the visibility of authority and to emphasize consensus as the operative mode.*
>
> —William Litzinger et al., 1970*

Formal dual-reporting mechanisms create slow, sticky alignment. Consider the contrasting case: A distributed chapter of media specialists across a global CPG enterprise doubled the effectiveness of their multibillion-dollar media investment without reconfiguring a single reporting relationship. Their lightweight structure prioritized expertise rather than authority and achieved what elaborate matrix relationships rarely deliver: real results on a short timeline.

The matrix structure persists because groups often assume that effective

---

* William Litzinger et al., "The Manned Spacecraft Center in Houston: The Practice of Matrix Management," *International Review of Administrative Sciences* 36, no. 1 (1970): 2–8, https://journals .sagepub.com/doi/10.1177/002085237003600101. This is one of the earliest papers on matrix management; recall that the matrix was designed for many companies to build rockets that took people into space. The consequences of poor integration were high, so consensus was *essential*.

coordination must come from formal authority. This assumption leads companies to design their structures around predefined relationships rather than allowing natural collaboration to emerge. As a result, informal networks become limited to casual knowledge sharing, while the "real work" is controlled by hierarchy.[37]

Making a matrix structure effective requires organizations to excel at things that are genuinely difficult: smooth communication across departments; clear roles that everyone understands; politics-free conflict resolution; managers who can handle competing demands without bias. Since most individuals (let alone organizations!) struggle to master these skills, common problems emerge: meetings where no clear decisions are made; strategy sessions that secretly become battles over resources; employees feeling trapped between conflicting performance demands.

Consultants are aware of these problems, but their usual advice is simply to add more rules or layers of management. Unfortunately, these additions make coordination even more complicated without solving the basic issue: balancing specialized teams' independence with the organization's need for integrated results.

THEREFORE...

Chapters are an effective middle ground between traditional departments and fully independent practitioners.[38] They connect people with similar skills across different teams, forming communities focused on improving their craft rather than controlling their work. You can think of chapters as blending ideas from ROLE-SOUL DISTINCTION (8) and NETWORK OF TEAMS (13). Instead of grouping people by who their manager is, chapters bring people together around shared areas of expertise, allowing them to stay part of their main team while benefiting from a broader community. This helps teams avoid the extremes of rigid hierarchy or unstructured collaboration.

Large Bank

Purpose: Help people control their financial future through accessible, ethical money services.

Risk Experts

Build better risk models that satisfy regulators while providing strategic insights.
- Members come from trading, banking, retail, and regulatory teams.
- Share knowledge across different countries and regulations.
- Set standards for checking and validating risk models.
- Build expertise in new risk areas (climate, cyber, political).

Customer Experience

Create smooth experiences that turn transactions into trusted relationships.
- Deliver consistent experiences across wealth management, personal banking, and business services.
- Design interaction guidelines that work within regulations.
- Share insights about customer behavior across all touchpoints.
- Build expertise in how people make financial decisions.

Algorithmic Ethics

Make sure automated systems reflect company values while improving efficiency.
- Create frameworks for making algorithms transparent.
- Develop methods to detect unintended bias in automated systems.
- Set ethical standards for using data in machine learning.
- Connect technical experts with ethics specialists.

Midsize Manufacturing

Purpose: Strengthen local manufacturing through distributed production and materials innovation.

Production Improvement

Develop methods to continuously improve distributed manufacturing.
• Connect experts across different production locations.
• Maintain standards for process efficiency and quality.
• Build expertise communities around specific material challenges.
• Help transfer knowledge between established and new facilities.

Sustainable Design

Transform product development through reusable design and material recovery.
• Create design standards that maximize component reuse.
• Develop expertise in design-for-disassembly and reverse logistics.
• Share knowledge about material life cycle and sustainable alternatives.
• Coordinate expertise in sustainable business models.

Advanced Manufacturing

Expand capabilities through new manufacturing technologies.
• Connect traditional craft knowledge with digital fabrication.
• Set standards for 3D printing quality and integration with traditional methods.
• Develop capabilities in coordinating distributed production.
• Share knowledge about material-specific innovations.

Small Healthcare
Purpose: Make healthcare more accessible through community-centered models and prevention.

Care Continuity

Design seamless care paths that cross traditional boundaries.
- Set standards for information sharing during care transitions.
- Develop expertise in coordinating care across different providers.
- Create methods for measuring how well continuity of care works.
- Share knowledge for developing cross-discipline care protocols.

Prevention

Reimagine healthcare to prioritize prevention through environment and behavior.
- Connect clinical prevention experts with community systems.
- Develop frameworks for measuring prevention effectiveness.
- Set standards for ethically applying behavioral insights.
- Share knowledge across clinical, community, and policy areas.

Health Equity Group

Identify and remove barriers to equal health outcomes.
- Develop methods for detecting outcome disparities and finding root causes.
- Set standards for inclusive service design.
- Build expertise communities around specific equity challenges.
- Create frameworks for measuring equity progress.

Implementing Chapters should feel natural: Start by identifying areas of expertise that are essential, then establish lightweight ways to organize these groups, typically through CONSENT & CONSENSUS (10); find leaders through EMERGENT LEADERSHIP (58), guiding conversations, helping set standards, and encouraging learning; allow Chapters to adapt based on real needs, following the principle of DISSOLVABILITY (9). Regular HEALTH CHECKS (59) help ensure Chapters remain effective and aligned with their original purpose.

●▼◢■✳◆

Chapters' strength comes from balancing consistency with flexibility. They promote common practices without forcing everyone to do things exactly the same way.* By clearly separating networks of expertise from management structures, Chapters embody EXPANDED AVAILABLE POWER (4). When combined with TRANSPARENCY (32) and EXPERIMENTATION (62), Chapters help organizations build a resilient network of knowledge—one that stays aligned but still encourages innovation. This allows organizations to evolve away from rigid structures toward networks of dynamic capabilities, shifting coordination from top-down control to distributed intelligence.

---

* You could call this approach "minimum viable governance."

23 Domains, Assets & Standards

What do you own?

Clear ownership is essential.

Without it, teams waste energy negotiating responsibilities, waiting for approvals, and navigating unclear boundaries. Work stalls, frustrations grow, and good people disengage. But many organizations still operate in this foggy state, where accountability doesn't match authority and responsibilities overlap confusingly.

Imagine a common scenario: A product launch meeting dissolves into confusion. Marketing thought engineering owned the landing page; engineering expected designs from creative; legal is worried about data compliance; but nobody knows who has final say. This confusion leads to delays, finger-pointing, and missed opportunities.

THEREFORE...

Domains, Assets & Standards clears up confusion by giving teams explicit ownership over defined areas of responsibility, resources, and guiding principles. Each dimension solves a specific kind of ambiguity and confusion, and it's a tool for structuring work.

DOMAINS

Domains define exactly what teams control and decide. For example, at Spotify, squads clearly own specific features like "Search Experience," meaning they decide everything from design to delivery within their domain without constant approvals.* This is a *domain,* and it aligns closely with TRUE PURPOSE (1) by connecting each team's work to outcomes they fully control and care about.

Domains are also a powerful tool for team design. Teams can be organized around well-defined domain boundaries to minimize interdependencies and to manage cognitive load effectively. Ideally, domains cover end-to-end responsibility for a *particular value stream* or *business capability.*

A useful way to determine whether something is a domain—and whether it's the right size—is to look for a *coherent set of responsibilities* that produces a *distinct value outcome* or capability for the organization, ideally one that a single team can handle without constant cross-team dependencies. If multiple teams need to share day-to-day authority over what feels like the same domain, that's a sign it may be too large or too vague; you'll see frequent coordination overhead, misalignment, or finger-pointing about who owns which piece. Conversely, if the domain is so narrow that the team is underutilized (for instance, just one small slice of a broader capability), it may be artificially constrained. The scope of a domain should fit the cognitive load a team can manage by being large enough to make a meaningful contribution but not so sprawling that the team can't maintain situational awareness.

In terms of PACE LAYERS (11), most team-level domains live at the layer of annual operating plans (one to two years) or functions and capabilities as sources of competitive advantage (two to five years) rather than short-term outputs or decade-long strategic bets, so think in terms of ongoing product features, core functions, or operational processes that evolve year over year. Of course, if you're tackling domains like "user authentication" or "logistics management," these might straddle different time horizons—some activities change rapidly (e.g., adding a new feature for an upcoming release), while others, like overall system architecture,

---

* Kniberg and Ivarsson, "Scaling Agile @ Spotify." This is now 13 years old, so things will have changed somewhat, but Spotify does still operate according to these principles.

evolve more slowly. The key is that each domain should be defined so teams can own it for the foreseeable future, continuously improving and adapting it without excessive coordination burden.

ASSETS

Assets are valuable resources that need clear stewardship rather than complete control. For instance, GitHub (the software, not the company) assigns specific code areas to individual users as *assets*. Users steward these resources, maintaining/improving their security, quality, and effectiveness, even though others may *use* them.[39] Protecting assets effectively requires STRUCTURAL & PSYCHOLOGICAL SAFETY (3) so stewards feel empowered in their roles.

STANDARDS

Standards provide shared guidelines that teams follow without losing autonomy. Design systems (e.g., Google's Material Design, IBM's Carbon Design, Salesforce's Lightning Design System) are excellent examples of this, as are brand guidelines. They're consistent principles for design or brand development that provide the constraints to fuel good creativity. Standards support RULE OF LAW (2) and SELF-MANAGED TEAMS (18) by ensuring consistency without micromanagement. With more high-quality standards in place, it's easier to pull off:

- DISTRIBUTED MANAGEMENT (14), because we know what good looks like;
- NETWORK OF TEAMS (13), because we don't have to worry if people are going in the right direction;
- DO THE RIGHT THING (26), because we expressed what we meant by "right";
- LEAN TEAMS (19) and SELF-MANAGED TEAMS (18), because the standard can be a good stand-in for a human or a manager.

APPLICATION

Start by identifying areas of recurring confusion or friction. Clearly define:

- Domains: Where does a team's decision-making authority begin and end?
- Assets: Which resources need dedicated stewardship?
- Standards: What shared guidelines or principles should teams follow?

Global Retailer
Purpose: Make sustainable living accessible and affordable.

Domain Examples
- **E-Commerce Experience:** Full authority over website design, checkout flow, and customer experience optimization.
- **Supply-Chain Management:** Full ownership of global sourcing, logistics, and inventory management processes.

Asset Examples
- **Customer Data Platform:** Stewards all customer data, ensuring security, accuracy, and compliance with privacy regulations.
- **Sustainability Guidelines:** Maintains and updates standards for sourcing materials sustainably across global operations.

Standard Examples
- **Customer Experience Principles:** Guidelines that ensure consistency in customer interactions online and in stores worldwide.
- **Ethical Sourcing Practices:** Company-wide principles for selecting suppliers and materials to meet sustainability goals.

Renewable Energy Firm
Purpose: Accelerate the world's transition to clean energy.

Domain Examples
- **Energy Storage Solutions:** Full decision-making over battery technology research, development, and production methods.
- **Regional Project Delivery:** Authority over planning, constructing, and operating energy projects within defined regions.

Asset Examples
- **Smart-Grid Technology:** Maintains and protects proprietary smart-grid infrastructure, facilitating reliable integration across projects.
- **Patents and Intellectual Property:** Manages and protects innovations in renewable technology.

Standard Examples
- **Safety and Reliability Standards:** Establish guidelines ensuring consistent safety, performance, and maintenance practices across all facilities.
- **Environmental Impact Guidelines:** Clear criteria to ensure educational offerings remain accessible to learners of all backgrounds and abilities.

Digital Education Provider
Purpose: Democratize access to high-quality education.

Domain Examples
- **Course Development:** Complete control over course content creation, delivery methods, and curriculum innovation.
- **Learning Analytics:** Complete responsibility for data analytics, measuring student engagement, and improving learning outcomes.

Asset Examples
- **Content Repository:** Responsible for maintaining the integrity, accessibility, and quality of the centralized digital content library.
- **Student Privacy Protocols:** Ensures compliance with global privacy standards for protecting student data.

Standard Examples
- **Pedagogical Best Practices:** Shared principles for designing effective and engaging educational content across courses and platforms.
- **Accessibility and Inclusion Standards:** Clear standards to minimize environmental impact and maximize sustainability across projects.

●▼◢■✿♠

Once identified, assign ownership based on expertise and capability. Document and communicate these assignments clearly and transparently. Use patterns like TEAM CHARTER (43) and WORK IN PUBLIC (50) to keep roles and responsibilities visible. This is self-reinforcing: It's easier to have a good charter, and to publicize your work, if you know that you own the domain and someone else isn't going to swoop in and redirect your work.

Regularly revisit and refine these assignments. Resolve disputes or overlaps through STRUCTURED DECISION-MAKING (30) or CONSENT & CONSENSUS (10), ensuring teams maintain autonomy while cooperating effectively.

24 *Upward Representation*

Structural integrity
Structural authority

A hospital introduces a new electronic health record system, selected by executives who've never used it. Frontline nurses struggle with clunky interfaces that double documentation time, while patients wait longer for care. Despite numerous complaints, concerns never reach decision-makers. The project is declared a success based on implementation metrics, while care quality suffers.[40]

This disconnect between decision-makers and those implementing decisions plagues organizations of all types. Traditional hierarchies act like information filters, with each layer removing critical context before messages reach the top. This results in leaders making consequential decisions based on sanitized, incomplete information.[41]

Without structured representation, teams can become voiceless within their own organizations. Valuable ideas wither on the vine. Preventable problems fester. The RULE OF LAW (2) exists on paper, but in practice, different standards apply to frontline teams versus leadership. Despite claims of TRANSPARENCY (32), teams lack visibility into how decisions are made. Over time, this erodes STRUCTURAL & PSYCHOLOGICAL SAFETY (3), as speaking up seems futile or even risky.

Consider Pixar's approach to their film development process.* Rather than re-

---

* Also mentioned as a method for establishing STRUCTURAL & PSYCHOLOGICAL SAFETY (3). These meetings set the stage for this pattern to be useful.

lying solely on executive decisions, they established a "Braintrust" where directors elect representatives from their teams to participate in critical review sessions.[42] These representatives—animators, story artists, technical directors—bring unfiltered frontline perspectives that executives would otherwise miss. This practice has become central to Pixar's creative success, ensuring that decisions reflect the wisdom of those closest to the work.

THEREFORE...

Implement Upward Representation by having every team elect a representative to participate in meetings at the next-highest level of the organization. These representatives serve as conduits for team concerns, priorities, and feedback, ensuring frontline voices directly influence leadership decisions.

At Buurtzorg, the renowned Dutch healthcare organization, nurses work in self-managing teams of 10–12 people. Each team elects a representative to regional councils, where issues affecting multiple teams are addressed. These representatives aren't managers—they're practicing nurses with full client loads who maintain their primary role while carrying team concerns upward. This structure has helped Buurtzorg achieve remarkable client satisfaction while reducing care costs by 40%.[43]

Airbnb goes a step further, using its Host Advisory Board to integrate host perspectives into its strategic decision-making. This board comprises hosts from around the world who regularly engage with Airbnb's leadership, ensuring that the experiences and insights of hosts directly influence company policies and initiatives.[44]

APPLICATION

The key elements of Upward Representation include:

Elected Roles

Representatives are chosen democratically by their teams using ELECTIONS (15), ensuring they have the team's trust. The election process should be simple but formal, with clear terms of service (typically 6–12 months) and responsibilities.

Leader Accountability
Leaders commit to considering representative input in decision-making through STRUCTURED DECISION-MAKING (30). While final authority may rest with leaders, they must demonstrate how representative feedback influenced outcomes.

Structured Presence
Representatives participate in all relevant higher-level meetings, where they have equal speaking rights.* This presence can't be optional or occasional; it has to be built into the agendas and the invite lists.

Two-Way Communication
Representatives faithfully convey team concerns upward while bringing context and decisions back to their teams, creating TRANSPARENCY (32) in both directions. This responsibility requires regular team check-ins and updates.

The pattern works in harmony with DISTRIBUTED MANAGEMENT (14) and SELF-MANAGED TEAMS (18), creating an organization where authority and information flow freely. It is also an exceptional opportunity for EMERGENT LEADERSHIP (58); consider using MEETING ROLES (51) to help representatives know how to show up in the moments that matter.

---

* You might consider an alternative setup here—perhaps the representatives have a certain way that they're asked to participate that isn't equal but satisfies the general principle.

25 *Team Incentives*

Individual rewards fragment teams

Incentives are typically structured around individual performance, creating an inherent tension between personal gain and collective success. Even when teams succeed together, the rewards often flow to individuals based on their perceived contributions or hierarchical position. This individualistic approach made sense in an industrial era where work could be cleanly divided and measured, but it breaks down in today's interconnected knowledge work environment.*

Furthermore, attempts to measure individual contributions within team settings are often arbitrary and political, consuming enormous organizational energy while producing questionable results.

The reality is that most meaningful work is inherently collaborative. No significant project or innovation comes from a single person working in isolation. When we pretend otherwise through our incentive structures, we create destructive competition and undermine the very teamwork we claim to value.[45]

THEREFORE...

Structure all incentives—monetary rewards, recognition, opportunities for growth—at the team level, with equal distribution among team members or

---

* See NETWORK OF TEAMS (13) and SELF-MANAGED TEAMS (18).

application of another mutually agreed-upon sharing scheme, via CONSENT & CONSENSUS (10). As a result, team members succeed or fail together.

The mechanism is simple: When the team achieves its goals or creates value, everyone on the team benefits equally. This could apply to bonuses, profit sharing, equity, or nonmonetary rewards. The key is that the reward structure makes it impossible for individuals to win at the expense of their teammates.

Exceptions to this system will arise. But any deviation from equal distribution must be explicitly agreed upon by the team in advance, using clear criteria that everyone understands and accepts. This preserves a principle of **shared destiny** while allowing teams to adapt the model to their specific context. With fairness and equity as a starting point, team members are more likely to recognize true star performance, perhaps as driven by DISTRIBUTED MANAGEMENT (14) and according to roles described in the TEAM CHARTER (43). Regular METRICS REVIEWS (36) are often a forcing function for teams to understand who is contributing more than their fair share to the outcomes of the team.

APPLICATION

Implementation starts with creating a NETWORK OF TEAMS (13) and measurable team OBJECTIVES & KEY RESULTS (28). Teams must be real units with shared accountability, not arbitrary groupings. Clear DOMAINS, ASSETS & STANDARDS (23) will help here, so that contributions to given outcomes are obvious; active BOUNDARY MANAGEMENT (67) is key. Key steps include:

1. Establish clear team-level metrics and goals that align with broader organizational objectives;
2. Create transparent formulas for how team success translates into rewards;
3. Develop processes for teams to decide on any deviation from equal distribution;
4. Ensure leadership consistently reinforces team-first messaging and behavior.

For larger organizations, consider creating nested team structures where rewards cascade from organizational success to unit success to team success. This maintains a principle of **collective incentives** while acknowledging different scales of contribution.

Team Incentives align individual and collective interests, shifting focus from personal credit to team success. This reduces politics and increases collaboration as reward structures make knowledge sharing a default "way to win." Over time, teams become more cohesive and adaptable, reorganizing based on work needs rather than career concerns. A collaborative culture emerges where collective achievement beats out individual heroics.

Purely Individual Rewards ⟶ **Purely Communitarian**

Purely Individual Rewards					Purely Communitarian
Commission-based sales bonuses tie sales to individual volume. This creates no shared reward, encourages internal competition, and keeps metrics purely personal.	In a call center where 80% of bonus is individual (e.g., conversion) and 20% is team (e.g., CSAT), personal targets dominate and the small team incentive yields only light collaboration.	In a matrix org with 50% of incentive compensation coming from functional goals and 50% coming from project goals, loyalty splits between craft and business unit; collaboration rises, but priorities can clash.	A product team with a collective release bonus plus a small peer-voted "star" kicker puts most reward on team success while recognizing standout contributions through transparent, pre-agreed rules.	Whole Foods-style gain-sharing distributes bonuses equally across the store team, building cohesion and shared accountability while limiting differentiation for top performers and minimizing internal competition.	In Wikipedia/open-source/community models with no financial reward, contributors are driven by intrinsic motivation; success hinges on shared purpose and community norms, with little formal structure.

DIRECTION

26 Do the Right Thing

Only worry about doing them right once you're certain they're the right things

We often optimize for efficiency and excellence in execution—"doing things right"—while losing sight of whether we're doing the right things at all. Teams will perfectly execute the wrong priorities. We build "flawless" products that have no market. We'll meticulously follow processes—or hold people to processes—that seem important but create no value. The pressure to demonstrate competence and progress overrides the real question: Are we doing the things that matter? (And how do we know that's the case?)[1]

This is hard enough for an individual human, where aspirations of productivity are mixed with varying attitudes, attention spans, and abilities. Knowing whether every one of the thousands of people in a large organization is, in fact, spending their time in the *best possible way* at any given moment gets exponentially more difficult as organizations scale.[2] Layers of metrics, objectives, and incentives can obscure the ultimate impact of work, to say nothing of the structural impact of hierarchy on information quality.*

Knowing is hard enough. Deciding is often much more challenging. Boston Consulting Group's *Your Strategy Needs a Strategy* shows there isn't a one-size-fits-all direction: Environments can be classical, adaptive, visionary, shaping, or in renewal, and each calls for a different playbook.[3]

Doing things right only really matters in a few situations:

---

* See NETWORK OF TEAMS (13) for more on this, and for a good "fix."

- If you're doing the right thing;
- If you're working in an industry or problem space saddled with unavoidable, systemic risk (if you're building an airplane, doing things the right way is pretty important);[4]
- If you're in a situation where the right way has been known for more than 50 years.

THEREFORE ...

When it comes to directing the work of organizations, teams, and individuals, overinvest in systems that help teams do the right thing, tempered by a healthy understanding of the general unknowability of the future.[5]

SYSTEM 1: HAVE ONE PERSON DECIDE WHAT THE RIGHT THING IS[6]

The easiest—and in some situations, best—possible way to do this is to have an individual person decide. At a certain point of organizational scale, this becomes impossible for one human, but the upsides of this approach outweigh the downsides in many conditions; this is why many of the most spectacular case studies in business point back to a single person using their taste and high standards to drive the operation in a particular direction. How do you know who this person should be? If it's not obvious, consider ELECTIONS (15) to use the collective wisdom of a group to pick an individual to make the key call. That individual can use ADVICE (31) to make a wiser decision. When it comes to "what to do," this is generally preferable to using CONSENT & CONSENSUS (10).

What if the problem space is too hairy for one person to be a reliable indicator of what the next smartest thing to do might be?

SYSTEM 2: FORMALIZE GOOD DIRECTION

As organizations grow, the intuitive taste of a single person becomes insufficient to navigate big, challenging, multifactor decisions. Formalizing a way to provide good direction by putting structured systems in place is a good alternative that allows teams to *independently* evaluate what work matters most without constant leadership oversight.

This formalization has three dimensions: value definition, decision protocols, and enablement. **Value definition** clarifies what "right" looks like by making it explicit. **Decision protocols** establish consistent frameworks for evaluating work, while ensuring regular course corrections rather than annual planning cycles. **Enablement** creates the support for teams to question directions and pivot when needed.

Value Definition	Decision Protocols	Enablement
• Clear articulation of what constitutes "right" • Explicit connection to customer/stakeholder needs • Measurable impact criteria • Regular validation cycles	• Standard questions for evaluating potential work • Clear processes for stopping or redirecting effort • Mechanisms for surfacing and addressing misalignment • Regular review of ongoing commitments	• Recognition for avoiding wrong work • Safety for questioning established directions • Celebration of early course correction • Support for deeper purpose exploration
↓ ACTIVATED ↓	↓ ACTIVATED ↓	↓ ACTIVATED ↓
OBJECTIVES & KEY RESULTS (28) STRATEGY HEURISTIC (29) RELATIVE TARGETS (33) TEAM CHARTER (43)	ACTIVE STEERING (27) STRUCTURED DECISION-MAKING (30) ADVICE (31) CONFLICT RESOLUTION (39)	TRANSPARENCY (32) DEMOS (35) METRICS REVIEW (36)

SYSTEM 3: INTENTIONALLY SCAN THE ENVIRONMENT

Even with regular, formalized direction setting, you can miss critical context shifts. Perfect systems will fail if they operate in isolation from reality.*

---

* Consider using Simon Wardley's "Wardley Maps": Plot your value chain against stages of evolution so the team can "cross the river by feeling the stones," spotting where novelty, commodity, and strategic leverage actually sit.

Teams in fast-moving environments need to build in methods that detect shifts in customer needs, competitive landscapes, technological capabilities, and changing expectations before they become existential threats or missed opportunities. This goes beyond ad hoc market research or annual strategic reviews and makes situational awareness a part of daily operations.

Do this across three time horizons:

- Immediate horizon: Tracking customer feedback and usage patterns through METRICS REVIEW (36) and DEMO (35) sessions to identify immediate friction points and emerging needs
- Midrange horizon: Monitoring industry shifts, competitor moves, and adjacent market developments through structured intelligence gathering
- Distant horizon: Exploring weak signals of change in society, technology, economics, environment, and politics that could reshape fundamental assumptions

These signals are perfect partners to value definition activities and decision protocols (shown in the table on the previous page).

27 *Active Steering*

You'd never steer a ship annually

Multiyear plans, heavy up-front investments, and centralized decision-making: These approaches work in relatively stable environments, but they're no match for complexity, rapid change, and increasingly high customer standards. Long planning horizons create inertia, and centralized decision-making distances critical choices from the data and context needed to make them effectively.

These conventional approaches lock organizations into what we might call "Path A" thinking: making big, infrequent bets based on weak evidence, then committing substantial resources before knowing if they'll succeed. Teams conduct free-form interviews, build market projections, and leap directly to market launch—a high-risk path that leads to expensive failures.

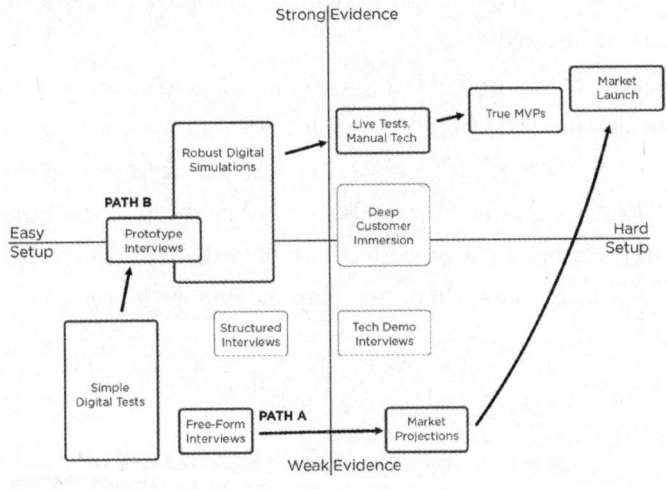

* Adapted from Alex Osterwalder's work.

This path is coupled with a fundamental misalignment between conviction and investment: Well-meaning executives pour company resources into initiatives that team members wouldn't personally bet on. This creates a culture where teams pursue and defend projects they don't truly believe in, simply because the planning process demanded it or because changing course would admit failure.

At the same time, leaders struggle to feel genuinely comfortable with smaller, more frequent decisions that can feel risky or inconsequential. Teams worry about losing control or creating chaos, and individuals may hesitate to make decisions for fear of blame if things go wrong. The result is organizational paralysis—either doubling down on failing big bets or avoiding decisive action entirely.

THEREFORE...

Actively steer by embedding decision-making capabilities at the edges of the organization, empowering teams to act on fresh, proximate data. This requires a shift in both mindset and systems, ensuring decisions are made in short, iterative cycles and based on the best available information.

This approach favors what might be called "Path B" decision-making: starting with simple digital tests, moving to prototype interviews and robust simulations, then progressing to live tests with real customers—all before major resource commitments. Each step builds stronger evidence, making later investments less risky and more likely to succeed.

Where'd this come from? Dave Snowden's Cynefin framework highlighted how different decision environments require different approaches, with complex domains demanding probe-sense-respond cycles.[7] The lean startup methodology, developed by Eric Ries in the early 2010s, established the build-measure-learn loop as a mechanism for rapid course correction.[8] Toyota's set-based concurrent engineering demonstrated how maintaining multiple options longer leads to better final decisions.[9]

APPLICATION

Active Steering thrives when decision-making is both *distributed* and *disciplined*. Organizations must push decision rights to the edges, empowering teams closest to customers, data, and markets to act swiftly and with confidence. This decentralization ensures that decisions are informed by the most relevant and immediate information, reducing delays and enabling frontline teams to respond directly to changes in the environment.

Align conviction with investment.
Create a matrix that maps the relationship between personal conviction ("What would you bet your own money on?") and organizational investment. Focus resources on initiatives where team conviction is high, and use small experiments for concepts with lower conviction.

Build an evidence ladder.
Define clear evidence thresholds that initiatives must pass before receiving additional investment. Start with low-cost tests that provide initial validation, then progressively increase investment as evidence strengthens.

Create rapid feedback loops.
Establish mechanisms for quickly capturing and responding to market signals, customer feedback, and performance data. Make these feedback channels available to decision-makers without filtering or delay.

Set clear guardrails.
Define boundaries within which teams can make autonomous decisions. These might include spending limits, brand guidelines, or ethical considerations that ensure decentralized decisions remain aligned with organizational values.

Implement nested decision cycles.
Create overlapping timeframes for review and adjustment—weekly for tactical decisions, monthly for operational choices, quarterly for strategic direction. Each cycle should include explicit moments to continue, adjust, or abandon initiatives. These can drive a smarter, more business-aligned CADENCE (65).

Active Steering connects to and reinforces other patterns. OBJECTIVES & KEY RESULTS (28) provide the framework for measuring progress during steering cycles. RELATIVE TARGETS (33) create more flexible benchmarks for assessing performance, allowing for smarter course corrections. The process of STRUC-TURED DECISION-MAKING (30) ensures that steering decisions are consistent and transparent, while METRICS REVIEW (36) provides the data needed to inform adjustments.

Implement this across different pace layers to create a dynamic, adaptive organization:

Organizations	At the organizational level, Active Steering replaces rigid, multiyear plans with dynamic, iterative planning. Leaders set the vision and guardrails while empowering teams to experiment and iterate within those boundaries. *Example: A retailer might replace a traditional annual budget process with quarterly investment reviews that reallocate resources based on shifting customer preferences and market conditions.*
Teams	Teams should be empowered to make tactical decisions without constantly escalating to leadership. This reduces bottlenecks and accelerates the ability to respond to real-time data. *Example: A customer support team might have the autonomy to offer immediate refunds or adjust policies based on customer feedback, rather than waiting for approval from senior management.*
Individuals	At the individual level, Active Steering requires a mindset shift toward ownership and accountability. Employees should feel empowered to make decisions within their scope, knowing they can adapt and course-correct if needed. *Example: A product manager might release an MVP (Minimum Viable Product) to customers for early feedback rather than waiting to perfect a full release.*

By making smaller, more frequent decisions, you will minimize the cost of mistakes and improve your ability to correct course. You will empower your teams by giving them the autonomy and ability to act and the support to iterate. Over time, you will build a culture of accountability, agility, and resilience.

28 *Objectives & Key Results*

Aspire, then calibrate

Goal setting is an annual ritual disconnected from daily work. Teams create elaborate plans that sit in rarely referenced and quickly outdated PowerPoint presentations. Long cycles, fixed targets, and hierarchical cascading of goals assume a level of stability and predictability that simply doesn't exist in today's environment.

Teams lose sight of larger purpose amid daily tasks, leading to misaligned efforts and wasted resources. Goals become either so vague they provide no direction ("Improve customer satisfaction") or so specific they constrain innovation ("Increase NPS by 2.3 points"). And then there's *sandbagging*, where teams set easily achievable targets to ensure success rather than pushing for breakthrough performance.

THEREFORE ...

Use Objectives & Key Results (OKRs) to provide a lightweight framework for setting, tracking, and adjusting goals that maintains both ambition and accountability. OKRs were pioneered at Intel in the 1970s when Andy Grove sought to solve the problem of goal alignment at scale. He developed a system that combined aspirational objectives with concrete measures of success.* The approach gained wider adoption when John Doerr introduced it to Google in 1999, where it became fundamental to their management system and helped drive their exceptional growth while maintaining focus.[10] The system has the following two core components.

---

* Andrew S. Grove, *High Output Management* (Vintage, 1995), 150–4. Grove describes his "Objectives and Key Results" discipline for cascading goals at Intel—widely regarded as the first published account of OKRs.

Objectives

Qualitative, inspirational goals that articulate what you want to achieve. They should feel somewhat uncomfortable and motivate teams to stretch beyond business-as-usual performance. For example: "Make our product the undisputed leader in ease of use" or "Transform our customer service from a cost center to a growth driver."

Key Results

Key results are specific, measurable outcomes that indicate progress toward the objective. Each objective typically has three to five key results that together provide a balanced picture of success. Key results should be ambitious but achievable with extraordinary effort—targeting 70% completion rather than 100%.

The power of OKRs comes from their connection to CADENCE (65)—typically quarterly goal setting with monthly check-ins—and their TRANSPARENCY (32), with all OKRs visible across the organization. This creates natural alignment while maintaining the flexibility to adjust as circumstances change.

APPLICATION

1. **Start at the top.** Leadership teams should set company-level OKRs first, providing clear direction while leaving room for teams to determine how they'll contribute. These top-level OKRs should connect directly to your TRUE PURPOSE (1).
2. **Start small.** Start with one or two key teams for a quarter before expanding. This allows you to refine the process and demonstrate value before scaling.
3. **Start a rhythm.** Create regular cadences for OKR activities:
   a. Quarterly: Set new OKRs through a collaborative process.
   b. Monthly: Conduct light-touch progress reviews and adjustments.
   c. End of quarter: Grade results and capture learnings.

Create transparency

Use a shared platform (start with a simple spreadsheet before trying any sort of dedicated software) to make all OKRs visible across the organization. This visibility supports TRANSPARENCY (32) and enables cross-team alignment.

Separate from compensation

Do not connect OKR achievement with compensation. Otherwise, you will not get stretch goals that create more value at 70% completion than easy targets hit at 100%. You will get sandbagging instead. People have mortgages, lives, and families.

Avoid a rigid cascade

You will be tempted to connect every team's Key Results to their sub-teams' Objectives, creating a cascade from the top to the bottom of the organization. This is tempting because it is obvious. That doesn't mean it's a good idea. You will spend more time worrying about the completeness of your framework than actually doing work.

PRODUCT DEVELOPMENT TEAM

	Good OKR	Bad OKR
Objective	Deliver an exceptional mobile user experience.	Enhance user satisfaction with the mobile app.
Key Results	Improve app store rating from 4.1 to 4.6 stars.	Gather more positive feedback from users.
	Reduce average page load time from 3 seconds to 1 second.	Regularly update and maintain app stability.
	Decrease crash rates from 2% to less than 0.5%.	Improve user interface and performance.

MARKETING TEAM

	Good OKR	Bad OKR
Objective	Expand brand visibility and attract qualified leads.	Increase audience engagement and brand awareness.
Key Results	Increase organic website traffic by 40% compared to last quarter.	Consistently publish new marketing content.
	Generate 500 new email subscribers from targeted campaigns.	Grow overall website traffic.
	Increase conversion rate from visitors to trial sign-ups by 15%.	Improve brand presence across social platforms.

CUSTOMER SUPPORT TEAM

	Good OKR	Bad OKR
Objective	Achieve outstanding customer satisfaction through swift support.	Provide responsive, high-quality customer service.
Key Results	Improve customer satisfaction score (CSAT) from 82% to 92%.	Ensure faster response times for customer inquiries.
	Reduce average ticket response time from 8 hours to under 4 hours.	Enhance overall customer satisfaction ratings.
	Resolve at least 70% of support requests on the first interaction.	Continuously work on improving ticket resolution processes.

When combined with ACTIVE STEERING (27), OKRs provide the framework for regular course correction while maintaining strategic direction. The transparent nature of OKRs supports TRANSPARENCY (32) and enables PULL UPDATES (34), as leaders can directly access information about team progress. OKRs also provide clear guidance for BACKLOG MANAGEMENT (37), helping teams prioritize work that contributes to key objectives.

For teams using STRATEGY HEURISTIC (29), OKRs provide a way to operationalize these strategic principles into specific, measurable goals. Similarly, the measurable nature of Key Results supports METRICS REVIEW (36), giving teams concrete data points to review regularly.

29 *Strategy Heuristic*

Make strategy useful

That lengthy, well-researched strategy document isn't going to be read all the way through. It's certainly not going to be internalized by the people on the front lines delivering to customers. Put another way: A big strategy doc doesn't have product-market fit. Teams need simple, memorable ways to make decisions that align with organizational direction, and Annual_Strategy_v75_Dave Edit _FINAL FINAL.pptx is giving them the exact opposite thing.

Strategy exists to help people make better decisions faster. To help them DO THE RIGHT THING (26). But most strategic output ends up slowing down decision-making. Leaders spend months crafting these documents, only to find they have minimal impact on day-to-day operations. Team members can't recall key strategic principles in the moment they need them most—in the room, with each other, working through what to do next.

Most strategic documents also try to be exhaustive rather than decisive. They avoid the hard trade-offs that define true strategy, favoring platitudes like "customer-focused" or "innovative" that offer no real guidance. Without clear priorities and explicit trade-offs, teams lack the filters needed to evaluate options against strategic intent. The results are inconsistent decisions, mixed signals about what matters, and wasted energy pursuing initiatives that don't align with core priorities.

THEREFORE ...

Transform strategy into simple decision-making rules—"heuristics"—that can be easily remembered and applied. These strategic heuristics take the form of clear trade-offs between two equally valuable options, making explicit what the organization will prioritize when forced to choose.

The core formula is: "[Priority A] even over [Priority B]"
Speed even over perfection
Customer satisfaction even over efficiency
Long-term value even over short-term gains

These heuristics serve as filters, helping teams quickly evaluate options against strategic priorities. They work because they acknowledge that both options have value, but they clearly state which one takes precedence when they conflict. Good heuristics cut through complexity by providing clear decision-making guidance in ambiguous situations.

Strategic heuristics have roots in the military concept of "commander's intent": the practice of distilling complex battle plans into clear, memorable guidance that subordinates can follow even when separated from command.

APPLICATION

Begin by identifying the key strategic challenges in your organization—areas where teams regularly struggle to make decisions between competing goods:

1. **Map decision points.** Document where teams face recurring trade-offs. Ask questions like: "Where do we regularly debate priorities?" or "What tensions arise in planning discussions?"
2. **Draft initial heuristics.** For each key tension, formulate two to three potential "even over" statements. Focus on genuine trade-offs between positive options, not obvious choices between good and bad.
3. **Test with scenarios.** Present realistic scenarios to teams and ask how the heuristics would guide their decisions. Refine the language until the heuristics consistently lead to the desired patterns of choice.

4. **Refine and prioritize.** Select three to five heuristics that address the most critical strategic tensions. Fewer is better—too many heuristics dilute their power.

5. **Socialize widely.** Share these heuristics in multiple formats (posters, cards, digital backgrounds) and reference them explicitly in decision-making contexts.

The heuristics become especially powerful when they are used in conjunction with STRUCTURED DECISION-MAKING (30). When teams face difficult choices, encouraging them to explicitly reference the relevant heuristics in their reasoning helps maintain strategic alignment. The simple format makes them easy to remember and apply, unlike complex strategic documents that gather dust.

Example: Healthtech Startup

Improve people's lives through personalized, proactive healthcare solutions.

Tensions

- **Innovation vs. Regulatory Compliance.** Rapid innovation can conflict with strict health regulations, challenging teams to balance groundbreaking ideas with mandated safety standards.
- **User Experience vs. Clinical Precision.** Exceptional, intuitive user experiences might sacrifice rigorous clinical standards, creating tension between ease of use and medical accuracy.
- **Rapid Expansion vs. Sustainable Growth.** Aggressively expanding market presence risks undermining long-term operational sustainability, forcing decisions about pace versus stability.

Smart but Forgettable Strategy

Commit to continuously pioneering innovative health solutions that dynamically adapt to regulatory frameworks and compliance guidelines across varying jurisdictions to simultaneously achieve user-friendly experiences without compromising clinical accuracy.

Strategy Heuristic

Clinical credibility even over speed to market

Example: Luxury Hospitality Brand

Create unforgettable experiences through meticulous attention to detail and exceptional service.

Tensions

- **Personalization vs. Operational Efficiency.** Deeply personalized guest services require more resources and complexity, creating tension with streamlined operations and cost efficiency.
- **Exclusivity vs. Revenue Maximization.** Maintaining an exclusive, premium brand identity conflicts with the temptation to broaden appeal for greater revenue.
- **Tradition vs. Modernization.** Staying true to heritage and tradition can limit the adoption of contemporary practices and technologies, raising difficult choices about identity versus evolution.

Smart but Forgettable Strategy

Strategically leverage operational efficiencies and cost-saving initiatives without diminishing our ability to deliver personalized, luxurious, and individually tailored guest experiences that preserve our legacy while embracing innovation.

Strategy Heuristic

Exceptional guest experience even over operational efficiency

Example: Renewable Energy Provider

Accelerate global sustainability by making renewable energy accessible and affordable.

Tensions

- **Scale vs. Community Integration.** Rapidly scaling renewable energy infrastructure can lead to overlooking specific local community needs and contexts.
- **Immediate Profitability vs. Long-Term Impact.** Prioritizing quick financial returns often conflicts with significant, long-term environmental and social impacts.

- **Technology Adoption vs. Cost Control.** Implementing cutting-edge renewable technologies frequently increases costs, creating tension with maintaining affordable solutions.

Smart but Forgettable Strategy

Rapidly scale global renewable energy infrastructure utilizing the latest technological innovations and methodologies to ensure maximum profitability and immediate return on investment while remaining mindful of long-term environmental objectives and local community considerations.

Strategy Heuristic

Long-term environmental impact even over short-term profitability

Strategy heuristics provide clear guidance for teams using the ADVICE (31) process, ensuring that input aligns with strategic priorities. For SELF-MANAGED TEAMS (18), heuristics create guardrails that enable autonomy while maintaining alignment. During ACTIVE STEERING (27), heuristics help teams make rapid course corrections that remain consistent with overall direction.

30 *Structured Decision-Making*

Create clarity, reduce politics

Most decision-making processes are informal and inconsistent.
Some decisions happen in hallway conversations.
Others in lengthy meetings.
Still others through email chains or chat threads.

This variability creates confusion, breeds mistrust, and often leads to decisions being revisited or undermined because stakeholders don't trust how they were made.

Thousands of decisions are made every day, ranging from minor operational choices to major strategic moves. Without a reliable, transparent process, the quality and legitimacy of these decisions suffer, regardless of whether the goal is consent or consensus.

There are deeper issues too. Without clear structure, many voices go unheard. Louder or more senior voices tend to dominate, and valuable perspectives get missed. Decisions lack the benefit of diverse thinking, and implementation suffers because people don't feel their input was properly considered.

THEREFORE ...

Establish a clear, consistent group decision-making process applicable for both consent and consensus. This structured approach ensures STRUCTURAL

& PSYCHOLOGICAL SAFETY (3) and thorough consideration, and builds trust in outcomes. The goal is to create decisions clearly *safe enough to try* or *mutually agreed on by all*—see CONSENT & CONSENSUS (10)—encouraging EXPERIMENTATION (62). This pattern is mirrored and applied in CONFLICT RESOLUTION (39).

What follows are a handful of *rules of engagement* that tend to work well. You can modify them in a number of ways to achieve the same goal: a trusted, consistent way of deciding big issues.[11]

Sociocratic/Consent Decision-Making

1. **Present proposal clearly and succinctly.** Presenter shares their idea concisely, focusing on the essential elements of the actual decision and stating their desired outcome clearly.
2. **Ensure shared understanding through clarifying questions.** Audience asks questions, only—to increase their understanding. Presenter responds, others listen. Call-and-response, not discussion.
3. **Gather reactions through structured** ROUNDS (48). Each audience member shares their honest reactions to the proposal, without debate or conversation. Presenter takes notes but does not respond.
4. **Allow proposal refinement based on reactions.** Presenter can modify based on reactions and questions, while intending to keep the original idea alive. Focus is on substantive concerns.
5. **Test for objections.** For consent: "Is this safe to try, knowing we can adjust if necessary?"
6. **Integrate feedback to reach conclusion.** If there are objections or concerns, address these one at a time, making small adjustments that preserve the intent but make it safe for (or supported by) by the group.

CONSENSUS-DRIVEN DECISION-MAKING (QUAKER METHOD)

If the group is facing a particularly complex or emotionally charged decision, try a structured decision-making approach inspired by the Quaker consensus tradition:[12]

1. Sit in a circle where everyone can see each other.
2. Begin by silently reflecting to center the group.
3. Presenter calmly shares their proposal clearly and thoughtfully.
4. Facilitator (Quakers refer to these as "clerks") gently guides a discussion where participants freely share thoughts, striving for a sense of the group's direction.
5. Another brief silence, allowing thoughtful reconsideration.
6. Facilitator checks for unity or remaining concerns, gently probing until participants find alignment or clarity about necessary adjustments.

The general idea here is that there always is an underlying will of the group that can be felt by all members of the group. For Quakers, as I understand it, this roughly equates to *finding the will of God*, together. That might feel off-putting for secular folks, but it's still interesting to prioritize a method that helps you find, and build, a decision that is truly shared by all. This takes *time* but builds community.

GENERAL TIPS

For Facilitators	For Participants
Stay neutral: Facilitator should guide conversation without steering outcomes.	Express clear, actionable concerns: Frame objections constructively and propose solutions whenever possible.
Separate clarifying from debating: Prevent early debates during the questions phase.	Try thinking in terms of "What is safe-to-try?" Adopt an iterative mindset, knowing adjustments can be made based on real-world feedback.
Explicitly invite quieter voices: Use structured ROUNDS (48) to ensure everyone's input.	
Timebox each phase: Clearly define and enforce time limits to maintain energy and focus.	Practice active listening: Listen carefully during ROUNDS (48) and avoid responding immediately to what you hear.

31 *Advice*

Make feedback nonbinding to get more feedback

There are two dysfunctional extremes of decision-making: autocratic control where leaders make all key decisions and consensus-seeking that paralyzes action through endless discussion. Both approaches waste the collective intelligence of the organization while creating frustration and disengagement. Teams need a way to make decisions that balances individual autonomy with collective wisdom.

Advice is a middle path—one that preserves individual agency while ensuring decisions benefit from diverse perspectives and organizational knowledge. It creates the conditions for both the empowered action and thoughtful consideration that result in teams that DO THE RIGHT THING (26).

THEREFORE...

Codify a clear advice process[13] where anyone can make decisions that affect their work, provided they:

- Seek input from those who will be significantly impacted;
- Consult those with relevant expertise;
- Notify affected parties of the final decision.

The person closest to the work initiates and owns the decision. They must actively seek advice but are not bound to follow it—they simply must show they have genuinely considered the input received. The scope of consultation should match the scale and impact of the decision.

This preserves individual agency while ensuring decisions benefit from collective wisdom. It creates responsibility without bureaucracy and maintains speed while accessing diverse perspectives.

Advice as a way of working was popularized by Dennis Bakke in *Joy at Work*, based on his experience at AES Corporation.[14] Similar approaches emerged in self-managing organizations like Morning Star and Buurtzorg.[15] Each case demonstrated that nonbinding input could maintain decision quality and alignment without creating bureaucratic bottlenecks or diluting accountability.

Note that this is a process for using advice to make major business decisions, but it applies to feedback conversations as well. You can put this pattern into practice as a leader or colleague just by adding something like "What I'm about to share is my advice" before providing counsel to someone on their work. For this to be genuine, you've got to mean it; if you frame direction as advice, you'll erase any PSYCHOLOGICAL SAFETY (3) that you were trying to build up.

APPLICATION

Begin by clearly communicating the steps of the advice process to all team members:

1. Someone identifies an opportunity or problem within their DOMAIN (23).
2. They notify relevant parties that they are exploring a decision.
3. They actively seek input from those affected and those with expertise.
4. They carefully consider all advice received.
5. They make and communicate their decision, explaining how input was incorporated.

Start with smaller decisions to build trust and capability. Use tools that make it easy to document consultation and share decisions, which could be as simple as WHITEBOARD AT INTERSECTIONS (74).

GOOD ADVICE VS. BAD ADVICE

The quality of input received dramatically impacts the effectiveness of the advice process. Help your organization distinguish between good and bad advice:

Good Advice	Bad Advice
Is specific and actionable	Is vague or generic
Comes from relevant experience or expertise	Comes from unfounded assumptions
	Ignores practical constraints
Considers the decision-maker's context and constraints	Presents personal preferences as universal truths
Acknowledges trade-offs and limitations	Conflates facts with opinions
Separates facts from opinions	Attempts to control the decision indirectly
Respects the decision-maker's autonomy	

The onus for good advice is on the person giving it and for those who request it. Teach teams to use structured prompts that elicit quality input:

Good Advice Prompts	Bad Advice Prompts
"Based on your experience with [specific area], what risks should I consider?"	"What do you think?" (too vague)
	"Is this a good idea?" (binary, doesn't elicit depth)
"What factors am I missing in my analysis of [specific aspect]?"	"Do you approve of this?" (frames as approval, not advice)
"How might this decision impact your team's work on [project/process]?"	"Tell me if there are any issues." (puts burden on advisor to spot problems)
"What alternative approaches have you seen work in similar situations?"	"I was thinking of doing X unless you have objections." (defensive positioning)
"What would you prioritize differently, and why?"	

The advice process reshapes the context surrounding direction from multiple, sometimes competing perspectives by clearly vesting authority in an individual or team while maintaining accountability to the collective—and to making high-quality decisions. People learn to think more broadly about the implications of their decisions while feeling empowered to act. The quality of decisions improves as they benefit from diverse perspectives while maintaining the clarity and speed of individual ownership.

●▼◢■✿◗

The advice process also reinforces other patterns in the book. It makes TRANSPARENCY (32) more meaningful by ensuring information is actively used in decision-making. It supplements STRUCTURED DECISION-MAKING (30) by providing a method for incorporating diverse perspectives. For organizations implementing SELF-MANAGED TEAMS (18), the advice process creates the coordination mechanisms needed to maintain alignment without hierarchy.

> At August, we scaled up the Advice to a whole-of-company way of improving ourselves. We called it Getting Better on Purpose (GBOP), and it took a lot of time, but it was time well spent. Unlike most annual reviews!
>
> 1. Gather advice—Send a short survey to peers and clients; drop every named comment into a shared doc.
> 2. Reflect & synthesize—The receiver mines themes and drafts a personal improvement plan.
> 3. 1:1 check-ins—Meet each advisor, share the synthesis, and refine it with their counsel.
> 4. Full-circle workshop—Reconvene all advisors to turn the plan into mutual commitments for support.

32 Transparency

Opacity creates friction
(Sometimes that's good, but usually not)

Traditional organizations operate on a "need to know" basis, where information flows through prescribed channels and access is carefully controlled. This approach emerged from military and industrial models where information security and chain of command were everything. Leaders worried that too much transparency might create confusion, slow decision-making, or give competitors an advantage.

But when information is hidden, teams duplicate effort, miss opportunities for collaboration, and lack the context needed to make good decisions. The rise of digital tools and distributed work has made transparency not just *possible* but *essential*. Opacity also breeds mistrust and disengagement; in my experience, this effect is especially pronounced in an organization's most important, highest-performing individuals and teams. When people don't understand why decisions are made or how their work connects to larger goals, they become passengers rather than drivers.

THEREFORE...

Make transparency the default state. Everything from strategic decisions to daily work should be visible and accessible to all members of the organization, with exceptions made only for truly sensitive information (like personnel matters or proprietary data).

This transparency operates at three levels:

1. **Strategic:** Clear visibility into decision-making processes, rationales, and organizational direction
2. **Operational:** Open access to work in progress, team discussions, and resource allocation
3. **Cultural:** Shared understanding of how things really work, including writing down the unwritten rules and power dynamics

Information should not just be available but actively publicized in ways that make it discoverable and useful. This means creating systems for documenting decisions, sharing work in progress, and making organizational knowledge accessible.

The open-source software community pioneered transparent development processes in the 1990s,[16] demonstrating how public visibility could enhance quality and collaboration.[17] Companies like August, Buffer, and GitLab later brought these principles into business operations, publishing everything from salaries to financial metrics.[18] These experiments showed that transparency could coexist with competitive advantage while creating stronger stakeholder trust.

APPLICATION

Begin by auditing your current information landscape. Identify what information is currently restricted and why, looking for opportunities to make more information openly available.

Implement Transparency

1. Open documentation systems where work and decisions are visible by default. This might include public project-management boards, shared document repositories, or decision logs.
2. Public channels for team communication instead of DMs or emails. This shift supports WORK IN PUBLIC (50) and creates natural knowledge sharing.
3. Shared digital workspaces that allow anyone to see what teams are working on. This visibility enables better coordination and reduces duplication.
4. Regular forums where decisions and their rationale are openly discussed, supporting STRUCTURED DECISION-MAKING (30).

Create Support Structures

1. Clear guidelines for what should remain private (and why). These exceptions should be specific and justified.
2. Training on how to work transparently and use shared information systems. This builds the capabilities needed for a transparent culture.
3. Regular practices for sharing work in progress, not just finished products. This approach supports ITERATIVE SHIPPING (46) and encourages early feedback.
4. Mechanisms for surfacing and addressing information asymmetries. These safeguards help ensure that transparency doesn't create new power imbalances.

Transparency makes PULL UPDATES (34) possible by allowing leaders to access information directly rather than through filtered channels. It supports ADVICE (31) processes by ensuring people have the context needed to provide meaningful input. It underpins CONFLICT AS A RESOURCE (38) by bringing potential issues to the surface where they can be addressed productively.

Organizations with high transparency also find it easier to implement SELF-MANAGED TEAMS (18), as these teams can make better decisions when they have access to broader organizational context. Similarly, EXPANDED AVAILABLE POWER (4) becomes more feasible when information isn't used as a tool for control.

33 *Relative Targets*

The way we budget is especially broken

Organizations typically set absolute targets far in advance, creating inflexible performance goals that rapidly become outdated in the face of real-world changes. Teams find themselves chasing arbitrary numbers instead of responding dynamically to evolving conditions. This rigidity incentivizes unhelpful behaviors, including gaming metrics, negotiating lower targets for easier achievement, and siloed thinking, all at the expense of genuine organizational agility and strategic responsiveness.*

> When a measure becomes a target,
> it ceases to be a good measure.
> —Goodhart's law[19]

Rigid targets also push teams to compete rather than collaborate, drive innovation out of the org by punishing experimentation, and cause misalignment by emphasizing achievement of outdated objectives over meaningful responses to market realities.

---

* Good read on relative TSR in exec comp; this is now standard across much of the S&P 500. Why not do the same for targets within the firm? https://corpgov.law.harvard.edu/2024/09/09/relative-tsr-awards-challenges-and-trade-offs.

THEREFORE...

Set relative targets, drawing inspiration from "Beyond Budgeting" principles popularized by Bjarte Bogsnes.

Relative targets measure success against meaningful benchmarks, like comparable internal units, industry standards, external competitors, or historical performance trends instead of fixed goals. This approach shifts the focus from simply hitting a predetermined number to continually outperforming relevant benchmarks.

Select Meaningful Benchmarks	Identify internal peers or comparable units within the organization.
	Determine external benchmarks, including industry averages, market growth rates, or competitors' performance.
	Use historical data to assess continuous improvement.
Establish Clear Comparison Frameworks	Create simple, transparent ratios or indexes that teams can easily interpret.
	Utilize rolling averages to reduce volatility and highlight consistent performance trends.
	Implement peer rankings that allow immediate comparison without extensive analysis.*
Support with Real-Time, Transparent Data	Invest in accessible, real-time dashboards.
	Regularly update data to reflect the latest performance insights.
	Facilitate open discussions about performance trends to foster organizational learning.
Enable and Encourage Cross-Team Learning	Regularly schedule sessions for teams to exchange best practices based on benchmark insights.
	Recognize teams improving relative to peers or the market, incentivizing collaboration over competition.

Handelsbanken, a Swedish bank established in 1871, transitioned to a deeply decentralized structure mirroring what is described in NETWORK OF TEAMS (13)

---

* Google has an interesting example here, focused on System Reliability Engineering Error Budgets: https://sre.google/workbook/error-budget-policy.

by granting significant autonomy to local branches. This approach, often referred to internally as "The Handelsbanken Way," relies on trust, respect for individuals, and a customer-first attitude. But it is the relative target approach to budgeting that truly drives a performance culture within this decentralized model, as it shifts the focus from hitting arbitrary, fixed targets to continuously improving performance compared to peers. This encourages COOPERATION (12), adaptability, and ACTIVE STEERING (27) to local market conditions rather than internal competition or target negotiation.[20]

Equinor (Norway's—state-owned!—oil company) was one of the pioneers of the Beyond Budgeting approach. Even in a highly volatile, hard-to-control industry, they were able to entirely remove traditional budgeting from their process and replace it with dynamic, relative targets. In making this shift, Equinor has empowered its teams to respond more effectively to market fluctuations and internal changes. All this despite being heavily regulated and publicly traded.[21]

● ▼ ▰ ▣ ✵ ⬟

When paired with OBJECTIVES & KEY RESULTS (28), Relative Targets reinforce meaningful goal setting and genuine organizational learning. They directly support the STRATEGY HEURISTIC (29) by providing clear, adaptive guidelines for prioritizing strategic decisions. PULL UPDATES (34) and TRANSPARENCY (32) become more effective when teams have clear, dynamic benchmarks against which to measure real-time progress.

Shifting to relative targets immediately makes it easier to have productive conversations around feedback and development, and this significantly reduces the administrative overhead surrounding target negotiations. Relative targets also just make it easier to learn and adjust so that more teams are doing more of THE RIGHT THING (26).

Let's consider Relative Targets in three scenarios.

Telecom Company

Connect people seamlessly, ensuring effortless communication everywhere, all the time.

Level	Existing Static Metric	New Relative Target
Customer Service Agent	Calls resolved per day	Customer satisfaction *improvement* vs. team average
Network Operations Team	Network uptime % target (e.g., 99.9%)	Outage duration improvement relative to comparable regional teams
Full Org/Strategic Target	Annual revenue growth % target	Market share growth relative to primary competitors

Energy Company

Power communities sustainably and reliably, accelerating the transition to renewable energy.

Level	Existing Static Metric	New Relative Target
Field Engineer	Number of completed inspections per month	Improvement in inspection accuracy vs. peer engineers
Solar Installations Team	Total installations per quarter	Installation speed and cost efficiency relative to other regional teams
Full Org/Strategic Target	Total gigawatts of renewable capacity installed annually	Growth rate relative to overall industry renewable installation growth

Fast-Growing Beauty Company

Empower individuals to express their beauty through innovative, inclusive, and sustainable products.

Level	Existing Static Metric	New Relative Target
Product Designer	Total new products designed per year	User satisfaction ratings improvement vs. design team average
Digital Marketing Team	Campaign reach/impressions per month	Conversion rate improvement relative to industry benchmarks
Full Org/Strategic Target	Annual sales growth %	Sales growth rate compared to market-leading competitors

34 *Pull Updates*

Leaders: go get the update yourself

A VP downloads data into a spreadsheet,
creates charts,
pastes them into PowerPoint slides
with carefully worded bullet points,
and emails the file to 20 stakeholders.[22]
Meanwhile the data keeps changing.

Repeat.

Leaders rely on these carefully curated presentations and reports to understand what's happening on the ground. Teams spend countless hours preparing polished updates, sanitizing data, and crafting narratives that obscure rather than illuminate. This goes beyond PowerPoint theater: It's a "push" model of information flow where teams periodically package and send updates upward, creating artificial barriers between leaders and the actual work being done.

This isn't good enough. Reality demands more immediate, authentic visibility into operations. Real-time data is increasingly available, so organizations have an opportunity to flip this dynamic, pushing leaders to "pull" the information they need, when they need it, directly from the source.*

---

* An excellent example of this is Stripe API changelog. It offers one feed for breaking changes and upgrades developers can pull anytime (https://docs.stripe.com/changelog). Platform companies like Stripe generally *must* provide this level of access to pull updates, but still.

Otherwise, teams of smart, highly paid people will continue to waste valuable time preparing and formatting updates instead of doing actual work.

Especially when paired with absolute targets and a traditional management hierarchy, the filtered nature of pushed updates means leaders lose touch with ground truth.* They see only what teams choose to show them, often missing early warning signs or emerging opportunities.†

THEREFORE...

Pull Updates to reshape how information flows through the organization. Instead of waiting for periodic reports, leaders should use direct access to the tools, dashboards, and workspaces teams use daily. This might include project management software, analytics dashboards, customer feedback channels, or collaboration platforms.

The key principles include:

- Real-time access to raw data and work in progress
- Standardized dashboards that present key metrics without manual preparation
- Direct visibility into team communications and decision-making
- Self-service tools that allow leaders to drill down into areas of interest

Toyota's iconic *genchi genbutsu* practice illustrates what effective "pull updates" look like on the shop floor, where managers carve out daily *gemba* walks, stopping at each station's visual board—populated by the operators themselves—to ask "What problem are we solving? Where's the standard? When did we last miss *takt* time?" Because queue length, first-time-through rate, and Andon-cord pulls, which stop the production line when an employee notices a problem, are posted

---

* Also mentioned in NETWORK OF TEAMS (13).

† Aside here: This is one of the areas where consultants can be genuinely useful. Because they don't work at the company, there's less of an explicit requirement to soothe leaders to stay employed. This isn't always the case, but in my experience, we were always able to be more truthful to execs than the directors and managers who brought us in.

in real time right beside the work, executives fetch facts directly from the source rather than waiting for a slide deck.[23]

APPLICATION

Implementation begins with identifying the key information streams leaders need to access. Work with teams to ensure their daily tools and systems can surface relevant data in accessible ways.

This might involve:

- Creating standardized dashboards that automatically aggregate key metrics across projects or departments. These should require no manual preparation or formatting—they simply present live data.*
- Setting up shared digital workspaces where leaders can observe team discussions and decisions in real time. This might mean giving leaders access to project management tools, team chat channels, or development environments.
- Establishing clear protocols for what information should be readily available versus what might require additional context or privacy protection. Create a simple taxonomy of information types and appropriate access levels.
- Training leaders to pull the information they need rather than asking for custom reports. This skill development is crucial—many leaders are accustomed to having information packaged for them and may need guidance on how to navigate raw data sources effectively.
- Starting small with one or two key metrics or projects before expanding. Choose high-visibility areas where the benefits of real-time access will be immediately apparent.

Pull Updates depends on TRANSPARENCY (32) to make information visible and accessible. It supports ACTIVE STEERING (27) by providing the real-time data

---

* Tableau, I'm specifically *not* looking in your direction. The refresh time is just too slow.

needed for frequent course corrections. It makes METRICS REVIEW (36) interesting and gives WORK IN PUBLIC (50) an audience. Similarly, Pull Updates help
leaders practice ADVICE (31) more effectively by giving them the context needed
to provide meaningful input without controlling outcomes. This immediate transparency surfaces issues earlier and enables faster, more informed decision-making.
Leaders become more connected to day-to-day realities, while teams feel less pressure to manage impressions and can focus more on actual work.

35 Demos

Alignment through documentation, status reports,
and formal presentations is usually not alignment

There's a story of a technology team inside a large automaker where 200 people were working on a substantial new incentive program for dealers.* The output of the team's work would have a big impact on outcomes: better tracking of activity, better alignment of effort to opportunity, more sales. There was nothing special about this team, exactly: It contained all the normal capabilities that you'd expect from a scaled unit, like infrastructure services, information security, and business-aligned teams.

What's also unremarkable is that they hadn't delivered anything of value in five years.

You can imagine what the meetings were like between this team and the rest of the business.

The quarterly updates featured glossy slide decks filled with technical jargon and complex architecture diagrams, while business stakeholders sat stone-faced, mentally calculating the millions spent with nothing tangible to show.† Each meeting ended with vague promises about "upcoming milestones" that never materialized, while dealers continued using their decade-old systems.

---

* This story is true. You can probably find it online in video form, if you look hard enough. I'm leaving out the name of the organization to protect the (?) innocent.

† Assuming an average salary of around $150K per person, across five years, that's $150 million wasted (to say nothing about the additional costs that surround a team like this)! This number will probably strike you as either way too high or way too low depending on where you work.

This situation was fixed by applying many of the patterns in this book, but it's a *perfect* illustration of the failures of a document- and meeting-driven approach. This approach is about *representing* work rather than properly *demonstrating* it, leading to misalignment between those doing the work and those supporting or funding it.

Teams need more dynamic, authentic ways to share progress and gather feedback. The practice of regular demonstrations—showing real work in its current state—creates deeper understanding and stronger alignment than any status report could achieve.

No more sanitized updates that hide the messiness of real work, leading to unrealistic expectations and reduced trust. No more energy spent creating polished presentations rather than improving the actual work. No more "presentation culture," where looking good is more important than being good.

THEREFORE ...

Make demos the primary mechanisms for sharing progress, gathering feedback, and building alignment.

A true demo shows the actual work—the real service, the actual product, the functioning system—in its current state. When done consistently and authentically, demos reshape organizational culture around truth telling, COOPERATION (12), and EXPERIMENTATION (62).

Establish a demo-centric CADENCE (65) that makes showing real work a nonnegotiable part of how progress is shared. These demos should follow an ITERATIVE SHIPPING (46) approach: frequent (weekly or biweekly), open to anyone interested, and focused on actual functionality rather than planned features. Demoing real work pushes teams to DO THE RIGHT THING (26), aligning effort to true customer needs instead of speculative or outdated requirements.

DEMO MEETING AGENDA

Purpose: To show real work, get feedback, and align teams			
Show, don't tell	Keep it real	Prioritize feedback	Align through experience

Time	Activity	Purpose	Facilitator Notes
5 min	Welcome & Context	Set expectations and focus.	Clarify the goal: "We're here to see real work and learn." It's okay to show unfinished work.
20 min	Live Demo	Demonstrate actual work.	Actual products, services, or systems. What's working and what's not. Real scenarios, not abstract examples.
15 min	Feedback & Discussion	Gather reactions and questions.	Ask clear, simple questions: "What good things stood out?" "What questions or concerns do you have?" "What seems missing or unclear?"
5 min	Wrap-Up & Next Steps	Summarize insights and clarify actions.	Briefly summarize key points. Confirm immediate next steps and responsibilities. Set date and expectations for next demo.

SOUNDS GOOD, BUT WHAT DO I BRING TO THE MEETING?

Most teams struggle to translate their work into things that can be demoed, and a failure mode of this pattern is just demoing presentations (e.g., showing a presentation in edit mode to get feedback, rather than truly pitching the idea to stakeholders). Applying the TEAM/PROCESS AS PRODUCT (63) mindset helps teams continually refine what it means to "show the work," even in areas like HR, facilities, or finance.

Team	What & How to Demo	Notes
Product, Engineering *Easy*	Working builds, functional prototypes, actual systems Live interactive sessions showing real functionality	Focus on what works now, not what will work eventually; use real data; demonstrate failure modes.
Design *Easy*	Interactive prototypes, user journeys, visual systems Guided experiences with actual user interactions	Show design in context of use; demonstrate multiple states; reveal the system beyond single screens.
Marketing *Medium*	Actual campaigns, real content, real channels Live channel reviews, real audience interactions	Show performance data; demonstrate targeting mechanisms; reveal the full customer journey.
Facilities, Space *Medium*	Physical environments, actual usage, environmental metrics Guided tours, video of actual use, demonstration of features	Show spaces being used; demonstrate adaptability; reveal unexpected behaviors.
Legal, Compliance *Harder*	Process walk-throughs, actual documentation, real reviews Live process demonstrations, actual case walk-throughs	Use anonymized real scenarios; show time requirements; demonstrate decision frameworks.
Finance *Harder*	Working financial tools, actual analyses, decision frameworks Live data analysis, real-time forecast demonstrations	Use real company data; show edge cases; demonstrate how decisions would actually be made.
HR, People *Harder*	Process experiences, communication materials, actual tools Role-played experiences, real tool interactions	Demonstrate the emotional journey; show actual timeframes; use realistic scenarios.

●▼◢■✱⬟

Build the surrounding ecosystem that makes demos effective: Establish STRUC-
TURAL & PSYCHOLOGICAL SAFETY (3) so teams feel comfortable showing
incomplete or imperfect work. Embrace a visible FAIL WALL (69) to normalize experimentation and vulnerability, reinforcing trust that feedback supports improvement, not judgment. Finally, define clear PURPOSE, CUSTOMER, PLATFORM (16)
as context, anchoring demos to the strategic needs and real-world impact they're
meant to achieve.

36 *Metrics Review*

Start every meeting with a bit of data

It's a struggle to maintain consistent focus on what's most important. Most teams will track a handful of data points about their work or their business, while lacking a reliable approach to regularly reviewing and acting on this information. As a result, important signals get lost in the noise of daily operations, and teams drift from their intended practices and goals.

The metrics review pattern creates a deliberate space for teams to assess their performance, adherence to key practices, and progress toward objectives. When you stick to it, it is one of the most powerful forcing functions I've experienced for honest course correction.*

THEREFORE ...

At the beginning of one of your regular team meetings, spend a small amount of time reviewing both quantitative metrics and qualitative practices. This review should cover three key areas:

---

* If you want to *max out* this idea, check out the Amazon Weekly Business Review (WBR) process and related open-source app here, from Colin Bryar and Bill Carr, authors of *Working Backwards*: https://workingbackwards.com/wbr-app/sample-wbr-report.

What	How
Performance Metrics: Key indicators of team output and impact (e.g., sales numbers, customer satisfaction scores, project milestones)	Start with a quick review of dashboards or key numbers, but don't get lost in the data. The goal is to spot trends and identify areas needing attention; avoid spiraling on the measures by actively preventing discussion. Just look at the numbers for a while before you start justifying things.
Practice Adherence: Assessment of how well the team is following its established ways of working, e.g., "Are we WORKING IN PUBLIC (50)?" or "Are we using STRUCTURED DECISION-MAKING (30)?"	Move to a practice check-in, where team members briefly assess their adherence to key working methods. This can and should be as simple as a quick yes/no for each practice: "Did we maintain our KANBAN (55) board this week?" or "Did we hold our daily stand-ups?"
Mission Progress: Regular check-in on whether the team believes it's on track to achieve its broader objectives	End with the most important question: "Based on what we see, do we believe we're on track to achieve our mission?" This creates space for team members to voice concerns or suggestions early, before problems become critical.

The review should be brief, perhaps a maximum of 15 minutes and without becoming a full-fledged RETROSPECTIVE (66), but consistent. The attention to both quantitative and qualitative measures helps maintain alignment between daily work, DO THE RIGHT THING (26), and TRUE PURPOSE (1).[24] The regular cadence of review and reflection helps embed good practices more deeply into team operations, making it more likely that important working methods will stick even during busy or stressful periods.

37 *Backlog Management*

Know what you're not working on

Teams operate in silos, with work requests coming from multiple channels and priorities constantly shifting. Without a clear system for managing incoming work and current commitments, organizations default to reactive modes—responding to the loudest voice or latest crisis rather than strategically managing their capacity and focus.

Work enters through multiple channels (email, chat, hallway conversations) with no single source of truth. Teams take on too many concurrent projects, leading to context switching and delayed delivery. Stakeholders have no visibility into team capacity or priorities, leading to unrealistic expectations and constant interruptions. Important but non-urgent work gets perpetually delayed in favor of "emergency" requests. Teams struggle to make strategic decisions about what to work on next, defaulting to whatever seems most pressing in the moment.

Perhaps most damaging, the lack of visibility into what teams are actually working on prevents strategic conversations about trade-offs. When no one can see the full landscape of potential work, discussions about priorities remain abstract and disconnected from reality. Leaders can't make informed decisions about resource allocation because they can't see how current commitments align with organizational goals.

THEREFORE...

Establish a single, visible backlog that serves as the definitive source of truth for planned and potential work.* This backlog should be:

- **Accessible:** Visible to all stakeholders and team members
- **Prioritized:** Clearly showing what's next and what's on hold
- **Active:** Regularly reviewed and updated to reflect current reality
- **Bounded:** Limited in size to maintain focus and prevent overwhelming the team

The backlog is a key tool for managing work in progress (WIP) and setting expectations. Rather than maintaining multiple task lists or project plans, teams funnel all work through this single system, making it easier to manage capacity and communicate priorities.

The concept of managed backlogs emerged from software development practices in the early 2000s, particularly as part of Scrum and KANBAN (55) methodologies. However, unlike those specialized approaches, which often focus on technical estimation ceremonies and velocity calculations, strategic backlog management emphasizes transparency, prioritization, and cross-team coordination.

You don't need software to have a clear, reprioritizable backlog. You don't need to be working on software, either. You don't need ceremonies to manage your backlog, though they may help. Here's how:

---

* Read more about the basics of backlogs here: https://scrumguides.org/scrum-guide.html#scrum -artifacts.

CREATE TRANSPARENCY

Start by creating a simple, accessible backlog visible to everyone in the organization:

- Choose a platform that balances simplicity with sufficient detail (a physical board, spreadsheet, or purpose-built tool).
- Include key information: description, requestor, business value, dependencies, and status.
- Make it easily filterable and searchable to support different views and needs.
- Keep the interface intuitive enough that stakeholders can self-serve information.

ESTABLISH STRATEGIC FILTERING

Instead of elaborate estimation exercises, focus on strategic classification:

- Create clear criteria for backlog entry—not every request should make the cut.
- Develop simple classification schemes aligned with organizational priorities.
- Use STRATEGY HEURISTIC (29) principles to evaluate potential work.
- Explicitly mark items that you are "not doing now" but are worth keeping visible.

IMPLEMENT REGULAR RHYTHMS

Create lightweight cadences for backlog management:

- Brief weekly reviews (15–30 minutes) to assess new items and current priorities
- Monthly strategic reviews to ensure alignment with OBJECTIVES & KEY RESULTS (28)
- Quarterly purges to remove outdated items and refresh priorities
- Just-in-time refinement of upcoming work rather than extensive up-front planning

BUILD CROSS-TEAM COORDINATION

Use the backlog as a coordination tool across your NETWORK OF TEAMS (13):

- Create visibility into dependencies between teams.
- Establish clear handoff protocols when work crosses team boundaries.
- Use shared backlog reviews to identify potential conflicts or overlapping work.
- Implement visual indicators that show cross-team impacts.

MANAGE STAKEHOLDER RELATIONSHIPS

The backlog is a powerful tool for stakeholder management:

- Train stakeholders to consult the backlog before making new requests.
- Use the backlog in conversations about priorities and capacity.
- Help stakeholders understand trade-offs by showing what's displaced when new work enters.
- Establish clear paths for appropriate escalation when priorities conflict.

The most valuable aspect of backlog management is strategic transparency. When organizations can see their full work landscape, they make better decisions about where to invest energy and attention. This visibility makes conversations about priorities, capacity, and trade-offs meaningful.*

●▼◢■❀⬟

For teams implementing ACTIVE STEERING (27), the Backlog provides the inventory of potential adjustments. When combined with PULL UPDATES (34), stakeholders can directly observe work progress without requiring special reports. The consistent prioritization framework supports STRUCTURED DECISION-MAKING (30) by making trade-offs explicit rather than implicit.

---

* There's also a bunch of really good ways to do this that don't feel like a "traditional" backlog. Basecamp's *Shape Up* is a useful alternative (https://basecamp.com/shapeup).

38 *Conflict as a Resource*

A free, renewable source of energy

Organizations typically view conflict as a problem to be eliminated or, at best, a necessary evil to be managed. This perspective drives conflict underground, where it festers and creates dysfunction. Leaders pride themselves on "harmonious" teams where disagreements are rare, equating the absence of visible tension with health. But this approach misses the entire point of conflict at work: Healthy disagreement and productive tension are essential for innovation, learning, and growth. Without robust debate and the clash of diverse perspectives, teams default to mediocre compromises, miss critical insights, and fail to identify potential problems. The energy inherent in difference—different ideas, different approaches, different mental models—goes untapped.

This avoidance creates a culture of "nice" that breeds resentment. Important issues go unaddressed because raising them feels too risky. Innovation suffers as people hesitate to challenge existing ideas or propose radical alternatives. Decision-making gets compromised when crucial perspectives remain unvoiced. We lose the creative energy that productive conflict can generate.

Even when organizations recognize the value of healthy conflict, they often lack the structures to support it. Without clear processes for engaging in disagreement, attempts at "healthy debate" can quickly devolve into personal attacks or unproductive arguments. The absence of shared protocols for handling tension makes every conflict feel personally threatening rather than professionally valuable.

THEREFORE...

Transform conflict from a threat into a resource with mindset shifts and structural scaffolding. Recognize that conflict is not just inevitable but actually valuable when engaged in skillfully. When conflict becomes a resource, teams can engage in rigorous debate while maintaining strong relationships, and organizations can use tension as a driver of positive change rather than a source of dysfunction.*

The roots of this approach can be traced to Mary Parker Follett's "constructive conflict" concept developed in the 1920s.[25] Her pioneering work illustrated how conflicts could be integrated rather than dominated or compromised, yielding solutions superior to what any individual could devise alone. Later advances in negotiation theory from the Harvard Negotiation Project reinforced how separating people from problems enables more productive engagement with differences.[26]

To implement this pattern effectively:

1. Create explicit distinctions between productive conflict (focused on ideas, issues, and opportunities) and destructive conflict (centered on personalities, politics, or power). This clarity helps teams engage with the right kind of disagreement while avoiding unhealthy dynamics.

2. Establish specific CONFLICT RESOLUTION (39) protocols for raising and exploring disagreements. For example, designate certain meetings as "challenge sessions," where critical thinking is explicitly encouraged, or create structured formats for presenting alternative perspectives.

3. Develop shared language for engaging in productive conflict. This might include phrases like "I'd like to offer a different perspective" that signal constructive disagreement rather than personal attack.

4. Actively model and reward productive conflict behaviors. Leaders must demonstrate comfort with disagreement, actively solicit opposing views,

---

* Amazon's Leadership Principle "Have Backbone; Disagree and Commit" is an explicit norm for surfacing disagreement (https://www.aboutamazon.com/about-us/leadership-principles). At Netflix, they refer to this as "Farming for Dissent"; you wouldn't farm something you didn't see as a resource (https://jobs.netflix.com/culture)!

and show how conflicts can lead to better outcomes. Publicly recognize those who raise important counterpoints or identify potential problems.

These approaches create *and require* STRUCTURAL & PSYCHOLOGICAL SAFETY (3), enabling people to take the interpersonal risks of honest disagreement. Embracing conflict as a resource also improves your NETWORK OF TEAMS (13) by enabling stronger coordination across different units. It enables UPWARD REPRESENTATION (24) by creating channels for concerns to surface constructively, and it supports ADVICE (31) processes by making feedback more robust and honest.

When successfully implemented, this pattern creates a virtuous cycle. Teams that experience the benefits of productive conflict—better decisions, more innovative solutions, stronger relationships—become more comfortable engaging in constructive disagreement. The organization develops greater capacity for complexity and innovation as diverse perspectives are not just tolerated but actively sought.

39 *Conflict Resolution*

Misalignment, managed

Conflict is natural and necessary in healthy organizations, driving innovation and growth. The challenge is how it's handled. Most organizations default to hierarchical escalation, leaving root causes unaddressed and creating dependency on managers. Flatter organizations often lack structured ways to resolve disagreements, allowing conflicts to linger and damage trust.

And you surely can't use CONFLICT AS A RESOURCE (38) without some way to harness the energy.

THEREFORE...

Establish a structured conflict resolution process that emphasizes direct communication and accountability, supported by staged escalation, as follows.*

---

* This is based on Morning Star's process: Employees start conflict resolution through direct dialogue, then move to peer mediation and panel reviews, successfully resolving issues ranging from minor disputes to major disagreements, with the CEO as the Stage 4 authority figure.

STAGE 1: DIRECT DIALOGUE (15–30 MIN)

Parties first attempt face-to-face conversation focused on behaviors, impact, and desired outcomes, rather than blame.

Time	Activity	Purpose
2 min	Introduction	Clearly state the issue and intention for resolution.
5 min each	Facts & Impacts	Each party explains their perspective, sticking to facts and observed behaviors.
5 min	Desired Outcomes	Discuss and clearly state what each party needs for resolution.
5 min	Agreement & Next Steps	Document agreed actions and timelines.

STAGE 2: PEER MEDIATION (30–45 MIN)

If direct dialogue stalls, engage a trusted peer to facilitate without imposing solutions.

Time	Activity	Purpose
5 min	Mediator Introduction	Mediator explains their neutral role.
5 min each	Issue Restatement	Each party restates their perspective briefly.
20 min	Mediator-Led Dialogue	Mediator guides conversation toward mutual understanding and workable solutions.
10 min	Agreement & Documentation	Clarify agreed resolutions, document them, and outline clear next steps.

STAGE 3: PANEL REVIEW (45–60 MIN)

Unresolved issues move to a small panel of respected peers to mediate and suggest resolutions aligned with organizational values.

Time	Activity	Purpose
10 min	Panel Introduction	Panel introduces themselves and restates guidelines.
10 min each	Present Perspectives	Each party presents their case without interruption.
15 min	Panel Q&A	Panel seeks clarification.
15 min	Panel Discussion	Panel facilitates discussion toward a mutually acceptable resolution.
10 min	Panel Recommendation	Panel clearly states a recommended solution and next steps.

STAGE 4: FINAL ARBITRATION

Rarely used, but available—escalate to a trusted authority figure for a binding decision; agenda is the same as Stage 3, but with the authority figure in place of the panel, no discussion, and a binding decision as a result.

Clearly document the process and ensure all team members are trained in basic conflict-resolution skills, emphasizing STRUCTURAL & PSYCHOLOGICAL SAFETY (3) to ensure honest communication. Encourage TRANSPARENCY (32) by openly tracking conflict outcomes and addressing systemic patterns rather than isolated incidents. Conduct periodic reviews of the conflict process effectiveness, capturing insights for EXPERIMENTATION (62).

40 *Colleague Letter of Understanding*

Get, and stay, on the same page (literally)

Expectations among colleagues are often implicit, leading to misunderstandings and friction. When people work together, they bring different assumptions about responsibilities, communication styles, and working preferences. Without a framework for making these explicit, teams waste energy navigating unclear boundaries and unspoken expectations.

We've all experienced the frustration: You thought your colleague would handle a task, but they assumed it was yours. You expected daily updates, while they planned to check in weekly. You prefer direct feedback, while they soften criticism to avoid offense. These misalignments create unnecessary tension, damage trust, and reduce productivity. Not because of bad intentions, but because you never talked about expectations.

In most organizations, working relationships develop haphazardly, with colleagues discovering each other's preferences through trial and error. Teams often only discuss expectations when they're not being met, turning what could be constructive alignment into confrontation. The lack of a format for establishing working agreements means important details remain unaddressed until they cause problems.

THEREFORE ...

The Colleague Letter of Understanding (CLOU) makes hidden assumptions clear, mutually agreed-upon parameters for working relationships. It serves as a living document that captures how colleagues will work together, support each other, and handle potential conflicts.

This document is created collaboratively, reviewed regularly, and updated as needed. It serves not as a binding contract but as a shared reference point for building stronger working relationships.

CLOUs were developed at Morning Star to formalize peer-to-peer commitments in their self-managed organization. Agile methodologies have introduced similar working agreements to help teams align on process expectations. And academic research tells us that even informal contracts drive better workplace relationships.*

APPLICATION

Begin by scheduling dedicated time for colleagues to discuss and document their working relationship.† The initial conversation should cover:

Working Preferences

- When and how are you most productive? (For instance: *I do my best creative work in the morning and prefer focused time for analysis in afternoons.*)
- What communication channels work best for different needs? (For example: *Use Slack for quick questions, email for items needing documentation, and calls for complex discussions.*)
- How do you prefer to receive and process information? (Such as: *I need time to process information before responding to proposals.*)
- What meeting formats support your best thinking? (Perhaps: *I appreciate agendas in advance and time to prepare.*)

---

* For more on these, check out Gary Hamel's "First, Let's Fire All the Managers" from 2011, also referenced elsewhere in this book. Any doc on Scrum will help with working agreements, but those by Ken Schwaber and Jeff Sutherland are probably best. For overall *contracting*, check out Denise Rousseau's *Psychological Contracts in Organizations: Understanding Written and Unwritten Agreements* from 1995.

† When? According to your CADENCE (65), but at least on an annual basis.

Collaboration Framework

- What decisions can you make independently vs. together? (*You can make design decisions independently, but let's review user flows together.*)
- How will you handle role boundaries and overlaps? (*When customer issues involve both our areas, I'll take the first pass and tag you where needed.*)
- What does effective resource sharing look like? (*We'll review shared resource needs in our weekly check-in.*)
- How will you escalate issues when needed? (*If we can't resolve a disagreement in one conversation, we'll involve Maya as a thought partner.*)

Support Structure

- How do you prefer to receive feedback? (*I value direct feedback delivered privately [with specific examples].*)
- What check-in rhythm works for your partnership? (*Let's have a structured 15-minute check-in every Monday and informal touchpoints as needed.*)
- How will you approach problem-solving together? (*When issues arise, let's first clarify the problem before jumping to solutions.*)
- What does mutual support for growth look like? (*I'd like your perspective on my client presentations, and I'm happy to review your project plans.*)

The document should be succinct (one or two pages) and use clear, specific language. Avoid generic statements like "maintain good communication" in favor of specific agreements like "respond to urgent Slack messages within two hours during workdays." In my experience, this is usually best between two individual humans, but it would also work well among teams (and become a Team Letter of Understanding, or TLOU).*

---

* Haier, for example, expands this practice into a series of contracts between its thousands of microenterprises. Each month, thousands of bids are made for hundreds of potential contracts, all stored in their LOGBOOK (57), known as Workbench. Read more here: https://globalfocusmagazine.com/the-emc-contract-as-a-smart-coordination-mechanism.

TEMPLATE EXAMPLE

Colleague Letter of Understanding		
Between	[Name 1]	[Name 2]
Next Review	[Date, typically 3–6 months later]	
Our Working Relationship	Purpose: We're collaborating to [specific shared objective]. This document outlines how we'll work together effectively to achieve that goal.	
Working Rhythms	[Name 1] works best [early morning/late evening/etc.] and prefers [communication preference].	[Name 2] works best [time period] and prefers [communication preference].
	We'll have scheduled check-ins [frequency and format]. For urgent matters, we'll [specific protocol].	
Decision Rights	[Name 1] will make decisions about [areas] independently.	[Name 2] will make decisions about [areas] independently.
	We'll collaborate on decisions regarding [areas]. We'll resolve disagreements by [specific approach].	
Communication Agreements	For feedback, [Name 1] prefers [approach].	For feedback, [Name 2] prefers [approach].
	For project updates, we'll use [tool/method/frequency]. Expected response times: [specifics for different channels/priorities] Meeting preferences: [preparation needs, facilitation styles, follow-up expectations]	
Success Measures	We'll know our working relationship is successful when [observable outcomes]. We'll assess our collaboration through [specific method and timing].	
Signatures*		

The document should be reviewed quarterly and updated as needed, with both parties agreeing to changes. Keep it accessible to both parties and reference it during regular check-ins.

---

* Yes. Sign it!

By implementing CLOUs, organizations create a foundation for stronger, more intentional working relationships. Teams move faster and collaborate more effectively because expectations are clear and agreed upon. The practice of regularly discussing and updating these agreements builds trust and PSYCHOLOGICAL SAFETY (3), as colleagues become more comfortable having direct conversations about their working relationships.

This practice normalizes explicit communication about working styles and expectations. It reduces interpersonal friction, accelerates onboarding of new working relationships, and creates a more resilient organization where relationship challenges are addressed systematically *and* personally. The result is a more mature, professional environment where strong working relationships are built by design.

The Colleague Letter of Understanding creates clear expectations that support STRUCTURED DECISION-MAKING (30) by clarifying who makes which decisions. It enhances CONFLICT AS A RESOURCE (38) by establishing parameters for productive disagreement. For teams implementing DISTRIBUTED MANAGEMENT (14), CLOUs create the peer agreements necessary for coordination without hierarchy. The practice also provides a structured format for the ADVICE (31) process, clarifying when and how colleagues should seek input from each other. When combined with regular METRICS REVIEWS (36), CLOUs can include specific agreements about how colleagues will review and respond to performance data together.

41 *Open Space Technology*

Most workshops are truly terrible, and we may as well throw away the agenda

Detailed agendas, careful speaker selections, and rigid schedules reflect an industrial mindset that values predictability over emergence, and this reflects a deep mistrust of groups' ability to self-organize productively. This mistrust becomes self-fulfilling: Participants learn to wait for direction → "someone else" is in charge → passive audience/active speaker dynamic → decreased engagement → exhausted organizers.

You know this. You've felt it.

And anyone who's attended a conference knows that the most valuable moments often happen in hallways, during coffee breaks, and at dinner—wherever people naturally gather to discuss what really matters to them. (This is true for cities, too, and is a core reason why cities produce more intellectual and social capital than the suburbs.)

So there's a paradox here: The more tightly we control group gatherings, the more we diminish their value. We need approaches that harness rather than suppress the inherent self-organizing capacity of human systems.

THEREFORE ...

Don't design your workshop.*

---

* Forgive me, because OST is a kind of workshop *design*. You know what I mean: Don't spend a bunch of time finessing the agenda.

Use Open Space Technology (we'll use OST and Open Space interchangeably from here on out) instead, especially when a NETWORK OF TEAMS (13) is facing a challenge that threatens its ability to achieve its TRUE PURPOSE (1).

But it's also great as a way to facilitate a quarterly offsite for teams ranging from five to 2,000 people, provided you can fit them all into one place.

OST, created by Harrison Owen, provides a radically different approach based on a few simple rules that enable and encourage self-organization.[27] The format creates a marketplace of conversation and *work* where participants generate their own agenda and freely move between discussions based on interest and potential contribution.

Owen describes four principles and one law that give Open Space a structure.

Four Principles

1. Whoever comes are the right people.
2. Whatever happens is the only thing that could have.
3. When it starts is the right time.
4. When it's over, it's over.

The Law of Two Feet

If you find yourself in a situation where you are neither learning nor contributing, you have a responsibility to move somewhere else.

CRAFTING THE INVITATION*

The success of Open Space begins with a powerful invitation that draws forth participation and passion. A good invitation includes a compelling theme and clear boundaries.

---

* A note for a future edition: I think that *invitation* might be a pattern unto itself.

1. A THEME THAT MATTERS

Frame as an open-ended question or challenge	Make it broad enough to allow emergence	Ensure it connects to real urgency or passion
"What's the future we want to create for our industry?"	"What challenges and opportunities demand our collective attention?"	"How might we revolutionize patient care?"

2. CLEAR BOUNDARIES

When & Where	Who	What
Specify the exact timeframe (start/end).	Clarify who should attend.	Outline any constraints or guardrails.
Define physical or virtual space.		State what will happen with the outputs.

Sample Invitation

Our industry faces unprecedented change. Traditional approaches aren't enough anymore, and no one person or team has all the answers. We're inviting everyone who cares about our future to join a two-day gathering exploring: "How might we reinvent ourselves for the next decade?"

This isn't a traditional conference. You'll help create the agenda based on what you believe needs to be discussed. Come prepared to raise the questions that keep you up at night and to contribute to the conversations that call to you.

We'll gather at [location] from [dates/times]. Everything discussed will inform our strategic planning process, and you'll have the opportunity to lead initiatives that emerge.

Who should come? Anyone who feels pulled by this challenge and is willing to take responsibility for what they care about. If you're wondering if that includes you, it does.

Sample Agenda

Opening (30–45 minutes)

- Arrange chairs in a circle (no tables).
- Explain principles and law clearly.
- Define overall theme or question.
- Create blank agenda wall with time/space grid.
- Have materials ready for topic posting.

Marketplace Creation (30–45 minutes)

- Invite anyone to propose topics.
- Proposers write title, their name, and initial location.
- Post topics on agenda wall.
- Allow natural combining of similar topics.
- Participants sign up for sessions that interest them.

Sessions (Bulk of time; plan for 6–12 hours)

- Host multiple concurrent discussions in individual breakout rooms or areas within a larger plenary space.
- Proposer opens session by welcoming participants.
- Groups self-manage their discussions.
- Encourage movement between sessions.
- Capture key points and actions.
- Use "law of two feet" freely.

Closing (30–45 minutes)

- Return to full circle.
- Share key discoveries.
- Identify patterns and insights.
- Plan concrete next steps.
- Document commitments.

Supporting Elements

- FACILITATION (56) is important, but only with a light touch. Owen, in his TED Talk "Dancing with Shiva," explains that Open Space violates all the rules of good management. *No advanced agenda. No person in charge. No prior training. One facilitator who took long walks and naps and never intervened. Fifteen thousand percent improvement in productivity.*[28] Trust it. It works.

- Provide SPACE FOR WORK (72): Use breakout rooms or select a space large enough for multiple groups to have relatively private discussions.

- Provide visible documentation methods, like WHITEBOARDS AT INTERSECTIONS (74).

- Create a "news wall" for sharing insights across sessions and an "evening news" space for announcing changes.

- It's possible, but not exactly recommended, to try to do this remotely. This is an experience that works much better in person.

It's easy to find raving reviews for Open Space online, but I'll share my personal experience here as a strong recommendation to try this pattern *immediately.*

For many years at Undercurrent, we'd pause at the end of every trimester, shut down the business for two days, and run an offsite with the full team that we called Undercurrent University, or UCU. Every UCU had more or less the same topics, as driven by what we leaders thought was urgent for the business, based on what we were sensing, such as sales, allocations, or engagement. We made some progress as a group with top-down planning, but inevitably when another four months would go by, we'd still have the same problems.

Then we tried Open Space.

We solved problems that we'd been unable to solve. Four months later, the problems remained solved, and we moved on to a new, more interesting set of things to talk about.*

---

* If you're thinking that it's not going to work, you're wrong. I've done this dozens of times, and it's never not worked. Give it a try. Email me if you hate it: clay@cpj.fyi.

42 *Future Backward*

Break free from your constraints

Traditional strategic planning emphasizes linear progression and probable outcomes, limiting teams' ability to imagine truly new things. This narrow thinking leads to incrementality rather than breakthrough innovations. Most planning approaches start with current constraints and then project forward, which inevitably creates self-limiting futures that merely extend present conditions.

It's no wonder things generally stay the same.

The traditional approach is based on the idea that the future is a logical extension of the present. This forces teams to think within their existing mental models, making it nearly impossible to break free from current assumptions.

- Existing constraints and assumptions automatically limit future possibilities.
- Current problems dominate discussions, stifling creative thinking.
- Teams focus on feasible next steps rather than desired end states.
- Strategic planning becomes an exercise in extrapolating the present rather than imagining new possibilities.
- The richness of collective imagination remains untapped.

Most organizations can't escape the gravitational pull of their current reality. No matter how much they talk about innovation or transformation, their planning processes keep them tethered to incremental improvements rather than true reinvention.

THEREFORE...

Use the Future Backward method to create a structured process for teams to envision both utopian and dystopian futures, then work backward to connect these scenarios to the present. This technique deliberately breaks the tyranny of linear, forward-thinking planning by starting with divergent future states and working backward.

The method uses three time horizons:

- An **impossibly good** future (utopia) three to five years ahead
- An **impossibly bad** future (dystopia) three to five years ahead
- The **present state**

Teams first describe these states vividly, then create narrative bridges between them through a series of hypothetical events. This dual-path approach helps teams break free from present constraints while maintaining connection to current reality.*

Dave Snowden developed the Future Backwards method through his work at Cognitive Edge (now The Cynefin Company). It emerged from complexity science principles that recognize how small actions and decisions can lead to dramatically different outcomes in complex systems.[29]

APPLICATION

Like many lifelong games, sports, or skills, the ideas here are relatively simple but will get substantially better and easier with practice and preparation. Here's how to start:

---

* I'd argue that Amazon's "Press Release/Frequently Asked Questions" (PR/FAQ) practice, where projects kick off with an imagined press release from the future, demonstrating the consumer benefit created by the project, is an example of Future Backward applied to the whole enterprise. Read more about this excerpt from the aptly named *Working Backwards* by Colin Bryar and Bill Carr from 2021: https://www.aboutamazon.com/news/workplace/an-insider-look-at-amazons-culture-and-processes.

Preparation

You'll Need

- Large wall space or digital collaboration board (Miro works well)
- Large hexagonal sticky notes (5x8 inches or larger) in at least three colors (The shape, size, and color of these do make a difference in the way the exercise feels.)
- Regular sticky notes for capturing insights
- Markers for each participant
- Timer

Room Setup

- Clear wall space visible to all participants
- Five distinct areas marked on the wall:
  - Past events (leftmost)
  - Current state (center left)
  - Dystopia (top right)
  - Utopia (bottom right)
  - Space in between for backward paths

Facilitation Guidelines

1. Introduce the Process (10 minutes)

- Explain the purpose: breaking free from current constraints to imagine transformative possibilities.
- Describe the three time horizons and the backward mapping approach.
- Emphasize there are no wrong answers. The goal is to make sense of our world, together.

2. Generate Scenarios (45–60 minutes)

Start with the present state (15 minutes):

- Begin by documenting the current reality: "What are the defining characteristics of our situation today?"
- Have participants individually write elements of the present state on hexagonal notes (one color).
- Cluster related ideas in the center of the workspace.

Facilitation tip: Encourage descriptive statements rather than judgments. Ask "What would an objective observer notice?" rather than "What's wrong with our current state?"

Map events from the past year (15 minutes):

- Identify three or four key events or decisions from the past year that have shaped the present.
- Ask participants to work backward from today, rather than just naming events that happened.
- Work together to put these in order on the board, in a single line, starting with the current state.

Facilitation tip: This creates context for understanding how past patterns might influence future trajectories. Ask "Do you see any patterns in how we've arrived at our present state that might continue into the future?"

Describe utopia (15–20 minutes):

- Conduct a brief imagination exercise: "Close your eyes. Take three deep breaths. Imagine it's [date three to five years in the future]. Your organization has achieved extraordinary success beyond what seemed possible. What does that look like? What are people saying? What has fundamentally changed?"

- Have participants individually write elements of this utopian state on hexagonal notes (second color).
- Place these in the "Utopia" area of the workspace.

Facilitation tip: Don't rush this phase. Allow silence and thinking time. When energy wanes, prompt with questions like "What would your most demanding customer say about you in this future?" or "What headline would appear in your industry publication?"

Describe dystopia (15–20 minutes):

- Repeat the imagination exercise, but for the *impossibly bad* future.
- Guide visualization: "It's [same future date]. Everything that could go wrong has gone wrong. Your worst fears have materialized. What failed? What are people saying? What opportunities were missed?"
- Capture elements on the third color of hexagonal notes.
- Place these in the "Dystopia" area of the workspace.

3. Create Pathways (60 minutes)

Work backward from utopia (30 minutes):

- Start at the utopian future and ask: "What happened right before this that made this outcome possible?"
- Place this event on a new hexagonal note between utopia and present.
- Continue working backward: "And what happened before that?"
- Create a chain of four to six key events or decisions that connect back toward the present.

Facilitation tip: Don't help people figure out the path backward. Give them time to struggle with it. The cognitive work of creating the backward chain is where insights emerge. If they get stuck, ask, "What shift in thinking or behavior would have to happen for this future to become possible?"

Work backward from dystopia (30 minutes):

- Repeat the process for the dystopian future.
- Ask: "What critical mistake or missed opportunity led to this outcome?"
- Create a similar chain of four to six events.

Facilitation tip: Watch for events that appear in both the utopian and dystopian pathways but with opposite characteristics. These are often the most critical decision points.

4. Reflection and Synthesis (45–60 minutes)

Use 1-2-4-All format:

- Individual reflection (1 minute): Each person notes their key insights.
- Pairs discuss (2 minutes): Share most important observations.
- Groups of four expand (4 minutes): Identify patterns and implications.
- Whole group harvests key insights (all): Capture critical themes.

Facilitation tip: Focus the harvest on three questions: "What surprised you? What critical decision points did you identify? What does this suggest about actions we should take now?"

Look for patterns:

- Identify recurring themes across pathways.
- Note potential leverage points where small actions could create significant shifts.
- Highlight assumptions that appeared in both utopian and dystopian futures.

Facilitation tip: As facilitator, capture your own observations of patterns emerging during the exercise. Share these during the reflection phase to help the group see connections they might miss.

Facilitation Notes

- Budget more time than you think you'll need. This exercise typically takes three to four hours minimum for meaningful results. A half day is ideal.
- For large groups (15+), split into multiple small groups of five to seven people. If the room is large enough, they can work on different sections of the same wall. This creates richer content while keeping everyone engaged.
- Let silence work for you. When participants fall quiet, resist the urge to fill the space. Count silently to 20 before prompting further discussion.
- Capture nonlinear connections. If participants notice connections between events that aren't sequential, use string or drawn lines to make these relationships visible.
- Digital adaptation: If using Miro or similar tools (even in person), create a template with the five zones clearly marked. Digital tools can even enhance the in-person experience by making it easier to move and connect ideas, and sometimes they are your only option if you have 50 people and not enough breakout space.*
- Balanced timing approach: Depending on available time, choose between two approaches:
  - Deep dive (preferred): Have people reflect and discuss after each round of creation. This builds richer context and allows for course correction.
  - Expedited version: Complete all creation steps before reflection. This requires more skilled facilitation to help participants extract meaning from the completed exercise.
- End with commitments: Close by having each participant identify one action they'll take in the next week based on insights from the exercise.

Future Backward feels strange at first, but by the end of the session it will feel like magic. In my experience, you can throw away all of the output of the session, and the participants will do the things on the path to utopia, while avoiding the things on the path to dystopia. The shared language, the tangibility of the futures,

---

* Ask me how I know.

and the richer understanding of the current trajectory and potential alternatives—all of these build a smarter, savvier team.

This pattern works particularly well when combined with STRATEGY HEURISTIC (29), as the insights from Future Backward often reveal key tensions that can be formulated into strategic principles. The method also complements OBJECTIVES & KEY RESULTS (28) by helping teams set more ambitious and meaningful objectives that break free from current constraints. For teams implementing ACTIVE STEERING (27), Future Backward provides the broader context needed to guide iterative decision-making within a coherent strategic direction.

43 *Team Charter*

Write it down. Write it down!

Teams often begin work without clear alignment on fundamental questions about their purpose, scope, and ways of working. This ambiguity leads to confusion about priorities, decision rights, and responsibilities. While everyone may feel busy, the lack of shared understanding means efforts aren't necessarily focused on what matters most.

THEREFORE...

Create a clear team charter that explicitly defines five key elements:

1. TRUE PURPOSE (1)

Why does this team exist?	What unique value do we create?	What would be missing if we didn't exist?

2. FOCUS AREAS
INCLUDING STRATEGY HEURISTIC (29)

What specific work will we do?	What are our key priorities?	What is explicitly out of scope?

3. MEASURES

LIKE OBJECTIVES & KEY RESULTS (28) OR RELATIVE TARGETS (33) AND ASSESSED VIA METRICS REVIEW (36); USED TO APPLY TEAM INCENTIVES (25)

How will we know if we're successful?	What company metrics matter most to us?	What behaviors do we want to encourage for ourselves? For the organization as a whole?

4. DECISION RIGHTS

INCLUDING DOMAINS, ASSETS & STANDARDS (23)

What decisions can we make without anyone else's permission?	Where do we need to consult others?	What are our key dependencies?

5. ROLES

REFERENCING DISTRIBUTED MANAGEMENT (14) AND INCLUDING UPWARD REPRESENTATION (24). FILLED VIA ELECTIONS (15) AND USED BY THE TALENT MARKETPLACE (20).

What distinct roles do we need?	What are their core accountabilities?	How does this role interact with others on our team? With others outside our team?

It's a good idea to craft the team charter *with* the team that it governs. Begin with a focused workshop lasting two to three hours where the team collaboratively drafts each section. Use FACILITATION (56). Ask different team members to lead the discussion of different sections to build shared ownership. Test the charter by applying it to recent decisions or challenges—would it have provided clear guidance?*

Review the charter on a specified CADENCE (65) to ensure it remains relevant. Make updates based on what you've learned about how the team actually works. Share the charter with key stakeholders and use it to onboard new team members; WORK IN PUBLIC (50) so that others can find your charter easily and understand what your team does and does not do.

If you're starting from scratch, you'll want to run a small workshop with your team to create your charter for the first time.

STEP 1: GET CLEAR ON THE PURPOSE FOR THE TEAM†

This works best if you have a clear, consequential TRUE PURPOSE (1) for the team. Especially in larger organizations, teams don't have permission to write their own purpose, so doing this prep may require going to the next level of authority in the organization above the team and asking them for clarity on mission. Use the prompts above when thinking about your purpose.

STEP 2: CAPTURE THE WORK TO BE DONE

Write down all of the work that the team needs to do (not just what it's doing today) in order to achieve the mission. Try to break down the work to a task level. As an example, "Scheduling flights for vendor assessment" is better than "Travel," and "Selecting which content gets presented to execs" is better than "Exec decks."

When you do this right, you're going to have a lot of tasks. The best tool we

---

* Atlassian's "Working Agreements" play is a good guide if you're looking for more (https://www .atlassian.com/team-playbook/plays/working-agreements)!

† A version of this content originally appeared on my blog, at cpj.fyi, circa 2021. I've been running this specific process since 2015, and I know that it works very well.

EXAMPLE CHARTER

Team	Design Systems	
Purpose	Enable rapid, high-quality product development across the organization by creating and maintaining a cohesive design system that makes it easier to build consistent, accessible user experiences.	
Focus areas	• Design system strategy and road map • Core component library development • Design tokens and foundations • Documentation and guidelines • Usage analytics and adoption metrics	Out of Scope • Individual product design decisions • Feature-specific components • Marketing or brand design • Design sprint facilitation
Measures	Core • Component adoption rate across products • Time saved per new feature development • System consistency score • Documentation usage/satisfaction • Design debt-reduction rate	Behavioral • Proactive contribution from product teams • Cross-functional collaboration quality • Knowledge-sharing effectiveness
Decision rights	Autonomous • Component architecture and implementation • Documentation standards • Release scheduling • Technical stack choices • Internal team processes	Consultative • Major design-language changes (consult product design leads) • Breaking changes (consult engineering leads) • Resource allocation (consult design director) • Cross-team processes (consult affected teams)
Roles	Design systems lead: Strategic direction and stakeholder alignment	
	Senior design systems designer: Design integrity and user experience	
	Design systems engineer: Technical implementation and maintenance	
	Documentation specialist: Knowledge accessibility and adoption	
Review schedule	• Monthly metrics review • Quarterly charter adjustment • Semiannual role evaluation • Annual strategic alignment	

have for capturing a team's full scope of work is a spreadsheet—not Post-its or Miro boards.* You're looking for ease of manipulation—clustering things, tagging things, adding richer data to a bunch of tasks at once—and spreadsheets make this dead simple. A Google Sheet is best, but a Notion database or Airtable base will work well; the key here is something that many people can edit together in real time. Ideally, assign this prep work to each individual person on the team, and have them put all of their individual work in a single document. It's easier to cover all the ground on this task when you have a bit of space to think by yourself.

Especially for the corporate teams out there, there are a handful of "kinds of tasks" that you don't want to forget. Use these as prompts when you're capturing work:

- What do we do to serve our customers?
- What work is required to guide other teams or direct reports?
- What goes into our team's partnership with other firms?
- How do we surface data to leadership?

STEP 3: GROUP THE WORK INTO ROLES

If you're working in a spreadsheet, the fastest way to do this is to go row by row and tag each work element with a brief handle. This is where you can start using broader terms like "Travel" or "Exec Decks." When you're done tagging, do a quick alphabetical sort based on the row that contains all the tags. Patterns should emerge.

If you want to do this as an in-person workshop, transpose everything from the shared spreadsheet onto Post-it notes and ask the group to cluster related work. Consider clustering based on customer type, functional category, or required expertise. Patterns should emerge.

After you've tagged or clustered, you need to name each group. Once you name these clusters, you've got your starting set of roles. Naming roles is probably worth breaking down in a separate guide—semantics are important!—but to start, try using a pattern that begins with [Function/Capability/Workstream] and ends with [Style or Involvement]; Finance Guide; Strategy Adviser; Partner Liase-er; etc.

---

* Miro's ever-improving AI summaries are useful here, though!

STEP 4: ADD MEANINGFUL DEFINITION TO THE ROLES

To start, just rewrite the rows in the spreadsheet to follow a common format, where each row begins with a verb. These form the starter set of expectations for the roles you just named.

Some of the expectations will begin with a very special verb: *deciding*. Look out for these—they can form the backbone of clear decision rights on the team. When you assign one of these expectations to a role, try actually letting that role make the call for a short while, rather than trying to involve everyone on the team.

STEP 5: ASSIGN PEOPLE TO THE ROLES

Allow multiple people to fill a single role, and allow individual people to fill a variety of roles. This makes each individual role, and each individual expectation, a little less important—and a little more collective. This is good up to a point: It encourages a more robust discussion of what's actually important for the team, but can lead to *if it's everyone's job, it's nobody's job-itis.* When you notice the latter creeping in, take that as an invitation to break down a role a bit further to get more specific about authority and accountability.

On a traditional team, where there's a clear team lead, this is the moment for the leader to step forward and use their positional authority to assign people to roles. It can be helpful to set a reasonable time limit to these assignments. Try quarterly time limits to start.

PRACTICE

44 *Check In & Out*

What's got your attention?

Meetings often begin abruptly and end without closure, with participants mentally elsewhere. This hidden tax on productivity stems from poor transitions between activities, where distractions, emotions, and unresolved thoughts from previous interactions affect current engagement.

Groups have been *checking in* with each other to start sessions since forever, but several studies of high-stress operational environments have proven the importance of this extremely simple pattern (that every meeting, project, or general group moment should be bookended by a check-in and checkout). Whether you're a helicopter crew heading out to an oil rig on the North Sea, or surgeons about to start an emergency operation, context sharing before getting down to business has been proven to reduce mistakes and improve outcomes.[1]

THEREFORE...

Begin and end every significant group interaction with intentional check-in and checkout rounds.* Each person briefly shares without interruption:

---

* Jim and Michele McCarthy's "Core Protocols" are worth some additional exploration if this resonates with you. Find them here: https://liveingreatness.com.

Check-in	Checkout
Current state of mind, distractions, or hopes for the session	Reflections, learnings, or unresolved tensions

The simple act of listening—truly listening—to each person before diving into work may be the most powerful inclusion tool available to teams.

If you're a leader or facilitator...	If you're a participant...
Model appropriate vulnerability first to set the tone.	Come prepared to share honestly but concisely.
Keep check-ins brief (30–60 seconds per person).	Listen fully to others without planning your response.
Use a consistent order (clockwise/name list) to reduce anxiety about "who goes next."	Respect the no-commentary guideline.
	Practice appropriate vulnerability. Share what would be helpful for others to know.
Protect the space from interruptions or commentary.	Honor your own boundaries. Pass if truly needed, but challenge yourself to participate.
Offer simple, clear prompts that invite authentic sharing.	
Acknowledge but don't problem-solve issues that arise during check-in.	Use checkout to acknowledge unresolved items that need follow-up.

Check In & Out builds on STRUCTURAL & PSYCHOLOGICAL SAFETY (3) by creating a *predictable* space for authentic expression. It is usually practiced through ROUNDS (48) and supports CONFLICT AS A RESOURCE (38) by surfacing tensions early before they escalate. It's a perfect kickoff for any meeting, but especially an ACTION MEETING (47), and it can sometimes help inform an ADAPTIVE AGENDA (49) or be used as a type of ad hoc HEALTH CHECK (59). It's best with FACILITATION (56), but over time, groups will self-organize around this practice.

45 *Only Important Notes*

Capture the essence

Teams spend hours meticulously documenting meeting conversations but struggle to find the decisions that actually matter. Meeting notes are graveyards—massive documents where important information goes to die.*

For some reason, we want meeting notes (and, for that matter, emails and DMs) to be transcripts. *AI is going to do the transcript for us anyway.* So don't try to document everything that was said.

THEREFORE...

When it comes to meetings, capture only three things:

Decisions made and why
Actions with clear owners
Changes to existing work

Everything else is noise.

---

* If we're being honest, it's not just meeting notes. Even your perfectly polished, deeply researched PowerPoints are likely gathering dust, unread by those who are probably interested but just don't have time.

IMPLEMENTATION

1. Setup: Designate a dedicated notetaker. Share an **empty template** before starting.

2. During meetings: When something sounds like a decision, **speak up**: "Are we deciding *X*? Let's capture that." Don't transcribe discussions. Summarize the outcomes.

3. After meetings: **Immediately** share notes. Don't spend more than five minutes cleaning them up.

When it's working, people reference meeting notes before asking questions, decisions don't need to be relitigated, actions actually happen, and future discussions build on past decisions instead of rehashing them.

TEMPLATE

Meeting	[Title] - [Date]
Attendees	[Names]
Decided	[Specific decision]
Why	[Reason, in 140 characters or fewer]
Actions	[Name] will [specific action] by [date]
Changes	[System/document/process] to [new state]

DEALING WITH PUSHBACK

"But we'll lose context!"

No, you won't. And you weren't using that context anyway. Record meetings if you need full context, but keep your notes focused only on decisions, changes, and actions.

"But everything actually is important!"

No, it's not. Force yourself to distinguish between interesting discussions and actual decisions and actions.

"We need more detail!"
Link to supporting documents rather than copying content into notes.

EXPERIMENT

For your next three meetings, only write down decisions, actions, or changes. Compare completion of action items to your previous approach.

Only Important Notes works well with ACTION MEETING (47) for generating clear next steps, STRUCTURED DECISION-MAKING (30) for making better decisions worth documenting, and TRANSPARENCY (32) for sharing decisions widely after they're made, and it helps make LOGBOOK (57) more useful by limiting entries to things that truly matter.

46 *Iterative Shipping*

The only way to make better work is with good feedback

Knowledge workers spend months perfecting work before showing it to anyone. Projects disappear into black holes of "almost ready" for quarters at a time. When they finally emerge, they're often disconnected from what's actually needed. Meanwhile, stakeholders grow increasingly anxious without visibility.

This "perfect *then* ship" mentality creates a deadly cycle: extended isolation → misaligned work → late-stage feedback → painful revisions → missed deadlines → lost trust.

THEREFORE...

Ship small, meaningful pieces *weekly*.* Break large deliverables into "minimum testable ideas": the smallest unit that can generate useful feedback. Share rough thinking with stakeholders early and often, using lightweight formats: one-pagers, mock-ups, prototypes, or outlines.†

---

* This post from Public Digital, "No prizes for week notes" is exactly on the money: https://public
  .digital/pd-insights/blog/2019/08/no-prizes-for-weeknotes. Parabol, a company that makes software that would help with many of the patterns contained in this book, has been doing a Friday Ship since it was founded a little more than eight years ago: https://www.parabol.co/friday-ship.
† Read *much more* about this in GitLab's Values (emphasis on the Iteration section): https://
  handbook.gitlab.com/handbook/values/#iteration.

WEEKLY SHIPPING CADENCE (65)

Monday	Tuesday	Wednesday	Thursday	Friday
Frame key questions and hypotheses.	Develop and test thinking.	Develop and test thinking.	Develop and test thinking.	Ship something that moves understanding forward. One-page summary Basic prototype Simple visualization Draft framework Key findings

IMPLEMENTATION

1. **Start small:** Pick one important project. Break it into weekly *minimum testable* pieces.
2. **Set expectations:** Tell stakeholders, "We'll share progress each Friday. It will be rough, and that's intentional. We want your input before going too far."
3. **Frame feedback:** When sharing work, include specific questions: "Does this approach address your core need?" or "Which of these three directions feels most promising?"
4. **Create the habit:** Schedule recurring Friday shipping meetings or demos to create a forcing function.

When it's working: Work consistently moves forward in visible increments; stakeholders provide input that reshapes direction early, when changes are still easy; teams avoid extended periods of misalignment; quality improves through successive iterations; sense of progress sustains motivation; trust builds through transparency.

DEALING WITH PUSHBACK

"But it's not ready yet!"
It's never ready. Share your thinking, not just polished outputs.

"What if they hate it?"
Better to learn that now than after three more months of work.

"We need more time to get it right."
You'll get it right through iteration, not isolation.

EXPERIMENT

Take your largest current project. Identify something (anything!) you could share *this Friday* that would generate useful feedback. Even if it's just a one-page summary of your current thinking. Share it.

Works well with: WORK IN PUBLIC (50) for creating transparency around in-progress work; ONLY IMPORTANT NOTES (45) for capturing feedback efficiently; ACTIVE STEERING (27) for getting work out of teams more frequently; DEMOS (35) for showcasing working versions rather than discussing abstract plans.

47 *Action Meeting*

Meet about the work separately from the work

The average team wastes hours weekly in unfocused meetings.* Status updates drag on while real work waits. People report meaningless unchanged statuses to the group instead of actually doing something about the blocked projects. The room fills with passive listeners as one person dominates. These meetings end without clear next steps, creating an endless cycle of talking without progress.

Daily stand-ups are ritualized micromanagement: "What did you do yesterday? What will you do today? Any blockers?" This approach treats professionals like they need daily supervision rather than focusing on what *actually* needs coordination.

THEREFORE ...

Replace status meetings with a single, focused 30–45-minute Action Meeting each week.† In time, you can get this down to 15 minutes. Use this precise format that separates updates from processing and drives toward clear, assigned actions. You will think this format and facilitation style is too restrictive.‡ Just try it.

---

* There are many studies available on this, but you don't need a study to know this is true. It is true.

† This one is inspired by Holacracy's Tactical Meeting, but removes a few things to keep it to the core of the pattern: https://www.holacracy.org/r/tactical-meetings.

‡ This is one case where the format should be rigid, as separate from the agenda, which is built in the room. If you're having a hard time with it, call me: 312-576-0600.

ACTION MEETING FORMAT

1. Check In (2–3 minutes)	Quick ROUND (48): "What has your attention?" No discussion. Just listening.
2. Review Prior Actions (2–10 minutes)	Read last week's action list. Each owner reports: "Complete" or "Not complete." No explanations, excuses, or discussion.
3. Build Agenda (2–3 minutes)	• Do not create a predefined agenda of items to resolve. Build it live. • Each person adds agenda items as single words or short phrases. • Write items publicly where everyone can see; optionally add the initials of the person who added the item for easier facilitation. No discussion of items during this phase. Seriously. Do not talk about the items as you're creating the agenda.
4. Process Agenda (5–35 minutes)*	Take each item in order. For each item: • Proposer describes the tension/issue in one sentence. • Facilitator asks: "What do you need?" • Direct interaction to address the need. • Capture specific actions or projects. • Facilitator asks: "Did you get what you need?" • When yes, move to next item. If no, facilitator asks again: "What do you need?" Keep tight timeboxes (10 seconds–2 minutes per item). Focus on actions, not discussion.
5. Close (2–3 minutes)	Review all new actions captured. Run a quick closing ROUND (48): "Share a reflection on this meeting."

---

* It's only ever 35 minutes if the group has never done it before. Well-practiced groups can take down 30–40 items in 5 minutes. For real!

IMPLEMENTATION

1. Assign/ELECT (15) two MEETING ROLES (51): FACILITATOR (56), who runs the process, and scribe, who captures actions.
2. Create a shared document for tracking actions.
3. Schedule a consistent weekly time.
4. Facilitator keeps strict timeboxes and prevents discussion during updates.
5. Always ask "What do you need?" Don't ask any other question. You will be tempted. Don't get creative.
6. When processing agenda items, allow discussion ONLY until the need is clear.
7. Focus relentlessly on generating next actions, not solving problems in the room. Use patterns like PAIRING (54) and FLOW STATE WORK (61) for this; your goal is to maximize time available to actually work—not try to squeeze a solution into a status meeting.
8. When someone starts problem-solving, redirect: "What's the next action?"

When it's working: Every issue turns into an explicit next action with an owner; updates take seconds, not minutes; people bring real issues, not status reports; the team develops rhythm and momentum; issues get resolved through action between meetings.

ADDRESSING PUSHBACK/PROBLEMS

"People give long updates."
Interrupt politely: "To keep our pace, can you just tell us complete or not complete? We can discuss why later if needed."

"We try to solve problems in the meeting."
Redirect: "This sounds like a longer conversation. What's the next action to move this forward?" If you're absolutely stuck on solving within the boundaries of this kind of meeting, consider the Level 10 Meeting from Entrepreneurial Operating System (EOS); its agenda devotes 60 minutes to identifying, discussing, and solving problems.* I still think you should save this for separate, smaller sessions after an Action Meeting, though!

---

* Read more here: https://www.eosworldwide.com/blog/the-level-10-meeting.

"Some people dominate the agenda."
Talk to them after the meeting and ask them not to do what they did.

EXPERIMENT

Replace all your status meetings with one Action Meeting. Run it strictly by this format for one month. Measure total meeting time before and after.

Works well with: CHECK IN & OUT (44) for grounding the meeting; ONLY IMPORTANT NOTES (45) for capturing just the essential actions; BACKLOG MANAGEMENT (37) and KANBAN (55) to track the work in progress; STRATEGY HEURISTIC (29) to guide the work in between meetings so that stand-ups are less necessary.

48 Rounds

The simplest hack for inclusion is listening

In most discussions, a few voices dominate while the quieter, often wiser perspectives remain unheard. Traditional open discussion formats naturally amplify power dynamics, and even raising hands or speaker stacks can be dominated by the same confident, sometimes privileged voices.

THEREFORE...

Structure group dialogue as rounds, where each person speaks in turn, without interruption or immediate response.[2] Make it safe to pass. The power lies in the prompt: the specific question that guides each person's contribution.

How to Run a Round

- Clearly state the prompt. Explain: "We'll go around the circle. Each person speaks briefly without interruption. It's fine to pass. We will come back to you."
- Begin with yourself or designate a starter.
- Move in a consistent direction.
- Thank each person after they speak.
- Don't comment on contributions or allow others to respond until the round completes.
- Come back to those who passed.

When to Use Rounds

- Opening and closing meetings with a CHECK IN & OUT (44) to ground everyone
- Making important decisions to ensure all perspectives are heard
- Breaking through stuck conversations by shifting the format
- Reflecting on completed work before moving to the next phase
- Surfacing concerns or tensions that might otherwise remain hidden
- Building STRUCTURAL & PSYCHOLOGICAL SAFETY (3) by creating space for every voice

Foundations

What principle or value feels most relevant to our current situation?

What assumption might we be making that could be limiting our thinking?

What would our purpose suggest we do in this situation?

Structuring

What's one boundary that needs clarification in our current structure?

Where do you see unnecessary friction in our current way of working?

What's one role or responsibility that's unclear right now?

Direction

What would success look like for this initiative in one year?

What question, if answered, would most help us move forward?

What concern about our direction hasn't been voiced yet?

Practice

What practice or habit would most improve our effectiveness right now?

What's one thing we should start doing in our meetings?

What's one thing you've seen another team do that we should adopt?

Learning

What's one thing you've learned recently that changed your thinking?
Where have you seen us make the same mistake twice?
What feedback have you received that we should all hear?

Decision-Making

What would need to be true for you to fully support this direction?
What risk do you see that others might have missed?
On a scale of 1–4, how confident are you in this approach, and why?*

Problem Identifying

What's one thing that feels harder than it should be?
What conversation are we not having that we should be having?
What's something you've been hesitant to bring up?

Problem-Solving

What's an adjacent field or discipline that might have solved this problem?
What constraints are we treating as fixed that might actually be flexible?
If you had a magic wand to remove one obstacle, what would it be?

Reflection

What moment made you feel most energized this week?
Where did you see one of our values in action recently?
What's something small that happened that we might have missed but should
    celebrate?

---

* 1: If we do this, I'd quit; 4: If we don't do this, I'd quit. We also use this in HEALTH CHECK (59).

Closing

What's one action you're taking away from this conversation?
What support do you need in the coming week?
What are you grateful for from today's discussion?

Creativity*

What if we reversed our core assumption on this topic?
If we had to solve this problem without technology, what would we do?
What existing product or service from a different industry could inspire us?

Feedback

What's one thing I'm doing well that I should continue?
What's one blind spot you think I might have?
How could I better support you in your work?

Conflict Resolution

What need of yours isn't being met in the current situation?
What's one thing you appreciate about the perspective you disagree with?
What shared goal do you think everyone in this conflict cares about?

Works well with: ACTION MEETING (47) for building and processing agenda items; CONFLICT AS A RESOURCE (38) for surfacing diverse perspectives; HAVE ONE CONVERSATION (53) for maintaining focus during complex discussions; CURIOSITY (5) for digging deeper.

---

* I recommend Brian Eno's Oblique Strategies for more. One of my favorites of these strategies that isn't good for a round: "Make an exhaustive list of everything you might do and do the last thing on the list." So good.

49 *Adaptive Agenda*

Don't force it

Meeting agendas are created days in advance and followed rigidly regardless of what's actually happening.* Critical emerging issues get delayed to future meetings while teams trudge through pre-planned topics that are no longer urgent. The loudest or most senior voices dominate the prioritization process, and the team's real needs get sidelined.

There's also the politics of agendas: Who gets to decide what's discussed is often an open secret, and it has a substantial impact on what the organization ends up prioritizing. In many organizations, getting your item on the agenda requires political capital or seniority. Junior team members, new voices, or those from underrepresented groups often struggle to get their concerns addressed because they lack the juice to get on the agenda in the first place.

THEREFORE ...

Create adaptive agendas that evolve in real time based on current needs. Make the agenda visible to everyone and treat it as a living thing that changes as circumstances change.† The idea here is not to have *zero agenda*, but instead to have a

---

* If they get created at all, which is its own problem! Don't not have an agenda.
† Lean Coffee is a great example of this in practice: https://leancoffee.org.

trustworthy mechanism that allows for responsiveness, inclusion, and adaptation to what's actually happening in the team or in the business.

Gather & Process	**Begin with a dedicated gathering phase (5–10 minutes):** Everyone contributes topics needing discussion.
	Items are captured as brief bullet points without discussion. All voices have equal opportunity.
	Follow with quick prioritization (2–3 minutes): Sequence items based on urgency, dependencies, and energy.
	Process in priority order with flexibility to reorder.
	Explicitly defer items that can't be addressed.
Physical Board	**Create a simple board with three columns:** To Discuss, Discussing, and Resolved.
	Write topics on sticky notes that physically move across the board.
	Keep the board visible in your team space all week.
	Anyone can add items anytime, not just during meetings.
	Start meetings by quickly reviewing and prioritizing what's on the board.
Time Bound	**Begin with timeboxes for categories rather than specific topics:** **10 min**—Immediate operational needs **15 min**—Short-term tactical issues **15 min**—Forward-looking strategic topics
	Within each category, collect and prioritize specific items in real time.
	Allow for shifting time between categories based on current needs.
Energy Based	**Sort topics into three zones:** Urgent, Important, and Energizing.
	Begin with 1–2 urgent items to create momentum.
	Follow with an energizing item to boost engagement.
	Tackle important items in the middle when energy is highest.
	Close with another energizing item to end on a positive note.

IMPLEMENTATION

Make It Visible

- Use a whiteboard, digital board, or shared screen that everyone can see.
- For remote teams, use collaborative tools like Miro, Trello, or Google Docs.
- Update in real time as you go, not after the fact.

Keep It Flexible

- Review and adjust priorities at natural transition points.
- Explicitly ask: "Is this still the most important thing to discuss?"
- Be willing to completely abandon the planned agenda when circumstances change.

Democratize the Agenda

- Use ROUNDS (48) when gathering agenda items to ensure everyone contributes.
- Consider silent generation of topics to avoid anchoring on the first ideas.
- Rotate responsibility for maintaining the agenda.
- Explicitly invite contributions from quieter team members.
- Create multiple channels for adding items (digital, physical, before/during meetings).
- Establish a norm that anyone can add items regardless of role or seniority.

When it's working: The team spends time on what matters most right now, not what seemed important days ago; new information shifts priorities without drama; everyone, not just the meeting leader, feels ownership of the agenda; the team maintains forward momentum while remaining responsive.

●▼◢■❋⬢

Works well with: ONLY IMPORTANT NOTES (45) for capturing decisions as they emerge; ACTION MEETING (47), which uses a specific type of adaptive agenda; HAVE ONE CONVERSATION (53) to maintain focus on the current agenda item; DO THE RIGHT THING (26) by connecting the agenda to what people are actually sensing.

50 *Work in Public*

If your kitchen is too tidy, nobody's gonna help you cook

Knowledge work happens behind closed doors, with outputs emerging only when deemed ready. Documents hide in personal folders, decisions in private messages, and work slides into a series of big reveals.

Duplication of effort (the real source of waste!).

Slow feedback cycles.

An endless stream of "can you share that doc with me?" messages.

These are self-imposed bottlenecks that we have to fix *ourselves*.

THEREFORE...

Make work accessible from the start. Default to open, shared workspaces where everything is visible to the team. Treat private work as the exception that requires justification, not the rule.

MAKE WORK PUBLIC

1. Establish Common Spaces	Create a well-organized team drive with clear folder structures. Use naming conventions everyone understands (YYYYMMDD-ProjectName-DocumentType). Maintain shared bookmarks to frequently accessed spaces. Document the system so new members can navigate immediately.
2. Draft in Shared Documents	Start new docs directly in shared spaces, not personal drives. Use collaborative tools that show real-time edits (Google Docs, Notion, etc.). Write short context notes at the top explaining what you're creating and why. Don't put DRAFT in document titles. Everything is a draft.
3. Make Status Visible	Use visible project boards (digital or physical) showing all work in progress. Update task status in real time, not just during meetings. Flag blocked items immediately rather than waiting for check-ins. Make dependencies between tasks explicit.
4. Move Conversations from Private to Public	Default to team channels instead of DMs for work discussions. When useful information emerges in private chats, summarize in public channels. Use threads to maintain context while keeping channels navigable. Tag specific people when their attention is needed instead of going private.

5. Create Working Session Habits	Schedule regular open working hours where people work alongside each other.
	Share screens during complex tasks so others can learn or provide input.
	Narrate your work occasionally: "I'm tackling X issue using Y approach."
	Normalize asking for help and offering support in the open.
6. Build Public Documentation Reflexes	Document decisions in shared spaces immediately, not later.
	Capture meeting notes directly in team wikis, not personal notebooks.
	Screenshot whiteboards and add to shared spaces before erasing.
	Update documentation as you go, not as a separate activity.

IMPLEMENTATION

Start with Infrastructure

- Audit current tool usage and identify barriers to public work.
- Choose tools that make sharing the path of least resistance.
- Create templates that live in shared spaces for common documents.
- Set up automated reminders to move private work public.

Shift Team Norms

- Review recent work and ask: "Could someone new understand our current priorities by looking at our shared spaces?"
- Explicitly praise public documentation and sharing.
- When asking for status, always check public spaces first.
- Respond to private requests with "Could we discuss this in the channel so others can benefit?"

Address Resistance

- Acknowledge legitimate privacy concerns (HR, sensitive feedback).
- Create clear guidelines for what should remain private.
- Address perfectionism: "Sharing early work shows confidence, not weakness."
- Emphasize learning benefits: "Your draft helps others understand how you think."

When it's working: Team members can find what they need without asking; context doesn't get lost when people are out; new team members can get up to speed faster; work naturally builds on previous efforts instead of re-creating them; feedback comes earlier, when changes are easier to make; "Who has the latest version?" questions disappear; people feel connected to the broader context of work.

DEALING WITH PROBLEMS

"We'll clean it up later."
Later never comes. Take two minutes to organize as you go.

"Let me just finish this first."
Share now. Perfect later.

"It's faster to do it myself."
It's slower for the team when you do.

"I'll just DM this question."
Someone else probably has the same question.

EXPERIMENT

For one week, try this radical approach: If it isn't in the shared space, it doesn't exist. Don't reference docs, decisions, or discussions that aren't accessible to everyone. Notice how quickly this forces better public work habits.

●▼◢■❋⬟

Works well with: TRANSPARENCY (32) for the philosophical foundation of open work; ONLY IMPORTANT NOTES (45) for making this possible for everyone to do; ITERATIVE SHIPPING (46) for sharing work early and often; PROCESS ON THE WALL (68) for capturing decisions in accessible places.

51 *Meeting Roles*

Know which hat you're wearing

Meetings drift into chaos because no one is explicitly responsible for their success. The loudest voices dominate, discussions meander, and vital information vanishes into the ether. Organizations assume meetings will somehow run themselves, yet we rarely clarify who's responsible for what.

The standard approach of *only* assigning a meeting owner, and leaving everything else up to chance, leads to confused accountability and missed opportunities. When one person (usually the most senior) tries to handle content, process, and documentation simultaneously, they fail at all three.

THEREFORE...

Distribute meeting responsibilities across explicitly defined roles that operate in service to the group. Make these roles visible at the start of the meeting, rotate them regularly to build organizational capability, and select people based on required skills rather than hierarchy.

FACILITATOR

Holds the process, not the content. Manages time, guides discussion flow, and maintains balanced participation, like a conductor helping the group produce its best thinking.

Let's hear from someone who hasn't spoken yet. We have 10 minutes left for this topic. I notice we're getting off track.

SCRIBE

Captures decisions, actions, and key points in real time through active synthesis that helps the group see its emerging understanding. (If it's just taking verbatim notes, you're doing it wrong.)

I've captured this decision as X. Who owns this action item? Can I clarify what we just decided?

TIMEKEEPER

Tracks time separately from the facilitator, gives warnings, and helps maintain momentum.

We have five minutes remaining on this topic. That's our time for this section. Should we extend this discussion or move on?

OBSERVER

Doesn't participate in content but watches group dynamics and provides process feedback at the end.

I noticed some people didn't get a chance to speak. The energy shifted when we discussed X. We seemed to make decisions quickly after hearing from certain voices.

THINKING HATS ROLES

Based on Edward de Bono's Six Thinking Hats framework:[3]

White Hat (Facts & Data)	Focuses purely on information, data, and facts without interpretation or opinion. *Here are the numbers we currently have. What data is missing that we need before deciding? Factually speaking, our current situation is X.*
Red Hat (Emotions & Intuition)	Brings emotional intelligence and gut feelings into the discussion without needing rational justification. *My intuition says this approach feels risky. I'm excited about this direction. I have a concern I can't quite articulate yet.*
Black Hat (Caution & Critique)	Identifies risks, problems, and potential failures to strengthen ideas. *This could fail if X. We haven't addressed this critical weakness. The legal implications concern me.*
Yellow Hat (Benefits & Optimism)	Focuses on value, benefits, and why something might work. *The opportunity here is X. This could solve several problems at once. The best aspect of this approach is X.*
Green Hat (Creativity & Alternatives)	Generates new ideas, possibilities, and alternative approaches. *What if we approached this completely differently? Here's a wild idea that might spark something. Let's consider three entirely new options.*
Blue Hat (Process & Meta Thinking)	Manages the thinking process itself and ensures productive use of the other hats. *Let's shift to Yellow Hat thinking for the next five minutes. We need more creative options—can we use Green Hat thinking? What thinking approach would be most useful right now?*

CONTRARIAN

Deliberately takes the opposite position to test the strength of arguments and reveal hidden assumptions.

Let me argue against what seems like the consensus. What if the exact opposite is true? I'll challenge this idea to help us strengthen it.

SCOPE

Keeps the discussion within defined boundaries and prevents scope creep.

That's interesting but outside what we need to decide today. Let's add that to the parking lot for future discussion. Are we still addressing our key question?

IMPACT

Consistently asks about downstream effects and consequences of ideas.

How will this affect our other teams? What's the potential impact on our customers? Who might be unintentionally harmed by this approach?

ELEPHANT

Names unspoken tensions, taboo topics, or uncomfortable truths that others avoid mentioning.

I think there's something we're all avoiding. Can we talk about the real issue here? I'm noticing we keep talking around this topic.

HISTORY

Provides organizational memory, reminding the group of past decisions, attempts, and context.

We tried something similar last year and here's what happened. This reminds me of our previous approach where we learned X. For context, this issue has come up before in these circumstances . . .

BACK CHANNEL

Watches chat, messages, or other digital communication happening alongside the main conversation.

There are questions coming in through the chat. Several people in the chat are expressing concern about X. Let me surface what's happening in our digital back channel.

DECISION TRACKER

Specifically focuses on identifying when decisions are being made and ensuring clarity around them.

Did we just make a decision? Let me restate it. Are we deciding this now or still exploring? For clarity, the decision we just made is X.

DECIDER (FOR CONSENSUS-CHALLENGED MEETINGS)

Has clear authority to make final decisions when discussion reaches an impasse.

I've heard the perspectives and here's my decision. We need to move forward, so we'll proceed with option B. The decision timeframe requires us to conclude now.

NEXT STEPPER

Ensures every discussion concludes with clear action items and ownership.

What are our next steps on this? Who's taking ownership of this action? When will this be done, and how will we know?

SAFETY

Specifically attends to group dynamics that might inhibit open participation.

That's an interesting idea. Can you tell us more? I appreciate you raising that difficult point. There are no bad ideas at this stage.

SPONSOR VOICE (FOR WORKSHOPS/WORKING SESSIONS)

Speaks to the broader organizational context and decision-making constraints.

Here's why this work matters to the organization. These are the constraints we need to work within. This is how decisions will be made after our session.

TRANSLATOR (FOR CROSS-FUNCTIONAL MEETINGS)

Bridges technical and non-technical perspectives by translating between different domains.

Let me explain what that technical term means in business impact. The business need translates to these technical requirements. Here's what this would actually mean for our systems.

REMOTE ADVOCATE (FOR HYBRID MEETINGS)

Ensures remote participants are fully included in discussions.

Let's check if our remote folks have input. I noticed someone online has their hand up. Can we adjust the camera so remote participants can see the whiteboard?

NEW JOINER BUDDY (FOR TEAM MEETINGS WITH RECENT HIRES)

Provides context and background for discussions that reference history unknown to new team members.

For context, this refers to a project from last quarter. Let me quickly explain that reference for those who joined recently. That acronym stands for . . .

IMPLEMENTATION

Try these roles. Try them yourself! Start with the basics, like facilitator and scribe. Add them to your TEAM CHARTER (43) if they prove important and powerful. Make them visible, or call them out intentionally. Debrief and rotate, according to RETROSPECTIVES (66), LENGTH LIMIT (64), and ELECTIONS (15).

When it's working: Meetings have clearer purpose and more balanced participation; different perspectives emerge naturally through role distribution; people speak from multiple viewpoints rather than fixed positions; the quality of thinking improves as specialized lenses are applied; meetings become more self-aware with built-in process improvement; teams develop a sophisticated vocabulary for different thinking modes; meeting outcomes improve without relying on hierarchical authority.

EXPERIMENT

For your next significant meeting, try giving one person a specific role. When that works, add another. Keep trying new roles.

DEALING WITH PUSHBACK AND PROBLEMS

"Isn't this artificial and forced?"
Initially, yes. Like any new practice, it feels awkward at first. Start with just two or three roles until they become natural, then expand.

"Won't this make meetings longer?"
Quite the opposite. Clear roles create focus and prevent the circular conversations that waste time. The initial investment pays off quickly.

"What if someone is bad at their assigned role?"
That's valuable information! Role rotation reveals development needs and hidden talents. Support people with coaching rather than avoiding assignments.

"Do we need all these roles in every meeting?"
Absolutely not. Match roles to your meeting purpose and team size. A quick decision meeting might only need a facilitator, devil's advocate, and decision tracker.

Works well with: CHECK IN & OUT (44) for grounding the meeting; ROUNDS (48) for ensuring all voices are heard; HAVE ONE CONVERSATION (53) for maintaining focus; ONLY IMPORTANT NOTES (45) for effective documentation; FACILITATION (56) for developing process leadership skills that help with EMERGENT LEADERSHIP (58). You can document this in your TEAM CHARTER (43).

52 Triage

What on earth do we do next?

Without a clear system for evaluating what deserves attention, teams default to either addressing everything (burning people out) or focusing solely on whatever seems urgent (creating strategic drift).

The problem is the lack of a consistent framework for quickly assessing whether something deserves action, who should handle it, and how to route it appropriately.

THEREFORE...

Implement a simple triage system that starts with one fundamental question:

"Can this team take action?"

A simple decision tree, like this one that is inspired by David Allen's *Getting Things Done*, prevents wasteful analysis paralysis while ensuring important matters get routed to the right people.[4]

Yes The team can and should address this, based on our TRUE PURPOSE (1).		No The team shouldn't address this, because:		
Less than two-minute tasks	**More than two-minute tasks**	**We would need authority**	**It's clearly someone else's responsibility**	**It's not aligned to our company** PURPOSE (1)
Do immediately.	Capture and track systematically.	We should act but lack permission, so our action is to **go get permission**.	Someone else should do this, so our action is to **find them, and tell them it's their job**.	Nobody should do this, so our action is to **delete or disregard**.

IMPLEMENTATION

Add this to your ACTION MEETING (47) process. Use it in your one-on-ones with teammates. Post the decision tree where others can see and/or use it, perhaps near WHITEBOARDS AT INTERSECTIONS (74).

●▼◫▥✳⬠

Works well with: KANBAN (55) for visualizing triaged work items; ACTION MEET-ING (47) for structured follow-through; DOMAINS, ASSETS & STANDARDS (23) for clarifying team responsibilities; DISTRIBUTED MANAGEMENT (14) for empowering frontline triage; NETWORK OF TEAMS (13) for effective cross-team routing.

53 *Have One Conversation*

Parallel processing works in computers, not in meetings

We've all experienced it: One person speaks while others whisper to neighbors, check emails, or interrupt with tangential points. The room buzzes with fragmented attention, killing the group's collective intelligence and ability to make good decisions.[5]

When multiple conversations occur simultaneously, attention fractures, important insights get lost, quieter voices are silenced, and everyone's mental energy drains faster.

THEREFORE...

Establish "one conversation at a time" as a fundamental practice. Start meetings by explicitly stating this expectation and enforce it consistently. When side conversations emerge, intervene gently: "I notice we have multiple discussions happening. Let's bring it back to one conversation."

Employ simple tools like FACILITATION (56), a talking object that indicates who has the floor, or hand signals for those wishing to speak next. Create space for all voices through structured practices like ROUNDS (48), where you go person by person, or by maintaining a visible queue of who speaks next.

It might feel silly or remedial, but it's important. Protecting the space for a single conversation thread improves the meeting and builds the group's capacity for clear thinking and good collaboration.

●▼◢■✳◆

Have One Conversation provides the foundation for ACTION MEETING (47) and ROUNDS (48) by keeping discussion focused on agenda items and promoting a culture where each person can speak without interruption. The pattern is often maintained by skilled FACILITATION (56) and reinforced by clear MEETING ROLES (51). When combined with CHECK IN & OUT (44), it creates meetings where everyone feels heard.

54 *Pairing*

Two brains are better than one

Individual work seems good. It seems normal. The periodic reviews and handoffs are all part of how work is done. The knowledge silos, slow feedback loops, and increased risk of errors are all just part of the game.[6]

THEREFORE...

Have two people work together on the same task in defined intervals, with frequent rotation of pairs.[7] The pair actively collaborates—one person *drives* (does the actual work) while the other *navigates* (thinks strategically, spots issues, suggests approaches).

You can take this even further with something called mob programming (or, for non-programmers, mob working). Have a small group of three to five people, or an entire LEAN TEAM (19), work together on a single task, with one person driving while others collaborate on direction, taking turns at the keyboard at regular rotations.

IMPLEMENTATION

Basic Pairing

1. **Set clear roles.**
   - Driver: Has hands on keyboard/tools, focuses on immediate task
   - Navigator: Thinks ahead, spots issues, suggests approaches
   - Switch roles every 30–60 minutes.

2. **Create the right environment.**
   - Shared screen/workspace visible to both participants
   - Comfortable seating that allows side-by-side work
   - Minimal distractions

3. **Establish communication norms.**
   - Navigator asks questions rather than giving commands.
   - Regular check-ins: How's this approach working?
   - Explicit handoffs when switching roles

Mob Working

1. **Structure the session.**
   - Designate a facilitator to keep things on track.
   - Set a timer for driver rotation (5–15 minutes).
   - Use a "navigator stack" where people queue up ideas.

2. **Manage the dynamics.**
   - Everyone must agree on the next action.
   - Use "yes, and . . ." rather than "no, but . . ."
   - Capture alternative approaches to try later.

3. **Keep energy high.**
   - Take regular breaks (10 minutes every hour).
   - Switch problem-solving approaches when stuck.
   - Celebrate progress and learning moments.

DEALING WITH PUSHBACK AND PROBLEMS

"It feels slower."
It is slower initially, but faster overall when you account for fewer bugs, less rework, and knowledge sharing. Track cycle time, not just active development time.

"We're not good at navigating."
Create a simple navigator checklist: *What might go wrong? What are we missing? Is there a simpler way? How will we test this?*

"Some people dominate pairing sessions."
Use a timer for strict role switching and establish a "navigator stack" where people queue their ideas.

"It's exhausting."
It is! Take more frequent breaks, limit pairing to five to six hours per day, and vary who you pair with.

When it's working: Knowledge spreads rapidly through the team; quality problems are caught earlier; new team members become productive faster; work no longer stalls when someone is out; solutions incorporate multiple perspectives; the team develops shared approaches and standards.

EXPERIMENT

Try these simple experiments:

For teams new to pairing:	For experienced pairs:
1. Start with a single 2-hour pairing session per day.	1. Try a full-day mob session on a complex problem.
2. Begin with a clearly defined, medium-complexity task.	2. Include someone from outside the immediate team.
3. Use a 30-minute timer for role switching.	3. Rotate drivers every 8–10 minutes.
4. Debrief afterward: What worked? What was challenging?	4. Compare the solution quality with typical approaches.

●▽◢◼✳⬠

Works well with: LEAN TEAMS (19) for focused, collaborative work; GUILDS (21) for spreading knowledge beyond pairs; ITERATIVE SHIPPING (46) for rapid feedback cycles; CONFLICT AS A RESOURCE (38) for leveraging different perspectives; STRUCTURAL & PSYCHOLOGICAL SAFETY (3) for effective collaboration.

55 *Kanban*

Visualize your work

It feels impossible to balance workflow, manage capacity, and maintain predictable delivery. Work piles up unevenly. Some teams are drowning while others wait for handoffs. Everyone's busy, but nothing seems to be getting done. Starting new work seems easier than finishing what's in progress.

THEREFORE ...

Implement a visual Kanban board that makes work visible and explicitly limits work in progress (WIP). Break work into manageable items that move through clearly defined workflow stages with strict capacity limits at each stage.

Kanban, the Japanese word for "signboard" or "visual card," was developed at Toyota in the 1950s under the guidance of Taiichi Ohno, one of the key architects of the Toyota Production System (TPS). Originally, the term referred to a physical card system used on the factory floor to signal steps in the manufacturing process, helping teams control inventory levels, balance production flow, and reduce waste.*

The core mechanics are simple:

---

* Kanban emerged as part of Toyota's broader pursuit of Just-in-Time (JIT) manufacturing: a methodology designed to produce only what is needed, when it is needed, and in the amount needed, thereby minimizing inventory and inefficiencies. Ohno's work has been referenced elsewhere, but if you've missed those mentions, go back to his original writing on this topic. It's so good! Taiichi Ohno, *Toyota Production System: Beyond Large-Scale Production* (Portland, OR: Productivity Press, 1988).

- **Visualize the workflow.** Create columns representing each work stage.
- **Limit WIP.** Set maximum items allowed in each column.*
- **Pull (don't push) work.** Only start new work when capacity exists.*
- **Make policies explicit.** Define clear rules for moving items.
- **Improve collaboratively.** Use the visual system to identify bottlenecks.

IMPLEMENTATION

Problems with Kanban mostly arise when you try to complicate things. So . . .

1. Start Ridiculously Simple

Begin with just three columns:

To Do	Doing	Done
Work items not yet started	Work currently in progress (limit this!)	Completed work

Add a WIP limit to the *Doing* column (usually team size minus one). If you have a team of seven people, this means that you can only have six items in the *Doing* column. You'll see how this works in a moment. Make this visible to everyone. Physical boards work surprisingly well, but digital tools (Trello, Asana, Jira) are fine for distributed teams.

2. Define Clear Item Types

Create visual distinctions between different work types. Use different colors of Post-its, stickers, or tags in the digital space to mark different kinds of work.

---

* This great, old (2008!) presentation from David Anderson is a good reminder that it's not a real Kanban system if it doesn't physically limit the amount of work in the system: https://www.infoq .com/presentations/kanban-for-software.

♠	♦	♣	♥
Features or Deliverables	**Bugs/Defects**	**Technical Debt or Maintenance**	**Knowledge Acquisition**
Primary value-creating work	Quality issues requiring resolution	System improvement work	Learning tasks with deliverables

3. Establish Operating Rules

Post these rules directly on your board:

- No exceeding WIP limits without team consensus.
- Visually flag blocked items.
- Finish work in progress before starting new work.
- Everyone helps resolve bottlenecks before pulling new work.
- Move cards only when they're actually done.

4. Incorporate into Your CADENCE (65)

Establish these regular Kanban practices:

- Daily stand-up (10–15 min): Focus on flow, blockers, and helping—not status reports.*
- Prioritization meeting (30–60 min, weekly): Prioritize and prepare upcoming work.
- Review (30 min, biweekly): Analyze what was delivered and gather feedback.
- RETROSPECTIVE (66) (30 min, monthly): Assess and improve the Kanban system itself.

5. Measure What Matters

Kanban makes it simple to track a handful of key metrics to improve your flow:

- Lead time: Total time from request to delivery
- Cycle time: Time from starting work to completion
- Throughput: Number of items completed per time period

---

* You shouldn't need to do this if you're doing an ACTION MEETING (47), and the team commits to WORK IN PUBLIC (50).

- WIP: Current number of items in progress
- Blockers: Frequency and duration of impediments

DEALING WITH PUSHBACK AND PROBLEMS

"WIP limits are constantly broken."
Make breaking limits painful; require team consensus and capture root causes.

"Work items are too large and get stuck."
Break down items until they can flow through a column in one to three days.

"Emergency work constantly disrupts flow."
Create an expedite lane with explicit policies and track disruption impact.

"Columns become dumping grounds."
Tighten definitions of "done" and conduct regular cleanup sessions.

When it's working: Team members pull work when ready rather than having it assigned; bottlenecks become visible before they cause delays; predictions about delivery become more reliable; continuous improvement turns into a habit; work items reduce in size over time.

EXPERIMENT

Try this one-week experiment: Create a simple three-column board (To Do, Doing, Done), place all your current work on the board, and track how many items actually complete versus your normal pace.

Works well with: CURIOSITY (5) for understanding your participants and their motives and interests; ITERATIVE SHIPPING (46) for delivering smaller increments; TRIAGE (52) for managing input demand; ONLY IMPORTANT NOTES (45) for documenting policies; LEAN TEAMS (19) for rightsizing work capacity; CADENCE (65) for establishing regular rhythms.

56 Facilitation

Groups almost always need a little guidance

Teams rarely stumble into high-quality collaboration on their own. Without a designated steward of the process, three chronic forces take over:

- **Cognitive overload:** Conversation branches faster than anyone can track, so shared understanding fragments and decisions blur.
- **Social gravity:** Status, confidence, and airtime skew whose ideas shape the outcome, no matter the merit.
- **Inertia:** Pressure to "keep moving" rewards talking rather than thinking, favoring the first workable option over the best one.

As a result, we get circular debates, half-made decisions, silent dissent, "parking lots" that never see daylight, meetings that drain energy instead of creating it. These are artifacts of an **unfacilitated** process, where content owners are forced to juggle structure, psychology, and timekeeping while also defending their point of view.

THEREFORE...

Establish facilitation as a distinct and celebrated role separate from content leadership, building on what's described in MEETING ROLES (51). The facilitator focuses solely on process—designing and guiding how the group works together—while remaining neutral on content.

FACILITATING WELL

Opening a Session	Clarify purpose and desired outcomes.
	Establish or remind of working agreements.
	Use CHECK IN & OUT (44) to ground the group.
	Preview the process you'll be using.
Managing Participation	Use ROUNDS (48) to ensure all voices are heard.
	Create a speaker queue to manage who speaks next.
	Notice and invite quiet participants.
	Respectfully interrupt dominant voices.
	Use hand signals for common needs (agree, clarify, new topic).
Focusing the Conversation	Post the current topic/question where everyone can see it.
	Use a parking lot for important but tangential ideas.
	Gently redirect when conversations stray.
	Summarize progress and check for alignment.
	Name the elephant in the room when needed.
Making Decisions	Clarify how decisions will be made before discussing options.
	Test for consent: "Do you have any objections to this approach?"
	Test for consensus: "What would need to change for you to support this?"
	Use fist-to-five voting to quickly gauge agreement.*
	Ensure all concerns are heard, even if they don't change the decision.
	Document decisions visibly in real time.
Closing a Session	Summarize key points, decisions, and actions.
	Ensure actions have clear owners and deadlines.
	Use a quick reflection round on the process.
	Acknowledge contributions and progress.
	End on time (or get consent to continue).

---

* Or, if you're feeling spicy, the one-finger ("If we do this, I'd quit") to four-finger ("If we don't do this, I'd quit") test.

FACILITATION MOVES

Build your ability to employ these basic interventions:

Stacking: Create a visible speaking order so people don't have to interrupt.
I see hands from Jamie, then Aisha, then Marcus.

Redirecting: Gently steer the conversation back to the topic.
That's an interesting point for another conversation. For now, let's refocus on . . .

Elevating: Shift the discussion to a higher or more strategic level when stuck in details.
Let's step back and look at the bigger picture here.

Deepening: Ask for more depth when discussion stays superficial.
Can you say more about that? or *What's underneath that concern?*

Balancing: Actively seek alternative or missing perspectives.
We've heard several supportive views. Who sees potential downsides?

Clarifying: Test understanding without judgment.
Let me see if I understand . . . or *Are you saying that . . . ?*

Synthesizing: Combine and summarize multiple points into coherent themes.
I'm hearing three main themes in our discussion so far . . .

Process Checking: Pause to evaluate how the conversation is going.
How is this process working for everyone? Do we need to adjust?

COMMON PROBLEMS AND SOLUTIONS

Certain voices consistently dominate.
Use structured ROUNDS (48) and explicit turn taking; consider breaking into smaller groups.

Energy drops and engagement wanes.
Change modes (sitting to standing, discussion to silent writing, analytical to creative).

Conversation keeps cycling without progress.
Capture positions visibly, name the pattern, and suggest a different approach.

Synthesizing feels hard.
In my experience, this is a result of either (a) underpreparing and not knowing the subject material enough, or (b) not listening hard enough. Just because you are *neutral* as a facilitator doesn't mean you can be *empty*.

Signs It's Working: Meeting evaluations improve; more voices contribute regularly to discussions; the group makes better decisions with broader buy-in; difficult topics get addressed constructively; meetings end with clear next steps; people leave energized rather than drained.

EXPERIMENT

Try this in your next three meetings:

1. Designate a neutral facilitator who won't contribute to content.
2. Agree on two to three simple facilitation tools to use.
3. Allow the facilitator to interrupt process problems.
4. Debrief afterward: What worked? What was challenging?

Works well with: CHECK IN & OUT (44) for grounding the group; ROUNDS (48) for ensuring balanced participation; MEETING ROLES (51) to distribute other responsibilities; ONLY IMPORTANT NOTES (45) for capturing key points; HAVE ONE CONVERSATION (53) for maintaining focus.

LEARNING

57 Logbook

Your brain is hard to search*

Modern organizations exist as much in digital space as in physical reality, yet most still maintain their operating models—purposes, structures, roles, and decision rights—in static documents or, worse, only in the collective minds of their members.

While work increasingly flows through digital channels that enable unprecedented flexibility and speed, the underlying organizational architecture remains trapped in analog formats that resist adaptation. When NETWORK OF TEAMS (13) and TEAM/PROCESS AS PRODUCT (63) become your norm, this misalignment between digital operations and analog governance impedes progress.†

Important knowledge—who owns which decisions, what teams exist and why, what individuals are accountable for—remains implicit rather than explicit, hidden rather than accessible. This information asymmetry severely hampers coordination efforts; the cognitive load of maintaining mental models of complex structures eventually exceeds human capacity, especially as organizations scale.

The invisibility problem results in daily frustrations. Teams initiate redundant work because they cannot see parallel efforts. Decision processes stall when ownership boundaries remain ambiguous. Organizational memory fades as transitions occur without adequate knowledge transfer.

---

* For now!

† To say nothing for ACTIVE STEERING (27), ITERATIVE SHIPPING (46), and EXPERIMENTATION (62), which have the potential to generate a gigantic amount of data.

The situation worsens exponentially with growth. What functions adequately in a 10-person startup becomes dysfunctional at 50, and nearly impossible at 500. As Mike Arauz, one of my co-founders at August, noted in *First Round Review*, "In most organizations today, the answers to these questions . . . exist at best in static PowerPoint documents sitting on a senior manager's hard drive, and at worst are trapped in implicit assumptions inside the heads of all the people who need to work together."[1]

THEREFORE . . .

Put your operating model into a strongly typed digital artifact:* a searchable, accessible, and continuously evolvable representation of your organization's purpose, structure, roles, and governance.†

This will shift your organization from an implicit, cognitively overloaded system to an explicit, externally encoded one. Like code in a repository, your architecture can thus be inspected, discussed, improved, and versioned over time.‡ This digital manifestation creates a single source of truth that reduces coordination costs and enables real autonomy.§

While implementations vary, essential components of your Logbook would typically include:

- **Purpose and Direction:** The organization's overall TRUE PURPOSE (1), team-specific sub-missions aligned with PURPOSE, CUSTOMER,

---

* That is, not just a running, narrative-style log of things that happened but entries that have certain formatting and content expectations. This is a term borrowed from software engineering, but it applies here too.

† NASA maintains a publicly accessible Lessons Learned database capturing major mission data, technical findings, and decision rationales: https://llis.nasa.gov. Hopefully by the time you read this, it hasn't been deleted. In February 2025, things are *dark*.

‡ Individuals and teams that maintain their own Logbook are at a substantial advantage over their peers/competitors in a world where large language models help with instantaneous, context-rich memory. I keep my own diary of all of my meetings at Airbnb, and our internal AI is able to brief me before every meeting.

§ Doing this, by the way, makes it easier to actually spread the burden for managing the team, because more people know more about how the business operates. And vice versa.

PLATFORM (16), strategic priorities formulated as a STRATEGY HEU-RISTIC (29), and key metrics expressed through OBJECTIVES & KEY RESULTS (28).

- **Structural Elements:** Team definitions structured as a NETWORK OF TEAMS (13), team purposes articulated through a TEAM CHARTER (43), role descriptions that honor the ROLE-SOUL DISTINCTION (8), and reporting relationships that enable UPWARD REPRESENTATION (24).

- **Governance Mechanisms:** Decision rights clearly expressed through DOMAINS, ASSETS & STANDARDS (23), policies developed via CONSENT & CONSENSUS (10) and applied through RULE OF LAW (2), and approval processes based on STRUCTURED DECISION-MAKING (30).

- **Operational Guidelines:** Work processes visualized through KANBAN (55), meeting protocols using ACTION MEETING (47) formats, communication standards incorporating ROUNDS (48), and team agreements captured in a COLLEAGUE LETTER OF UNDERSTANDING (40) or TEAM CHARTER (43).

Next, you'll need somewhere to put this information. Options range from specialized organizational operating systems like GlassFrog or Sobol to adaptable general platforms like Google Drive, Microsoft Teams, Wordpress P2, or custom wikis. Don't get wrapped up in specific technologies; instead, look for tools with the ability to create a living, searchable document that's easily accessible to everyone in the organization.

The implementation process typically follows these phases:

- **Initial Documentation:** Begin with a dig, an archaeological process to capture your operating model's current state. This establishes what Edgar Schein would call the "visible artifacts" layer while acknowledging that perfection is unnecessary.[2]

- **Set Access Protocols:** These are clear expectations for who can edit what through DOMAINS, ASSETS & STANDARDS (23). This governance layer requires calibrated transparency—universal visibility with role-appropriate modification capabilities—creating ownership *across* organizational boundaries while maintaining consistency through RULE OF LAW (2).

- **Decide on Maintenance Rhythms:** Set a CADENCE (65) for adjusting the model, creating regular cycles for collective sense making and evolution. These rhythms should incorporate HEALTH CHECK (59) diagnostics, RETROSPECTIVES (66), and ACTIVE STEERING (27) protocols that enable responsive adaptation rather than rigid planning horizons.

- **Create Integration Points:** Connect your digital operating model to the tools people already use for daily work through WORK IN PUBLIC (50) principles. This prevents people from having to enter the same information twice or constantly switch between systems. Build these connections thoughtfully by having PLATFORM TEAMS (17) create integrations between your organizational model and project management tools, communication platforms, and documentation systems. Treat these integrations themselves as products that need ongoing improvement using TEAM/PROCESS AS PRODUCT (63) thinking. When information flows automatically between systems, you enable EXPERIMENTATION (62) by making organizational patterns and learning visible to everyone without extra effort.

This phased implementation creates what Stafford Beer, the British operational researcher who pioneered management cybernetics, calls a "viable system model"—an organizational architecture capable of sensing, responding to, and evolving with its environment through self-awareness and adaptation mechanisms.*

● ▼ ◢ ■ ✳ ◆

Logbook builds upon TRANSPARENCY (32) by making organizational structures explicitly visible, but it extends beyond information sharing to create a dynamic operating model. This visibility unlocks DISTRIBUTED MANAGEMENT (14) by democratizing access to organizational design—when everyone can see how the organization functions, authority can be meaningfully distributed without sacrificing coherence.

The sustainable competitive advantage of a digitized organization comes not from any single structure but from the ability to evolve structure continuously.

---

* Stafford Beer, *Brain of the Firm*, 2nd ed. (Wiley, 1981). Fun fact here: Beer designed some of the first data-driven operational "war rooms" to help Salvador Allende manage Chile's economy in the 1970s. Rabbit hole alert!

This evolutionary capacity depends on distributed sensing and response mecha-nisms—teams that can independently detect signals and initiate a change within their world while staying connected to the broader system.

The organization that can see itself most clearly can change itself most effectively.

58 *Emergent Leadership*

Leading > leaders

Most traditional leadership structures rely on clearly defined authority, hierarchical positions, and official titles. Managers lead teams because of their role rather than their expertise, insights, or suitability for every challenge. This approach often restricts leadership to a limited number of senior figures, creating rigid structures that struggle to respond quickly to changing conditions. As complexity and uncertainty increase, organizations that depend solely on formal leadership positions become slow, inflexible, and overly political. People feel discouraged from stepping forward to solve problems unless explicitly directed, waiting for direction instead of taking initiative.

THEREFORE...

Emergent Leadership offers a different approach. It encourages leadership to surface organically throughout the organization, driven not by formal positions but by who has the capability, insight, and energy to address particular challenges or opportunities. In this model, leadership is not restricted to those at the top; it is distributed widely, allowing anyone with relevant knowledge, skill, or passion to take initiative and guide the organization when needed.

This pattern is similar to, but not quite the same as, DISTRIBUTED MANAGEMENT (14), which explicitly assigns decision-making responsibilities across roles. Emergent Leadership thrives on spontaneous action, harnessing naturally occurring capabilities rather than relying on predetermined authority. This means developing clear DOMAINS (23) where leadership can emerge without permission. Teams need explicit authority to SELF-MANAGE (18) around challenges, with individuals stepping into and out of leadership roles based on what the situation demands. The reality is that not every leader will excel at every type of leadership, and that leadership is needed and valued in different ways at different PACE LAYERS (11). A CEO might make a dreadful frontline leader, and vice versa.

Pace Layer	Leadership Traits	Experience Needed
1. 90 Days		
Production & Execution	Quick decision-making, detail oriented, pragmatic problem-solving, high technical competence, tactical agility	Deep domain expertise, hands-on technical skills, sprint/project management, crisis management
2. 3–12 Months		
People Management & Training	Strong emotional intelligence, coaching ability, performance assessment skills, feedback expertise, team building	Team leadership experience, mentoring/coaching, performance management, conflict resolution
3. 1–2 Years		
Annual Operating Plans	Strategic thinking, resource-allocation skills, analytical mindset, balanced risk-taking, cross-functional awareness	Strategic planning, budget management, program/portfolio oversight, change management
4. 2–5 Years		
Functions & Capabilities as Sources of Advantage	Systems thinking, cross-functional expertise, design thinking, process optimization, organizational awareness	Multiple business functions, process/systems design, transformation initiatives, technical architecture
5. 5–10 Years		
Business Unit Strategy & Operating Model	Market orientation, innovation mindset, opportunity recognition, adaptability to disruption, business model expertise	P&L responsibility, market strategy development, competitive analysis, new business creation
6. 10–20 Years		
Corporate Mission & Values	Visionary thinking, purpose-driven leadership, cultural stewardship, long-term perspective, ethical foundation	Enterprise leadership, institutional knowledge, industry evolution awareness, cultural transformation

Beyond this recognition, a TALENT MARKETPLACE (20) will help potential leaders see where their capabilities might be valuable. This TRANSPARENCY (32) allows natural matching between leadership needs and leadership capacity, rather than relying on formal processes to make these connections.

●▼◢■✳⬟

Most importantly, organizations need to legitimize Emergent Leadership by acknowledging and supporting it when it appears. An excellent way to do this is with clear DOMAINS, ASSETS & STANDARDS (23) that individuals across the organization can control. A NETWORK OF TEAMS (13) means that there will be more open spots for legitimate leaders to bring their talents to bear. An organization of 10,000 people may have only 150 "senior leadership" spots available. If it were to break into a network of 1,000 teams, that number would increase by an order of magnitude. Adding UPWARD REPRESENTATION (24) doubles that figure.

59 *Health Check*

Waiting for symptoms is a symptom

Operating in cycles of crisis and recovery, with teams pushing through challenges until they break down or burn out, seems normal to most. It's only normal because traditional management approaches rely on lagging indicators like turnover, engagement surveys, or productivity metrics that surface issues only after damage is done. By then, fixing problems requires significant time and resources, and valuable team members may already be lost.[3]

The health of a team—its resilience, engagement, and capacity to deliver—needs continuous monitoring and adjustment.[4] This is especially crucial in environments where the pace of change is increasing, and teams face constantly shifting demands and pressures.[5]

THEREFORE ...

Implement structured, regular health checks that assess team vitality across key dimensions using clear metrics and facilitating open discussion.[6] These checks should occur at consistent intervals (typically monthly), and could be part of a regular team meeting on your CADENCE (65).

The easiest (and probably the best) way to do this is to simply ask the team to put up one, two, three, or four fingers, on the count of three, corresponding to an extremely spicy four-point scale.

One finger	Two fingers	Three fingers	Four fingers
If nothing changes, I'd quit.	We should make some changes.	We shouldn't make any changes.	If we change anything, I'd quit.

Do it on the count of three to ensure people aren't swayed by others. Use a four-point scale so there's no neutral option.

Team Energy & Sustainability

How sustainable is our current workload and pace over the next few months?

Mission Clarity & Alignment

How clear and aligned are we in this moment about our mission and individual roles?

Psychological Safety & Trust

How safe do you feel openly raising tough issues or mistakes with this team?*

Learning & Growth

Are you getting enough meaningful opportunities to grow and develop professionally?

Delivery Capability

Do we currently have what we need (tools, support, resources) to reliably deliver great work?

Then, talk about it.

---

* This is obviously pretty meta. If you ask this on a team and you get all threes and fours, you might not know if you (a) have great psychological safety, or (b) have terrible psychological safety. You're going to have to use your brain on this one.

●▼◢■✿◆

If you're in a position to lead, get ADVICE (31) from your teammates on what to change. Capture actions worth taking in your BACKLOG (37). Run an ACTION MEETING (47) to turn vague ideas into action. Run a real-time RETROSPECTIVE (66) if you need to dig deeper. Put the noteworthy failures on your FAIL WALL (69).

60 *Hack Day*

To break the rules, break the routine

Day-to-day bureaucracy, established processes, and the tyranny of daily deliverables cause ideas that could transform the business to wither in the shadows of the urgent but unimportant. Meetings create the illusion of progress while reinforcing existing power structures and thought patterns. Without deliberate intervention, even the most brilliant people produce mediocre outputs.

THEREFORE...

Institute regular Hack Days*—dedicated periods where normal work stops and people self-organize around projects they're passionate about. OPEN SPACE TECHNOLOGY (41) is one opinionated form of this. Hack Days typically last one or two days and welcome participation from all parts of the organization, not just technical teams, but they're also effective when stretched to an entire working week.

---

* Daniel H. Pink, *Drive: The Surprising Truth About What Motivates Us* (Riverhead, 2011). The most famous pop-management example of this is documented here and focuses on Atlassian's "FedEx Days" where employees have 24 hours to deliver. Clever! This seems to have become a regular practice through Atlassian's "ShipIt" days, which focus on much more than software: https://www.atlassian.com/company/shipit.

KEY ELEMENTS

Time bound	Self directed	Permission rich
Clear start and end.	Participants choose what to work on.	Normal constraints are temporarily suspended.
Prototype focused	**Inclusive**	**Celebratory**
Building beats planning; focus on ITERATIVE SHIPPING (46).	Open to all roles, levels, and perspectives.	All attempts are valued, not just successes.

ONE- TO TWO-DAY ADAPTIVE AGENDA (49)

Start by scheduling the event well in advance to ensure broad participation. Create an open platform (physical or digital) where people can post challenges and begin forming teams before the day itself.*

DAY 1: MORNING

Kickoff 9:00–9:30	Welcome and frame the purpose.
	Introduce available resources.
	Explain documentation expectations.
Team Formation & Challenge Selection 9:30–10:30	Quick pitches from challenge sponsors (roughly two minutes each).
	Self-organization into teams.
	Teams claim SPACE FOR WORK (72).
First Build Session 10:30–12:30	Teams dive into FLOW STATE WORK (61).
	Roaming experts available for consultation.

---

* There are no breaks in this agenda. I don't believe in breaks. People should take breaks when they need to. We're adults!

DAY 1: AFTERNOON

Working Lunch & Checkpoint 12:30–1:30	Optional two-minute progress shares. Resource requests and ad hoc problem-solving huddles with available experts.
Second Build Session 1:30–4:30	Continued FLOW STATE WORK (61) on prototypes. User testing if applicable.
Day 1 RETROSPECTIVES (66) 4:30–5:00	What's working/not working. Adjustments for Day 2, including identifying Day 2 focus areas. Celebration of early wins.

DAY 2: MORNING

Kickoff 9:00–9:30	Energy-building activity. Teams share Day 2 focus areas.
Build Session 9:30–12:30	Refinement of prototypes.

DAY 2: AFTERNOON

Working Lunch & Checkpoint 12:30–1:30	Progress share from teams that want feedback.
Final Build Session 1:30–3:30	Complete minimum viable prototypes and prep for DEMOS (35).
Show & Tell 3:30–5:00	50% of available time: short (5–10 minute) DEMOS (35) from each team, depending on how many teams there are. 40% of available time: audience feedback. 10% of available time: celebration of all efforts.
Next Steps & Closing 5:00–5:30	Process for advancing promising ideas. Recognition and celebration.

LONGER HACK DAYS/HACK WEEKS

With enough planning, it's possible to extend these Hack Days into intensive hack weeks that can be used for more focused, intentional transformations. Think *launching a new product, moving into a new category,* or *solving a big, entrenched problem.* Organizations like Mesa have built their entire business model around organizing efforts like these, with a special emphasis on bringing in outside experts who can accelerate *and* shift perspectives.*

In general, the flow looks something like this:

---

* mesa.do, out of Brazil. They're spectacular, and worth a meet.

Explore Days 1–2	• Problem immersion and reframing • User/stakeholder interviews • Competitive analysis • Challenge definition
Create Days 3–4	• Rapid prototyping • User testing cycles • Iteration and refinement • Implementation planning
Solidify & Hand Off Day 5	• Final prototypes • Documentation • Implementation road map • Accountability assignment

ESSENTIAL INGREDIENTS

Executive sponsorship without executive control creates the STRUCTURAL & PSYCHOLOGICAL SAFETY (3) necessary for genuine innovation. When leaders join as *participants*, they model vulnerability and signal that hierarchy is suspended for the duration of the Hack Days. Working alongside frontline staff during Hack Days will reveal issues you'd never have discovered through formal reports, so it's important to dig deep if you're in a seat of positional authority.

Physical environment matters because our spaces shape our thinking. The best Hack Days use SPACE FOR WORK (72) and HIDING PLACES (73) to create/use flexible zones for different work modes. Remove physical barriers between teams, provide abundant visualization tools, and ensure plenty of WHITEBOARDS AT INTERSECTIONS (74) where spontaneous collaboration occurs. The physical act of standing and moving activates imagination differently than sitting in meeting rooms, creating fresh perspectives and EMERGENT LEADERSHIP (58) from unexpected sources.

Documentation is nonnegotiable. LOGBOOK (57) principles apply here: What isn't captured is lost. Create templates in advance that make documentation feel like a natural part of the work rather than an administrative burden. The best learning comes not just from what was built but from how teams navigated obstacles and discovered new approaches. Consider individual printed pages with fields for team members/roles, problem statement, key insights discovered, solution overview, and implementation next steps.

Focus on feasibility instead of perfection to maintain momentum and maximize learning. The prototype's purpose isn't to be flawless, but to test assumptions and generate feedback. This principle connects directly to EXPERIMENTATION (62), valuing rapid learning cycles over polished deliverables. Teams should embrace a "yes, and" mindset, building on each other's ideas rather than prematurely judging them. This will help develop TEAM/PROCESS AS PRODUCT (63) thinking.

Support functions must participate to prevent post-event implementation barriers. When legal, finance, compliance, and IT teams join as enablers rather than gatekeepers, they develop firsthand understanding of challenges and can suggest viable alternatives rather than simply saying "no." This creates EXPANDED AVAILABLE POWER (4) by distributing decision-making authority during the event itself, rather than forcing solutions through approval gauntlets afterward.

61 *Flow State Work*

Deep > busy

Breakthrough work thrives on extended, distraction-free focus—what psychologists call "flow." Yet modern schedules and Slack pings make that state a luxury instead of the norm.

> RescueTime data scientists also calculated the *longest* interval that each user worked with no inbox checks or instant messaging. For half the users studied this longest uninterrupted interval was no more than forty minutes, with the most common length clocking in at a meager twenty minutes. More than two-thirds of the users never experienced an hour or more of uninterrupted time during the period studied.[7]

This is obviously not ideal.

Shallow work
Cognitively undemanding, logistical tasks, often performed while distracted
fill our days but rarely move the needle on what truly matters

Deep work

Professional activities performed in a state of distraction-free concentration that push cognitive capabilities to their limit
create breakthrough value and build rare, hard-to-replicate skills*

The solution seems obvious: Create space for uninterrupted focus—but actually doing this turns out to be remarkably difficult. Trying to protect deep work time collides with organizational cultures that prize response time. Meeting-heavy calendars fragment the day. It also feels good to be needed, to be in the meeting, to be busy.

THEREFORE...

Create deliberate structures, norms, and practices that protect deep, focused work as an organizational priority. Recognize that certain classes of problems, particularly those involving innovation, strategy, and complex analysis, can only be solved through sustained concentration. Design your environment, schedule, and communication protocols to enable regular states of flow both for individuals and entire teams.

CREATING CONDITIONS FOR FLOW

Design your environment to support cognitive best performance. Physical spaces signal expected behaviors. SPACE FOR WORK (72) principles apply directly here, so create designated deep work zones where conversation is prohibited and interruptions are taboo. Some organizations use visual signals (like small flags or lights) to indicate when someone is in flow state and shouldn't be disturbed. The physical environment should match the cognitive environment you wish to create, providing both HIDING PLACES (73) for concentration and collaborative spaces for when you emerge from deep work.

---

* Deep work connects directly to both personal satisfaction and organizational performance. A study from McKinsey found that executives who were able to achieve flow regularly were five times more productive than their distracted peers. That said, this statistic is hard to verify. It's attributed to Steven Kotler and references a private McKinsey study that spanned a decade. YMMV.

Establish time boundaries that protect focused attention. Flow requires un-interrupted time blocks of at least 90 minutes.* Adopt consistent focus hours or even focus days across teams, creating a CADENCE (65) that everyone respects. Treat these BOUNDARIES (67) with the same respect as crucial client meetings or exec-level planning sessions.

Create transition rituals that signal the brain to shift modes. Flow requires a deliberate transition. Develop consistent routines that signal "deep work begins now": closing email/messaging apps, clearing your physical workspace, putting phones in airplane mode, or even using specific music or sounds as a trigger. These small ceremonies prepare your mind for depth the same way pregame rituals prepare athletes for peak performance. Equally important are ending rituals that help you capture insights and create clean closure, allowing you to fully disconnect afterward.

FLOW AT THE TEAM LEVEL

While flow is often framed as an individual experience, organizations can systematically enable or disable it for entire teams. LEAN TEAMS (19) naturally support flow better than bloated ones, as they reduce coordination overhead and communication complexity. DISTRIBUTED MANAGEMENT (14) allows teams to self-regulate their work patterns without waiting for approval from distant authorities.

Establish shared norms around urgency and response times. Most workplace emergencies aren't truly urgent. They just feel that way due to lack of clear protocols. Create explicit agreements about what constitutes a genuine emergency (warranting interruption during deep work) versus what can wait, with defined response times for different communication channels (e.g., Slack messages within four hours, emails within 24 hours) to reduce the pressure for immediate responses. Try "urgent" and "FYI" email tags to reduce interruptions while ensuring truly time-sensitive matters still get attention.

---

* The minimum needed to reach real cognitive *depth*.

Build recovery into your rhythm. Flow is intense and depleting and cannot be sustained indefinitely. The most effective practitioners of deep work follow periods of intense focus with deliberate recovery. CADENCE (65) applies here: Alternate between focused individual work and collaborative sessions, between cognitive heavy lifting and lighter integrative tasks.

CHECK IN & OUT (44) **at the team level.** Start each day or week with brief check-ins where team members share their deep work priorities and when they'll be unavailable. End with checkouts where insights and progress are shared. Articulating your focus helps solidify your own commitment while setting appropriate expectations with teammates.

COMMON ANTI-PATTERNS

Watch for these familiar traps that look like productivity, but aren't:

The culture of continuous partial attention* treats immediate responsiveness as the highest virtue. Meetings interrupt deep work, messaging platforms demand instant replies, and employees are expected to be perpetually available. This environment systematically prevents flow from ever taking hold. The antidote is explicit permission—even encouragement—to disconnect, combined with clear protocols for what truly warrants interruption.

The activity trap confuses motion with progress, meetings with productivity, and responsiveness with effectiveness. Teams fall into this when they lack clear metrics for meaningful outcomes, instead defaulting to visible busyness as a proxy for contribution. METRICS REVIEW (36) helps escape this trap by focusing on impact rather than activity. When outcomes are transparent, the value of deep work is self-evident.

The multitasking myth persists despite overwhelming evidence that humans cannot effectively perform multiple cognitive tasks simultaneously. What appears

---

* A 1998 coinage by internet-era sociologist Linda Stone

as multitasking is actually rapid task switching, which degrades performance on all tasks. We inadvertently encourage this myth when we reward juggling ability rather than execution. BOUNDARY MANAGEMENT (67) helps establish clearer separation between different work modes and responsibilities.

BUILDING YOUR FLOW PRACTICE

Here's where to begin:

Start small. Even 30-minute focus blocks can build the mental muscles needed for deeper work. Gradually extend these periods as your capacity increases. Track your deep work hours to create accountability and visibility into your progress. Use the LENGTH LIMIT (64) pattern to constrain the scope of your deep work sessions, creating clear boundaries around both time and task.

Document your personal conditions for optimal flow: time of day, environmental factors, types of tasks, and mental state. This self-awareness helps you replicate successful flow states more consistently. The most effective practitioners are good at creating the conditions their unique cognitive style requires.

Combine deep work with RETROSPECTIVES (66) **to continuously refine your approach.** After focus sessions, briefly note what worked, what didn't, and how you might adjust next time. This creates a continuous improvement cycle for your personal flow practice.

62 Experimentation

Certainty shrinks possibility

You can't rely on annual strategies or quarterly plans when conditions shift daily. Instead, you need to develop the capacity for experimentation—the ability to *actually* test ideas, *actually* learn from results, and *actually* adapt your ongoing approach based on real data rather than assumptions.

THEREFORE...

Experimentation offers a practical alternative to committing up front to big plans and large investments based solely on guesses—by encouraging teams to rapidly and repeatedly test ideas at a small scale. Rather than seeing experiments as occasional special events, experimentation is embedded into the regular flow of daily work. It prioritizes quick learning, immediate feedback, and constant adjustment. This practice allows you to fail fast, fail cheaply, and learn effectively, dramatically reducing risk and increasing the organization's capacity to adapt quickly to changing conditions.

To begin practicing experimentation, start by clearly framing your ideas or projects as testable hypotheses. A good hypothesis explicitly states what you believe will happen, why, and how you'll know if it's true or false. For example, rather than saying, "Let's launch a new mobile app," frame it as, "If we provide customers with a simplified mobile app, we expect customer satisfaction to increase by 20 percent."

Clear hypotheses force clarity about why you're doing something and how you'll measure success or failure.*

Next, break down big, ambitious goals into smaller, actionable experiments that can be quickly tested. If your goal is to radically improve customer satisfaction, don't try to roll out a complete solution immediately.† Instead, run small experiments, like testing new customer service chat features with a limited group, offering simplified billing, or tweaking your onboarding experience. Each small experiment quickly reveals what works and what doesn't, allowing your team to continuously adjust direction based on real data instead of guesses.

---

* You can also do this with stakeholder or customer interviews. Don't just write an interview guide. Write the interview guide and add in what you think your customers are going to tell you. You've just doubled your knowledge, because you've exposed your biases to yourself.

† A really fun way to do this is to think about a thing you're working on and to make a grid where one axis is how much *company money* you'd bet on a thing, and the other axis is how much of *your own money* you'd bet on that thing. Use the same scale for each, and one end should be something small, like a coffee. The other end should be something relatively large, like ... your salary. Doing this will help you rethink the scale of your bets. Courtesy of user experience strategist Hias Wrba: https://x.com/ScreaminHias/status/1002835968364306432.

Something I Can Try Without Permission 100% chance of success Directly within my area of control	Achievable Change 70/30 chance of success Org has tools, but coordination needed	Radical/Important Change 50/50 chance of success Org would need significant shifts
PLAN THIS WAY →		← THINK THIS WAY
Treat other department heads like valued customers, and coach your directs to do the same (and hold them accountable).	Plan and run a series of workshops between your department and others that rely on yours, focused on shared performance improvement.	If we completely reorganize and focus on our most important business strategies and differentiators in market, we'll win.
Create a Slack channel to recognize cooperation happening within the department. Push directs to participate until this becomes routine.	Implement an annual award series for employees who model cooperation (each silo can nominate from other silos, and everyone votes).	If we create a new compensation plan incentivizing cooperation instead of competition between silos (and against "the business"), everything will be easier.
Start doing weekly pulse surveys with your team, and use the results to improve information sharing or delegation of work.	Work directly with a local artist/production house to develop short films, GIFs, or digital media that extend the brand.	If we switch agencies from current to a new/global partner, we'll have better resonance across our target audience.
Write down your own "operating principles" for your department, communicate them clearly, and collaborate with your team to integrate them daily.	Survey the team to assess how the existing vision/mission/ values are serving the org and how "true" they are in practice, and create a shared plan for improvement.	If we overhaul company vision/mission/values to match market needs, we'll hire better and accelerate our progress.
Say explicitly: "Not everyone should be a people manager, and that's OK." Collaborate with your team to identify alternative career paths.	Work with HR to redefine pay bands and incentive structures so your team isn't forced into an "up or out" career path.	If we change the entire company operating model to accommodate promotion paths that don't require people management, we'll keep top performers longer.
Share your social passions openly within your team to push authenticity (include these in your team's "how I work" files).	Help your team define their own social platforms, providing permission and support for public expression.	If we launch significant pro-social actions as a company based on employee votes, we'll fix a negative perception in the market.

Practically running an experiment involves four simple but critical steps:

1. Design	Clearly define your hypothesis, the specific action you're testing, the expected outcome, how you'll measure it, and the timeline for running the test. Usually, effective experiments run between a few days and a few weeks—long enough to gather useful data but short enough to allow quick learning.
2. Execute	Carry out the experiment exactly as planned. Resist the temptation to change things midway unless absolutely necessary, as consistency ensures clear learning.
3. Measure and Learn	Immediately after the experiment concludes, analyze the results objectively. Did the results match your hypothesis? Why or why not? Clearly document your learnings, whether the experiment succeeded or failed.
4. Adjust and Repeat	Use what you've learned to decide your next steps. Successful experiments may scale up slightly or inspire related tests. Failed experiments should inform new hypotheses or clarify misunderstandings. Every outcome should lead to another experiment, continuously refining your approach.

Building effective experimentation also means creating organizational structures that actively support small, frequent tests. Leaders must make it easier to run experiments than to simply implement assumptions without testing. Simplified processes for approving experiments, rapid resource allocation, and clear protocols for handling risks help teams experiment easily and frequently.

Additionally, experimentation requires a shift in how your organization views success and failure. Rather than punishing failure, leaders should publicly celebrate experiments, successful or not, that deliver clear learnings and progress toward TRUE PURPOSE (1). Use STRUCTURAL & PSYCHOLOGICAL SAFETY (3) to create a culture where failed experiments are openly discussed as valuable insights rather than concealed as embarrassments. Use a FAIL WALL (69) to reinforce this, and don't prevent those who try to learn from taking part in EMERGENT LEADERSHIP (58).

This openness about experimentation is all about getting smarter, not seeing who's best. So TEAM INCENTIVES (25) will be essential.

The main pitfalls of experimentation include overcomplicating the testing process, skipping clear hypothesis definition, or falling into the trap of experimentation for its own sake without clear learning goals. To avoid these pitfalls, keep experiments simple, focused, and clearly tied to measurable outcomes. Additionally, always track your results in your LOGBOOK (57) and connect them to your OBJECTIVES & KEY RESULTS (28). Ship them to customers, potentially, with ITERATIVE SHIPPING (46) and DEMOS (35).

You'll quickly notice dramatic improvements in adaptability and innovation after applying this pattern. Ideas will flow more freely, risk-taking will be safer, and decision-making will be easier and longer lasting. Teams will feel empowered, as their ideas will be validated through evidence rather than authority.

The best time to start this pattern was yesterday.

63 Team/Process as Product

Your interfaces are your intelligence

Everyone obsesses over customer-facing products, sweating every pixel and parsing every user interaction. Meanwhile, our internal teams operate like grubby medieval fiefdoms—opaque, idiosyncratic, and utterly dependent on tacit knowledge.* We've all been there: six months into a new job, still trying to figure out how to get IT to provision a laptop or how to navigate the finance department's byzantine reimbursement process. The chaos is both frustrating and expensive.†

THEREFORE...

Productize your team. Start treating your team like a product with real users, clear interfaces, and deliberate design choices.

1. MAP YOUR TEAM'S INTERFACES

Document every way other teams interact with yours. Think in terms of a contract between your team and the rest of the organization.

---

* Go read Franz Kafka's *The Castle* and track the resemblance to your own working experience.
† McKinsey estimates that employees spend nearly 20% of their time searching for information or colleagues who can help them complete basic tasks.

EXERCISE: INTERFACE MAPPING

1. Gather	Gather your team for a 90-minute workshop.
2. Generate	On a whiteboard, list all entry points to your team (requests, handoffs, dependencies).
3. Describe	For each entry point, document: • Input requirements (exactly what others must provide) • Processing time (be honest, not aspirational) • Output format (what they'll receive back) • Error states (what happens when things go wrong) • Support model (how users get help)
4. Prioritize	Identify your three most-used interfaces and your three most-problematic ones. (Once you've mapped these interfaces, you'll likely discover that 80% of frustration comes from 20% of your touchpoints. Focus there first!)

2. BUILD AND LAUNCH THE API

A team API (application programming interface) is simply the set of standardized ways other people can work with your team.[8] Think of it as your team's instruction manual. In the tech world, real APIs allow different software systems to communicate, like when a weather app on your phone requests data from a weather service. The weather service has a clear API that specifies: "If you send me a location, I'll send back the temperature, conditions, and forecast in this exact format." While technical teams will have actual code-based APIs, nontechnical teams need the same clarity about how others should interact with them. Your HR, finance, or marketing team API defines what information people need to provide, what they'll get back, how long it will take, and what happens when things go wrong. Build and launch these, ideally in a place where others can find them easily (see step five, "Design for Discoverability," on page 292).

Team Home Page *Create a single source of truth where anyone can find...*	• Mission and scope (what you do and don't do) • Team roster with clear roles • How-to guides for common requests • SLAs for different request types • Current workload and capacity
Request Management System *Don't rely on drive-by requests or Slack messages.*	• Create standardized intake forms. • Build a transparent queue visible to requesters. • Establish triage protocols with clear prioritization rules. • Set up automated acknowledgments and status updates. • Publish live metrics on throughput and cycle time.
Self-Service Tools *For every repetitive request, ask: "How can we make this self-service?"*	• Create templates for common deliverables. • Build decision trees to guide users through complex processes. • Develop calculators for estimates and forecasts. • Create diagnostic tools that solve common issues. • Automate approvals for low-risk requests.

3. VERSION YOUR PROCESSES

Just as software improves through iterations, your team processes should evolve through deliberate versions, not random drift.

Process Versioning in Practice

1. Document v1.0: Start by documenting current state, warts and all.
2. Test with users: Get feedback from actual internal customers.
3. Refine to v1.1: Make incremental improvements based on feedback.
4. Maintain a change log: Track what changed and why.
5. Communicate updates: Announce significant changes like you would product updates.
6. Deprecate old processes: Set end-of-life dates for outdated ways of working.

4. RUN USER RESEARCH

Stop assuming you know what other teams need from yours. Do proper user research.

Internal User Research Tactics

1. Friction logs: Ask partners to document every friction point when working with your team.
2. Process shadowing: Watch someone actually try to use your team's services.
3. Satisfaction surveys: Run quick pulse checks after interactions.
4. User testing: Before launching new processes, test them with real users.
5. Request analytics: Track which services are most/least used and why.

5. DESIGN FOR DISCOVERABILITY

Your team's services are worthless if people can't find them or don't know they exist.

Discoverability Techniques

1. Service catalog: Create a visual menu of everything your team offers.
2. Contextual embedding: Place links to your services where people need them.
3. New employee onboarding: Introduce key team interfaces during onboarding.
4. Office hours: Host regular, scheduled time for questions and help.
5. Internal marketing: Promote your team's capabilities through internal channels.

Experiment, Learn, and Improve

A proper product approach to a team or a process means that you'll be learning a *lot* more about how other teams are working with yours. It'll be jarring at first. You'll get a ton of questions and experience a fair share of failure: similar requests getting inconsistent responses; processes working differently depending on who you know; documentation feeling like it's perpetually out of date.

You will need to work at it.

●▼◢■❋◗

EXPERIMENTATION (62), HACK DAY (60), and LOGBOOK (57) are your best friends here, as are ITERATIVE SHIPPING (46) and KANBAN (55). They'll help you get smarter about your customers and actively prioritize the RIGHT THING (26). To that end, you may want to expose your BACKLOG MANAGEMENT (37) and METRICS REVIEW (36) to customers while you set RELATIVE TARGETS (33).

Remember, you're moving from a traditional, static approach to teaming and working to one where issues are *more apparent* but also easier to diagnose and fix. So stick with it, even if it feels less warm and fuzzy in the short term. The issues were always there, you just know about them now!

64 *Length Limit*

Constraint is the mother of emergence

Indefinite timelines for roles, projects, and commitments are somehow confused with stability.

Without clear temporal boundaries, initiatives drift, accountability weakens, and opportunities for reflection and renewal are lost. In a world of increasing uncertainty, the ability to adapt and evolve is crucial for survival. It'd be silly to leave this to chance.

THEREFORE...

Don't just embrace the idea that *someday,* what you're working on will DISSOLVE (9). Actually set time limits for everything—and stick to them. If the thing that you're working on *is working,* the time limit will give you a chance to re-up your commitment to the cause. If not, you have a built-in way to move forward and learn.

Pattern	Length Limit	Notes
ELECTIONS (15)	6–12 months	Ensures leadership renewal; avoids entrenched authority
SELF-MANAGED TEAMS (18)	12–18 months (before reassessment)	Provides regular reassessment of effectiveness and purpose alignment
TALENT MARKETPLACE (20)	3–6 months per rotation	Prevents stagnation; promotes active skill and career growth
CHAPTERS (22)	6–12 months (leadership and membership)	Freshness, avoidance of complacency
TEAM INCENTIVES (25)	Quarterly or semiannual review	Alignment, freshness, responsiveness
OBJECTIVES & KEY RESULTS (28)	Quarterly	Regular reflection, learning, and strategic realignment
PULL UPDATES (34)	Weekly	Prevents information overload
DEMOS (35)	Every 2 weeks	Frequent feedback, continuous iteration and improvement
BACKLOG MANAGEMENT (37)	Biweekly	Keeps it relevant, prioritized, manageable, and clear
COLLEAGUE LETTER OF UNDERSTANDING (40)	In force for 6–12 months	Frequent feedback, continuous iteration and improvement
TEAM CHARTER (43)	In force for 6–12 months	Frequent feedback, continuous iteration and improvement
ITERATIVE SHIPPING (46)	Weekly or biweekly	Reinforces rapid learning, continuous momentum; avoids stagnation
HEALTH CHECK (59)	Monthly (team), quarterly (organization)	Proactively identifies issues; maintains organizational responsiveness
HACK DAY (60)	1–2 days quarterly	Stimulates creativity and experimentation without risking burnout
EXPERIMENTATION (62)	1–4 weeks per experiment	Enables rapid feedback; minimizes risk; accelerates learning
LENGTH LIMIT (64)	Reviewed annually	Ensures limits themselves remain adaptive and relevant
RETROSPECTIVES (66)	60–90 mins every 2–4 weeks	Enables regular structured reflection, learning, and improvement
BOUNDARY MANAGEMENT (67)	Defined daily hours, weekly no-meeting blocks	Protects productivity; prevents burnout; sustains healthy boundaries

65 Cadence

It's hard to dance if you've got no rhythm

Lurching between frantic activity and exhausted recovery.

Letting work accumulate until it reaches a crisis point, followed by a heroic sprint that leaves teams depleted.

Entering every week with an understanding that the working rhythm will be, on one hand, completely new . . . and on the other a boring rerun. *8 AM–7 PM: 30 minutes back-to-back-to-back and work compressed into the after-dinner hours.*

This pattern might feel natural or inevitable. We know it creates unnecessary stress and reduces both quality and sustainability. Eliminating intensity doesn't make sense, though, especially if you're aligned with your work's purpose and have big dreams for what might be possible in the future world you're building. Instead of slowing down, we should create intentional rhythms that balance focus and renewal.

THEREFORE . . .

Establish clear cadences at multiple time scales, each serving distinct purposes, and stick to them over substantial amounts of time. Only change the cadence when you have good data to suggest you should, and don't make micro adjustments just because someone (even the boss!) can't attend a given time slot.

Let's repeat that last point, for clarity:

Don't change the cadence just because the boss can't attend a given time slot.

Keep the meeting. Run it the same way you always do.

Doing so will reinforce the team's belief in DISTRIBUTED MANAGEMENT (14) and EMERGENT LEADERSHIP (58). It will also be a lot easier if you lean into FACILITATION (56) or MEETING ROLES (51).

Daily	• Stand-ups for coordination (15 mins) • Long focus blocks for FLOW STATE WORK (61)
Weekly	• Planning and priority setting via an ACTION MEETING (47) • Progress reviews and adjustments, including HEALTH CHECKS (59) and RETROSPECTIVES (66) • Learning and reflection time
Monthly	• Strategic alignment checks • Capability development • Major releases* • Relationship maintenance
Quarterly	• Direction setting, with adjustments to STRATEGY HEURISTIC (29) • Capability building • Assessment and reassignment of roles, including an adjustment to the TEAM CHARTER (43) • Team renewal and adjustments to NETWORK OF TEAMS (13)
Annually	• Major direction adjustments—revisit vision and strategy with full team • Full capability and skills mapping—understand evolving team needs and growth paths • Deep system health review—examine core patterns, relationships, and ways of working

The key is matching the cadence to the natural rhythm of different types of work, rather than forcing everything into artificial time boxes.

---

* GitLab has been releasing monthly for 166 months straight (https://about.gitlab.com/releases)!

APPLICATION

Start by mapping your team's current patterns. Look for natural energy peaks and valleys and critical coordination points with other teams. Think about how quickly the team is able to learn and adjust. Build around real human renewal needs.*

Then design specific practices for each time horizon. Plot them on a calendar and stick to them according to the RULE OF LAW (2). Adjust them with extreme care, using CONSENT & CONSENSUS (10) and STRUCTURED DECISION-MAKING (30). Temper this with a clear understanding of DISSOLVABILITY (9). Consider capturing the results in your TEAM CHARTER (43).

In time, regular cadence will shift how everyone thinks about productivity and performance. Rather than seeing work as a constant sprint, teams intuit different energy states and how to use them effectively. This creates not just better sustainability but *actually* higher performance, as teams learn to match different types of work to appropriate rhythms. The organization develops temporal intelligence—the ability to work with rather than against natural cycles of effort and renewal.†

---

* Basecamp's *Shape Up* describes "Six Week Cycles" here: https://basecamp.com/shapeup/0.3 -chapter-01#six-week-cycles. Four weeks is too short. Six weeks is long enough.

† I imagine, and hope for, a world where every business has a feeling of seasonality. Not just summer all the time, if you catch my drift.

66 Retrospectives

The faster you go, the more often you need to learn

The postmortem, at the end of the project, to capture lessons learned, seems productive but prevents teams from identifying patterns and addressing systemic issues *within* the timeframe of the project. The pressure to deliver can make reflection feel like a luxury—and as a result, push it outside the timebox of the actual project—but without structured retrospection, teams repeat mistakes and miss opportunities for improvement.

When reflection does happen, it often focuses solely on problems or becomes a blame game, missing the opportunity to reinforce positive patterns and build on successes. The postmortem is doing what it says on the tin: The project is dead; why did it die?*

Retrospectives create intentional space for teams to step back, examine their work patterns, and deliberately evolve their practices.† Unlike casual discussions

---

* The practice of systematically reflecting on work and team effectiveness predates the Agile movement. Norman Kerth gets credit here for formalizing "project retrospectives" with his influential 2001 book, *Project Retrospectives: A Handbook for Team Reviews*. His approach was project-centric, usually involving post-project reviews. In 2001, retrospectives gained further momentum from Agile Manifesto principle 12: "At regular intervals, the team reflects on how to become more effective, then tunes and adjusts its behavior accordingly."

† Derby and Larsen, *Agile Retrospectives*. Esther Derby and Diana Larsen's 2006 book *Agile Retrospectives: Making Good Teams Great*, brought retrospectives fully into Agile teams' regular iteration cycles as frequent, short, incremental reviews.

or complaints aired in hallways, retrospectives provide a structured container for honest reflection and collective learning.

THEREFORE...

Retrospectives are regular, structured meetings where teams reflect on their work patterns and relationships. They should follow a clear format that balances appreciation with critique, and discussion with action, and ideally should be done the same way everywhere in your organization. That way everyone always knows how to participate, regardless of whether they've joined a new team or are on a team they've been on for years.

BASIC AGENDA

Retrospectives can follow a structured agenda, but it's usually best to have a principle-driven ADAPTIVE AGENDA (49) that follows this framework:

- **Successes first:** Start by identifying what's working well, creating psychological safety and recognizing positive patterns. The question "What worked?" is nearly perfect; it's also substantially better than starting with the faux-positive "Start" in "Start-stop-continue." (How many times does something like "Start being more accountable" come up? Too often.)
- **Challenges next:** Work through difficulties with curiosity rather than blame, focusing on systemic issues over individual actions. "Where did you get stuck?" centers individual experiences with the system.
- **Insights based on what's been discussed:** Look for patterns and connections between observations, drawing out deeper learnings about team dynamics and work processes. "What might we do next time?" opens the door to continuing good things, stopping bad things, and putting some new ideas in place.
- **Assign actions:** Identify specific, achievable improvements the team can implement, assigning clear ownership and timeframes. Switch directly into an ACTION MEETING (47) if that pattern is in play on your team.

CADENCE (65)

Different teams in different parts of the organization will have naturally different rhythms for retrospection. But in every case, the rhythm should be suited to the pace of the work rather than aligned to project timelines. Leadership teams, operating on big-picture issues, might adopt a quarterly rhythm. Purpose teams are well served by retrospecting monthly. Customer teams should do it every two weeks, and truly frontline teams (think call-center employees) will be well served by an even more frequent and probably shorter retrospective. In truly trying times, a daily retro will help a team learn at the speed of their shifting context.

Any team will benefit from a Retrospective practice, but it's particularly important for SELF-MANAGED TEAMS (18) and teams with shared INCENTIVES (25). Regular Retrospectives won't just improve the product. They'll help cement STRUCTURAL & PSYCHOLOGICAL SAFETY (3), promote COOPERATION (12), and provide intelligence for other patterns, like ELECTIONS (15), ACTIVE STEERING (27), and RELATIVE TARGETS (33). If a shared LOGBOOK (57) is in place,* then people can PULL UPDATES (34) to see how the organization is functioning. Truly good retros will use CONFLICT AS A RESOURCE (38) and FACILITATION (56), which both in their own way make it easier to call out issues in a group setting.

---

* Shout-out to my friend Jordan Husney's company Parabol, which makes retrospective software that is built with organizational intelligence in mind! It's very good, and you should use it.

67 *Boundary Management*

No boundaries = no accountability

We've successfully eliminated many boundaries at work.

Remote work, always-on messaging, flexible schedules—we were promised freedom but received chaos. Everyone's available everywhere, all the time. Your boss texts you at dinner, your colleagues Slack you on weekends, and Zoom meetings creep into every open slot on your calendar.

Burnout, resentment, blurred roles, and a frantic race toward exhaustion are the result.

THEREFORE...

Boundary Management restores order by making explicit what used to be implicit: clear rules around when, where, how, and how much you engage with work. Applying this pattern means treating boundaries as more than polite suggestions: Boundaries are deliberate walls you build to protect your energy, attention, and sanity.*

To get boundary management right, first acknowledge that every organization needs clear, defined, and respected boundaries around four key areas: **time, attention, roles,** and **relationships**.

---

* For further reading here, check out 2019's *It Doesn't Have to Be Crazy at Work* by David Heinemeier Hansson and Jason Fried; if you want proof that I'm right that this is a problem, check out *Digital Minimalism* by Cal Newport. But you know I'm right!

TIME BOUNDARIES

State when you are, and are not, expected to be working. If your workday is technically "9 to 5," but in practice is "9 to forever," your organization urgently needs clear agreements. Explicitly set and communicate protected working hours, and enforce them mercilessly.* Align this practice with clear CADENCE (65) and ensure explicit commitments via TEAM CHARTER (43). No exceptions unless it's genuinely urgent. Use TRIAGE (52) to clarify urgency. If a leader habitually ignores these boundaries, it's a violation of DO NO HARM (6) and signals a lack of STRUCTURAL & PSYCHOLOGICAL SAFETY (3).

Practically, create strict no-meeting hours (e.g., daily 2 PM–4 PM), or a full day per week without meetings, consistent with practices from FLOW STATE WORK (61).

ATTENTION BOUNDARIES

Recognize that not every message deserves immediate attention. Instant messaging and rapid email responses have trained us into constant interruption and distraction. Decide explicitly which messages require immediate responses and which can wait. Train leaders to PULL UPDATES (34) instead of DMing for a human response. Create clear response-time norms (e.g., "Slack responses within one working day; emails within two"). Resist the toxic notion that faster responses always equal better work. They don't. They break focus and drive lower-quality outcomes.

Practically, turn off noncritical notifications during deep work blocks. Train your teams that "quick questions" are never actually quick. Schedule them deliberately instead.

---

* In a 2012 post called "A fair working life," Brunello Cucinelli described the only hard-and-fast rule for running his company: "it is forbidden to work past the agreed working time." He expanded on that in a 2015 interview with Om Malik—https://om.co/2015/04/27/brunello-cucinelli-2/—where he defined the day as starting at 8 AM and ending at 5:30 PM, and that all emails should have two or fewer recipients.

ROLE BOUNDARIES

Clarify exactly who owns what responsibilities and decisions. Nothing kills productivity faster than unclear roles, duplicated effort, and everyone silently expecting someone else to handle important tasks. Without clear role boundaries, people trip over each other, argue silently through passive-aggressive emails, and ultimately fail to deliver. Explicitly define who decides, who contributes, and who gets informed. *Every single time.*

Practically, create simple, visible TEAM CHARTERS (43): Clearly write down who owns key decisions and tasks. Enforce these publicly.

RELATIONSHIP BOUNDARIES

Protect the line between professional collaboration and inappropriate personal demands. Leaders must model behaviors consistent with the values of WHOLENESS (7) and ensure interactions remain constructive and respectful, reinforcing STRUCTURAL & PSYCHOLOGICAL SAFETY (3) and CONFLICT RESOLUTION (39). Practically, leaders must visibly uphold these standards, using clear behavioral agreements like a COLLEAGUE LETTER OF UNDERSTANDING (40).

Boundaries only work if your leaders consistently model them. Hypocrisy kills boundaries. If your CEO claims weekends off-limits but floods inboxes Sunday night, your Boundary Management efforts collapse. Leaders must visibly and explicitly honor boundaries, aligning with DO THE RIGHT THING (26) and RULE OF LAW (2). Regular boundary checks are essential. Frequently revisit, renegotiate, and reinforce boundaries. Boundary management is continuous, supported by practices such as HEALTH CHECKS (59), CHECK IN & OUT (44), and ongoing cycles of EXPERIMENTATION (62).

SPACE

68 Process on the Wall

Digital tools hide work in browsers and apps, forcing teams to actively seek information about project status and progress. This creates unnecessary cognitive load and missed opportunities for collaboration.

Make work visible by using walls as active displays of current work and status.[1] Create clear zones showing work stages, current status, blockers, and team metrics. Use simple visual systems (cards, magnets, sticky notes) that anyone can update in seconds.[2]

When the process is physically visible, teams develop stronger shared understanding and catch issues earlier.[3] These Process Walls can be powerful tools for alignment and coordination, reducing the need for status meetings and creating natural moments for collaboration.

Key Elements

- Visible from most work areas
- Accessible for daily updates
- Large enough to show all active work
- Located where teams naturally gather
- Easy to modify and maintain

◆▼◢■✳◆

Process on the Wall amplifies WORK IN PUBLIC (50) by making tasks and progress visible to all, reinforcing TRANSPARENCY (32) to build trust and accelerate problem-solving. It naturally pairs with KANBAN (55). This real-time view helps with RETROSPECTIVES (66), making it easier to spot bottlenecks and celebrate wins. It aligns with TEAM/PROCESS AS PRODUCT (63), reminding everyone that workflow is a thing that can and should be changed when we learn more.

69 *Fail Wall*

Innovation requires failure,[4] but we hide evidence of setbacks and iterations, so we lose critical learning opportunities and develop risk-averse cultures.

A Fail Wall is a prominent, permanent space for documenting failures and their lessons.* Use a simple, consistent format that captures what was attempted, what happened, and what was learned. Include physical artifacts when possible. The wall should feel both serious (these are important lessons) and playful (failure is part of innovation).

Visible, valued failure moments make it easier for teams to experiment more boldly and learn faster. A Fail Wall signals that thoughtful risk-taking is safer than timid execution. New team members quickly understand that failure in service of learning is acceptable *and* expected.

Key Elements

- Visible location with high foot traffic
- Simple templates for capturing lessons
- Space for physical artifacts
- Regular rotation of content
- Clear focus on learning, not blame

---

* Aside here: I love that Bessemer Venture Partners openly shares their anti-portfolio (their "missed" investments, like Google and Apple, and lessons learned) at https://www.bvp.com/anti-portfolio. That's a *real* Fail Wall.

Fail Wall bolsters STRUCTURAL & PSYCHOLOGICAL SAFETY (3) by normalizing open discussions of mistakes rather than punishing them, transforming the tension of errors into CONFLICT AS A RESOURCE (38). It aligns with DO THE RIGHT THING (26), encouraging ethical action even (and especially) when outcomes fall short. It also reinforces EXPERIMENTATION (62) by publicly embracing missteps, deepening TRANSPARENCY (32).

Digital Analog: Fail Figma*

Keep a "Fails" frame in Figma, FigJam, Miro, or Notion, where teams post screenshots of flops plus a one-line lesson; review it at every retro to normalize risk.

---

* Shout-out to Tim Casasola for suggesting that I add digital versions of these space patterns. In some cases they're entirely unnecessary or too obvious to mention, but in a lot of cases they're helpful!

70 No Leadership Offices

Private offices for leaders send a powerful message about hierarchy and accessibility. They create artificial barriers to communication and reinforce outdated command-and-control structures.

Leaders should work in the same open environment as their teams, using the same variety of spaces based on their SPACE FOR WORK (72) or HIDING PLACES (73). If privacy is needed for sensitive conversations, it should be achieved through bookable rooms available to everyone.

When leadership is visibly accessible, communication improves and trust increases. The space demonstrates organizational values more convincingly than any mission statement.

●▼◢■✳◆

No Leadership Offices brings RULE OF LAW (2) to life by visually eliminating the notion that anyone stands outside or above organizational principles. It directly supports SELF-MANAGED TEAMS (18): When leaders share the same open space, teams feel freer to take initiative and own their work. EMERGENT LEADERSHIP (58) thrives in an environment where authority and ideas can come from any desk, not just from behind a door with a nameplate.

Digital Analog: Open DM Leadership

Leaders default to public Slack channels; private messages are rare and summarized back to the team in a searchable notes doc, erasing the digital corner office.

71 *No Assigned Desks*

Ownership of space makes borders in organizations visible. When people claim territory, they limit their exposure to new ideas and collaborations. Mobile teams report more cross-pollination of ideas and stronger networks across the organization. The space forces positive collisions that fixed seating would prevent.

Create a system of shared spaces that people select based on their work each day. Provide personal storage that moves easily, and establish clear protocols for cleaning and maintaining shared spaces. The key is making the system more convenient than fixed desks.

●▼◢■❋⬟

No Assigned Desks pairs well with MOVABLE EVERYTHING (75), making physical space an active participant in collaboration. It also supports BOUNDARY MANAGEMENT (67) by preventing rigid territorial lines between teams, while helping GUILDS (21), CHAPTERS (22), and a NETWORK OF TEAMS (13) to form more readily. *Break* this pattern in support of BOUNDARY MANAGEMENT (67).

Digital Analog: Temporary and Open Project Channels

Spin up temporary Slack/Teams channels for each initiative, archive them when the work ships, and let people "sit" where the action is instead of guarding territory.

72 *Space for Work*

Different types of work require fundamentally different spaces, but most offices provide only slight variations on a single theme: desks, or conference rooms, and *maybe* a designated boardroom for the most senior people.

Given the research on how flexible or specialized spaces can significantly improve cross-functional collaboration and performance, organizations should create distinct zones optimized for specific work modes.[5] Each should have appropriate acoustics, lighting, furniture, and tools. These aren't just different sizes of the same space but should be completely different environments.

SPACES FOR TEAMS

Zones optimized for group work: tables where small squads can cluster, stand-up areas for quick huddles, and corners suited for deeper discussion.[6] These areas help keep teams cohesive while still allowing cross-team serendipity.

Example: A "project nook" where a SELF-MANAGED TEAM (18) can gather, ensuring they have a semi-defined spot that anyone can join or observe.

SPACES FOR ELECTIONS (15)

For roles selected or ratified by a group, like in ELECTIONS (15), a shared area can serve as a transparent "polling station." This might look like a dedicated corner or a mini forum where ballots are cast physically or decisions are discussed in person.

SPACES FOR FLOW STATE WORK (61)

Quiet zones or "library spaces" offer an atmosphere conducive to deep concentration. While these areas don't have assigned desks, they're intentionally designed to minimize noise and interruption. People can pick a desk or couch and slip into deep focus, removing themselves from the buzz without permanently walling off from the rest of the team.[7]

SPACES FOR STRUCTURED DECISION-MAKING (30)

For formal decisions guided by STRUCTURED DECISION-MAKING (30), you'll need areas that lend themselves to systematic discussions and clear visual aids. Think large whiteboards, flexible seating arrangements for small breakouts, and a central space where proposals or data can be presented (this need not be digital!). Consider seating "in the round" so that everyone can see everyone else. Not assigning these spaces means any group can schedule or spontaneously occupy the room, ensuring the decision-making process is inclusive and open.

SPACES FOR CONFLICT AS A RESOURCE (38)

CONFLICT RESOLUTION (39) needs the right environment. A designated "peace room" or similar neutral territory can be used for difficult conversations, mediations, or stepping away from day-to-day rhythms to hash out disagreements. These should comfortably but intimately seat three people: the two people who are in conflict, and an optional facilitator or mediator.

SPACES TO WORK IN PUBLIC (50)

Encourage TRANSPARENCY (32) by having open tables or high-top counters where tasks are visibly in progress. Imagine a marketing team drafting copy on a giant whiteboard or a design group sketching wireframes. Being physically visible fosters spontaneous feedback and quick alignment across the organization.

SPACES FOR OPEN SPACE TECHNOLOGY (41) AND FUTURE BACKWARD (42)

Techniques like these require large, open areas where participants can move between breakout circles and collectively create emergent agendas. Unassigned, adaptable spaces adjacent to a larger plenary area make it easy to form subgroups, break off for side conversations, and then reconvene.

Digital Analog: Mode-Based Spaces

Create distinct digital rooms—quiet Zoom Focus, collaborative Miro, decision-making Loom recordings channel—available from a single shared list of links so everyone can switch context smoothly.

73 *Hiding Places*

Teams need spaces to retreat, think, and process. While open offices enable collaboration, the lack of protected spaces forces people to leave entirely when they need focus or privacy. This creates unnecessary disruption and signals that FLOW STATE WORK (61) isn't valued.

Create small, enclosed spaces throughout the workplace: phone booths, library nooks, meditation rooms. Position hiding places near but separate from primary work areas, like alcoves in a monastery. This allows people to step away briefly while remaining connected to the flow of work.

When hiding places are thoughtfully integrated, teams naturally develop sustainable rhythms between collaboration and focus. The space itself gives permission to retreat when needed, fostering both productivity and well-being.

Key Elements

- Readily available without booking
- Clearly designated for individual use
- Sound protected but visible
- Comfortable for 1–2 hours
- Free from screens or technology
- Distributed across different zones

Digital Analog: Respected Focus Tags

A calendar-driven "focus" status mutes notifications and drops you into a silent coworking room; teammates see you're head down and queue questions for later.

74 *Whiteboards at Intersections*

The best ideas often emerge from unplanned encounters, but most offices waste these moments of serendipity. Without tools for capture and development, insights evaporate.

Place whiteboards and capture tools wherever people naturally cross paths: hallway intersections, breakout areas, near coffee and water. When capture tools are ubiquitous, more ideas survive and evolve.

Key Elements

- Always visible and accessible
- Ready for immediate use
- Large enough for small groups
- Equipped with basic supplies
- Easy to photograph or digitize

Whiteboards at Intersections complements PROCESS ON THE WALL (68) by extending visual thinking beyond dedicated project spaces to everyday encounters, and it syncs with NO ASSIGNED DESKS (71)—when people roam, they're more likely to cross paths and co-create on these boards. Spontaneous contribution underpins EMERGENT LEADERSHIP (58): Anyone who grabs a marker can become the facilitator of a new idea.

Digital Analog: Live Cams

Set up a camera to take snaps of a whiteboard at given intervals, and auto-post to a #whiteboard channel that purges every two weeks to keep spontaneous ideas flowing.

75 Movable Everything

Fixed elements in a workspace are constraints on thinking and behavior. When everything is bolted down, teams subtly limit their imagination to what the space allows. Teams with truly movable spaces report higher creativity and more frequent collaboration.

Make everything movable except core structure and utilities. This includes not just furniture but also storage, displays, technology, and even lighting. Use industrial casters, lightweight materials, and modular components. Nothing should require more than two people to reconfigure.

Movable Everything supports NO ASSIGNED DESKS (71) and SPACE FOR WORK (72) by making physical environments fluid. When paired with WHITEBOARDS AT INTERSECTIONS (74) and PROCESS ON THE WALL (68), teams can quickly roll visual aids into place to capture insights. The ease of shifting layouts makes OPEN SPACE TECHNOLOGY (41) easier by matching ad hoc breakouts with ad hoc HIDING PLACES (73).

Looking Forward

What next?

Start by starting. Pick one nagging friction—meetings that sprawl, decisions that vanish into email, a team that never ships—and treat it like a design brief. Find one or more patterns that feel almost embarrassingly small for the job. ROUNDS (48) gives every voice airtime in a few minutes. KANBAN (55) replaces a status spreadsheet no one reads with a board everyone can see. CONSENT & CONSENSUS (10) keeps you from debating until the heat death of the universe. Win once, in one room, and earn the right to try the next pattern.

Wire the wins together. When ROUNDS (48) meets STRUCTURED DECISION-MAKING (30), meetings get both equitable and conclusive. Add LOG-BOOK (57) and you've baked a searchable memory into the workflow. A handful of patterns, well chosen and visibly linked, beat a 200-page transformation deck every time. They're also portable. Any of your colleagues (perhaps one across boundaries on another team) can follow the same path that you followed, even if they don't do it exactly the same way. Use the connection notes with each pattern as clues. They're there for a reason: Every pattern in this book emerged because it solved a common misfit with another.

Name it to tame it. Language is software for the social brain; the moment you give a hidden habit a name, a handle, a Post-it on the wall, a sarcastic Slack emoji, you create an edge people can grab. Now the thing can be moved, questioned, retired, or remixed. Back at Undercurrent we saw this in real time. We borrowed the Holacracy trick of labeling every accountability with the same "verb-object" syntax, and suddenly interns were proposing policy changes the partners hadn't thought of; vocabulary creates permission.

Keep an open lab notebook. Nothing kills momentum faster than hoarding lessons until they're perfect. Treat your workplace like an open-source project: Ship the patch notes while the code is still warm. That means public retros on Slack experiments, screenshots of Kanban flow, five-minute demos of a new NETWORK OF TEAMS (13) pilot, even when the metrics are wobbly. Early transparency attracts co-conspirators and surfaces gaps before they become material.

Have a working rhythm. One that I like:

- Friday afternoon: quick Loom video including what we tried, what broke, what we'll tweak next.
- Monday morning: a 10-minute ADVICE (31) round where anyone with context or consequences weighs in.
- Quarterly: a lightweight HEALTH CHECK (59) to see which patterns are still paying rent.

Mind the human cost. Use patterns to shorten cycles and guard the people doing the cycling. FLOW STATE WORK (61) without CADENCE (65) is just quiet burnout. A TALENT MARKETPLACE (20) without TEAM INCENTIVES (25) is just gig work in corporate attire. NO ASSIGNED DESKS (71) before anyone has STRUCTURAL & PSYCHOLOGICAL SAFETY (3) to sit somewhere new is an empty promise.

Keep the language alive. Christopher Alexander never claimed his 253 building patterns were final; he called them "seeds of a living language." Same here. Twelve months from now you'll have local variants I've never dreamed of: "Work from a Plane," "Agents Before Hires," "Silent Sprint Planning," "Draw It," "Dog-Walk 1:1s." Please send them my way—wins, flops, weird edge cases included. Post it in public with #hiddenpatterns and @ me: I am @clayparkerjones on nearly every social media platform. Every addition makes the whole garden tougher and more interesting.

If this book does its job, the second edition might even contradict half of what you've just read. That's progress.

See you in the field. I don't care whether you're a CEO plotting a NETWORK

OF TEAMS (13) rollout or a junior analyst sneaking a KANBAN (55) board onto the fridge. You have authority over the next small move. Use it. Tell me how it goes. We'll swap notes, steal shamelessly, and keep iterating until better ways of working stop being newsworthy and start being normal.

Thanks for reading, and more importantly, thanks in advance for trying. The language is yours now. Don't let it gather dust.

Acknowledgments

First, a huge thank-you to Katie Klumper—CEO of Black Glass—for championing this idea, wrangling the pitch process, and ultimately nudging the right people at the right moment to make this book a possibility. (McKenna Robenalt and Maureen Link: Thanks for being right next to me while testing a lot of this stuff out!)

I owe an equally outsized debt to my co-founders at August—Alix Zacharias, Erica Seldin, Mike Arauz, and Mark Raheja—whose willingness to experiment in public gave me the experiences that shaped these pages. To all the Undercurrenters, who spotted emerging patterns long before we had a name for them: Thank you for the real-time education in real-world systems thinking. (Especially to Alex Chung, who was always game to play with an interesting idea, and without whom this book probably never would have even gotten started.)

Early drafts are fragile things; Tim Casasola, Cara Moyer, Cullen MacDonald, and Mick McConnell read mine with the right mix of skepticism and generosity, saving you, dear reader, from at least four subpar metaphors and a dozen unnecessary footnotes. Similar thanks to Iain Roberts for the last-mile encouragement before I finished this thing one weekend in San Francisco.

I feel especially privileged to have had the opportunity to work with such brave clients along the way who tried these things, even when they felt a little funny, countercultural, or maybe even career-limiting. I owe you!

A final bow to the thinkers whose brains and work light me up: Christopher Alexander; Amy Edmondson; Naomi Stanford; Dave Snowden; Gary Hamel and Michele Zanini; Alison Coward; Rita McGrath; Henry Mintzberg; Richard Rumelt; Bree Groff; Geoffrey West; Bjarte Bogsnes; Bob Sutton and Huggy Rao; Aaron Dignan; Sam Spurlin; Dan Mezick; Danah Boyd; Stowe Boyd (unrelated, I think!); Matt Skelton and Manuel Pais; Carlota Perez; Simon Wardley; Linda Hill; Joost Minnaar and Pim de Morree; Teresa Amabile; Margaret Heffernan; Frances Frei and Anne Morriss; Esther Derby and Diana Larsen; Donella Meadows; Kim Scott; Claire Hughes Johnson; Lou Downe; Ryan Singer; Vishaan Chakrabarti . . . plus a legion of bloggers whose long-form rants and threads keep my curiosity going.

Notes

Front Matter

1. Deloitte Insights, "Purpose Is Everything: How Brands That Authentically Lead with Purpose Are Changing Business," October 15, 2019, https://web.archive.org/web/20250401044244/https://www2.deloitte.com/us/en/insights/topics/marketing-and-sales-operations/global-marketing-trends/2020/purpose-driven-companies.html. Deloitte's global research shows purpose-driven companies grow three times faster, gain higher market share, and report 30% more innovation and 40% better retention than purposeless peers, outperforming across trust, innovation, DEI adoption, and employee engagement.

2. BambooHR LLC, "The Great Gloom: Employees Are Unhappier Than Ever, According to Employee Happiness Index by BambooHR," press release, August 29, 2023. The study reports an 11% drop in employee eNPS from June 2022 to June 2023: nearly 15 times faster than the prior two-year decline.

3. Josh Bivens and Lawrence Mishel, "Understanding the Historic Divergence Between Productivity and a Typical Worker's Pay: Why It Matters and Why It's Real," *Economic Policy Institute*, September 2, 2015, https://www.epi.org/publication/understanding-the-historic-divergence-between-productivity-and-a-typical-workers-pay-why-it-matters-and-why-its-real. Using BLS data, the authors find that between 1973 and 2014, labor productivity grew 72.2%, while hourly compensation for the typical worker rose just 9.2%.

4. Christopher Alexander, Sara Ishikawa, and Murray Silverstein, *A Pattern Language: Towns, Buildings, Construction* (Oxford University Press, 1977).

Foundations

1. Ranjay Gulati, *Deep Purpose: The Heart and Soul of High-Performance Companies* (Harper Business, 2022).

2. Karl E. Weick, *Sensemaking in Organizations* (Sage, 1995).

3. Alan M. Saks, "Antecedents and Consequences of Employee Engagement," *Journal of Managerial Psychology* 21, no. 7 (2006): 600–19, https://doi.org/10.1108/02683940610690169.

4. L. L. Cummings and Philip Bromiley, "The Organizational Trust Inventory (OTI): Development and Validation," in *Trust in Organizations: Frontiers of Theory and Research*, ed. Roderick M. Kramer and Tom R. Tyler (Sage, 1996), 302–30.

5. Roderick M. Kramer, "Trust and Distrust in Organizations: Emerging Perspectives, Enduring Questions," *Annual Review of Psychology* 50 (1999): 569–98, https://doi.org/10.1146/annurev.psych.50.1.569.

6. "Ten Things We Know to Be True," Google, accessed February 2025, https://about.google/philosophy.

7. "Leadership Principles," Amazon, accessed February 2025, https://www.amazon.jobs/content/en/our-workplace/leadership-principles.

8. A. G. Lafley and Ram Charan, *The Game-Changer: How You Can Drive Revenue and Profit Growth with Innovation* (Crown Business, 2008).

9. Joseph A. Michelli, *The Starbucks Experience: 5 Principles for Turning Ordinary into Extraordinary* (McGraw Hill, 2007).

10. Joseph A. Michelli, *The New Gold Standard: 5 Leadership Principles for Creating a Legendary Customer Experience Courtesy of the Ritz-Carlton Hotel Company* (McGraw Hill, 2008).

11. Chris Argyris, "Skilled Incompetence," *Harvard Business Review* 64, no. 5 (1986): 74–9, https://hbr.org/1986/09/skilled-incompetence. Robert Merton called this phenomenon "trained incapacity" some years before.

12. Ed Catmull, "How Pixar Fosters Collective Creativity," *Harvard Business Review* 86, no. 9 (2008): 64–72, https://hbr.org/2008/09/how-pixar-fosters-collective-creativity.

13. Nicola Kelly et al., "Learning from Excellence in Healthcare: A New Approach to Incident Reporting," *Archives of Disease in Childhood* 101, no. 9 (2016): 788–92, https://doi.org/10.1136/archdischild-2015-310021; "Welcome to Learning from Excellence: A Call to Learn from What Works Well," Learning from Excellence, accessed February 2025, https://learningfromexcellence.com. (You might dive in to this last link to see how the programs are evolving over time.)

14. "Improving Patient Safety Culture—a Practical Guide," NHS England, last updated May 9, 2025, https://www.england.nhs.uk/long-read/improving-patient-safety-culture-a-practical-guide.

15. Alfred D. Chandler Jr., *Strategy and Structure: Chapters in the History of the American Industrial Enterprise* (MIT Press, 1969).

16. Danah Zohar, "Implementing Quantum Management: The RenDanHeyi/Zero Distance Business Model," in *Zero Distance* (Palgrave Macmillan, 2022), 55–70.

17. Steven Levy, *In the Plex: How Google Thinks, Works, and Shapes Our Lives* (Simon & Schuster, 2011).

18. Howard Schultz, *Onward: How Starbucks Fought for Its Life Without Losing Its Soul* (Rodale, 2011).

19. Yvon Chouinard, *Let My People Go Surfing: The Education of a Reluctant Businessman* (Penguin Books, 2016).

20. Anita Roddick, *Business as Unusual: My Entrepreneurial Journey, Profits with Principles* (Thorsons, 2001).

21. Alexandra Gibbs, "REI Pays Employees to Skip Black Friday and Head Outdoors," *CNBC*, October 27, 2015, https://www.cnbc.com/2015/10/27/rei-pays-employees-to-skip-black-friday-and-head-outdoors.html.

22. Arlie Russell Hochschild, *The Managed Heart: Commercialization of Human Feeling* (University of California Press, 1983).

23. Patricia Faison Hewlin, "Wearing the Cloak: Antecedents and Consequences of Creating Facades of Conformity," *Journal of Applied Psychology* 94, no. 3 (2009): 727–41, https://doi.org/10.1037/a0015228.

24. Amy Edmondson, "Psychological Safety and Learning Behavior in Work Teams," *Administrative Science Quarterly* 44, no. 2 (1999): 350–83, https://doi.org/10.2307/2666999.

25. Jeffrey Pfeffer, *SAS Institute: A Different Approach to Incentives and People Management Practices in the Software Industry* (Harvard Business School Publishing, 1998).

26. Tom Kelley and Jonathan Littman, *The Art of Innovation: Lessons in Creativity from IDEO, America's Leading Design Firm* (Crown Business, 2001).

27. Bob Chapman and Raj Sisodia, *Everybody Matters: The Extraordinary Power of Caring for Your People Like Family* (Portfolio, 2015).

28. William A. Kahn, "Psychological Conditions of Personal Engagement and Disengagement at Work," *The Academy of Management Journal* 33, no. 4 (1990): 692–724, https://journals.aom.org/doi/10.5465/256287.

29. Ronald Heifetz and Donald L. Laurie, "The Work of Leadership," *Harvard Business Review* 75, no. 1 (1997): 124–34, https://hbr.org/2001/12/the-work-of-leadership.

30. Blake E. Ashforth, *Role Transitions in Organizational Life: An Identity-Based Perspective* (Lawrence Erlbaum Associates, 2001).

31. Herminia Ibarra, *Working Identity: Unconventional Strategies for Reinventing Your Career* (Harvard Business School Press, 2003).

32. Jason Fried and David H. Hansson, *It Doesn't Have to Be Crazy at Work* (Harper Business, 2018).

33. Kelley and Littman, *The Art of Innovation*.

34. Reed Hastings and Erin Meyer, *No Rules Rules: Netflix and the Culture of Reinvention* (Penguin Press, 2020); "Netflix TechBlog," Medium, accessed February 2025, https://netflixtechblog.com. This is a particularly rich source for examples of retirings and deprecations.

35. Sam Kaner et al., *Facilitator's Guide to Participatory Decision-Making*, 3rd ed. (Jossey-Bass, 2014).

36. Irving L. Janis, *Groupthink: Psychological Studies of Policy Decisions and Fiascoes*, 2nd ed. (Houghton Mifflin, 1982).

37. John Buck Jr. and Sharon Villines, *We the People: Consenting to a Deeper Democracy* (Sociocracy.Info Press, 2007). This book is an absolute *must buy* if you're vibing with the ideas presented here so far.

38. Elliott Jaques, *Requisite Organization: The CEO's Guide to Creative Structure and Leadership* (Cason Hall, 1989); Ram Charan et al., *The Leadership Pipeline: How to Build the Leadership Powered Company*, 2nd ed. (Jossey-Bass, 2011).

39. Stewart Brand, *The Clock of the Long Now: Time and Responsibility* (Basic Books, 1999); Stewart Brand, *How Buildings Learn: What Happens After They're Built* (Penguin, 1995).

40. Jeffrey Liker, *The Toyota Way: 14 Management Principles from the World's Greatest Manufacturer* (McGraw Hill, 2004).

41. Colin Bryar and Bill Carr, *Working Backwards: Insights, Stories, and Secrets from Inside Amazon* (St. Martin's Press, 2021).

42. Dean Tjosvold, "The Conflict-Positive Organization: It Depends Upon Us," *Journal of Organizational Behavior* 29, no. 1 (2008): 19–28, https://doi.org/10.1002/job.473.

43. Ray Dalio, *Principles* (Simon & Schuster, 2017).

44. Valve Corporation, *Handbook for New Employees* (Valve Press, 2012), http://www.valvesoftware.com/company/Valve_Handbook_LowRes.pdf.

Structuring

1. "Overview Page: Deepwater Horizon Oil Spill," National Oceanic and Atmospheric Administration, accessed February 2025, https://response.restoration.noaa.gov/deepwater-horizon-oil-spill-case-study.

2. "Investigation Report Volume 1: Explosion and Fire at the Macondo Well," U.S. Chemical Safety and Hazard Investigation Board, June 5, 2014, https://www.csb.gov/assets/1/7/vol_1_final.pdf.

3. "Deep Water: The Gulf Oil Disaster and the Future of Offshore Drilling," National Commission on the BP Deepwater Horizon Oil Spill and Offshore Drilling, January 11, 2011, https://www.govinfo.gov/content/pkg/GPO-OILCOMMISSION/pdf/GPO-OILCOMMISSION.pdf.

4. Jay R. Galbraith, *Designing Complex Organizations* (Addison-Wesley, 1973).

5. General Stanley McChrystal et al., *Team of Teams: New Rules of Engagement for a Complex World* (Portfolio, 2015).

6.   Henrik Kniberg and Anders Ivarsson, "Scaling Agile @ Spotify," Crisp, October 2012, https://blog.crisp .se/wp-content/uploads/2012/11/SpotifyScaling.pdf.

7.   Gary Hamel, "First, Let's Fire All the Managers," *Harvard Business Review*, December 2011, https://hbr .org/2011/12/first-lets-fire-all-the-managers.

8.   "Roadmap," Are.na, accessed February 26, 2025, https://www.are.na/about#roadmap.

9.   "The Gore Story," Gore, accessed February 2025, https://www.gore.com/about/the-gore-story.

10.   "Stevey's Google Platforms Rant," GitHub Gist, published October 12, 2011, https://gist.github.com /chitchcock/1281611.

11.   Valve, *Handbook*.

12.   Henry Mintzberg, "The Manager's Job: Folklore and Fact," *Harvard Business Review* 53, no. 4 (1975), https://hbr.org/1990/03/the-managers-job-folklore-and-fact.

13.   Microsoft, "Work Trend Index: Will AI Fix Work?," May 9, 2023, https://www.microsoft.com/en-us /worklab/work-trend-index/will-ai-fix-work.

14.   Aaron De Smet et al., "Three Keys to Faster, Better Decisions," McKinsey Quarterly, May 1, 2019, https://www .mckinsey.com/capabilities/people-and-organizational-performance/our-insights/three-keys-to-faster-better-decisions.

15.   Microsoft, "2022 Work Trend Index Pulse: Hybrid Work Is Just Work. Are We Doing It Wrong?," September 22, 2022, https://assets-c4akfrf5b4d3f4b7.z01.azurefd.net/assets/2023/09/a81fcdeb-860a -44f2-aaeb-0525d38358ae-2022_Work_Trend_Index_Pulse_Report_Sep-3697v2.pdf.

16.   Gallup, "Twenty Percent of the World's Employees Experience Loneliness While Global Employee Engagement Stagnated and Employee Wellbeing Declined," press release, June 12, 2024, https://www.gallup .com/workplace/645758/state-of-the-global-workplace-2024-press-release.aspx.

17.   "Manager Hats," Cutlefish, accessed February 2025, https://publish.obsidian.md/cutlefish/Manager+Hats.

18.   Hastings and Meyer, *No Rules Rules*.

19.   Valve, *Handbook*.

20.   Gary Hamel, *The Future of Management* (Harvard Business School Press, 2007).

21.   Frederic Laloux, *Reinventing Organizations: A Guide to Creating Organizations Inspired by the Next Stage of Human Consciousness* (Nelson Parker, 2014).

22.   Ted J. Rau and Jerry Koch-Gonzalez, *Many Voices One Song: Shared Power with Sociocracy* (Sociocracy for All, 2018).

23.   Matthew Skelton and Manuel Pais, *Team Topologies: Organizing Business and Technology Teams for Fast Flow* (IT Revolution Press, 2019).

24.   Geoffrey G. Parker et al., *Platform Revolution: How Networked Markets Are Transforming the Economy— and How to Make Them Work for You* (W. W. Norton, 2016).

25.   David Weinberger, "Library as Platform," *Library Journal*, September 4, 2012, https://www.libraryjournal .com/story/by-david-weinberger.

26.   J. Richard Hackman, *Leading Teams: Setting the Stage for Great Performances* (Harvard Business School Press, 2002).

27.   Hackman, *Leading Teams*.

28.   Frederick P. Brooks Jr., *The Mythical Man-Month: Essays on Software Engineering, Anniversary Edition* (Addison-Wesley, 1995).

29.   Jeffrey Pfeffer and Robert I. Sutton, *Hard Facts, Dangerous Half-Truths, and Total Nonsense: Profiting from Evidence-Based Management* (Harvard Business Review Press, 2006).

30.   McChrystal et al., *Team of Teams*.

31. Deborah Ancona et al., *X-teams: How to Build Teams That Lead, Innovate, and Succeed* (Harvard Business Review Press, 2009).

32. Teresa Amabile and Steven Kramer, *The Progress Principle: Using Small Wins to Ignite Joy, Engagement, and Creativity at Work* (Harvard Business Review Press, 2011).

33. For further reading on this problem: McChrystal et al., *Team of Teams*; Jeff Wald, *The End of Jobs: The Rise of On-Demand Workers and Agile Corporations* (Post Hill Press, 2020); Laszlo Bock, *Work Rules!: Insights from Inside Google That Will Transform How You Live and Lead* (Twelve, 2015).

34. David Epstein, *Range: Why Generalists Triumph in a Specialized World* (Riverhead, 2019); Reid Hoffman et al., *The Alliance: Managing Talent in the Networked Age* (Harvard Business Review Press, 2014). Both useful here. People can do more than you think, and a new relationship with work is possible.

35. Gary Hamel and Michele Zanini, *Humanocracy: Creating Organizations as Amazing as the People Inside Them* (Harvard Business Review Press, 2020); Ram Charan et al., *Talent Wins: The New Playbook for Putting People First* (Harvard Business Review Press, 2018). Excellent reads here.

36. Stafford Beer, "What Is Cybernetics?" *Kybernetes* 31, no. 2 (2002): 209–19, https://doi.org/10.1108/03684920210417283.

37. Amy Kates and Jay R. Galbraith, *Designing Your Organization: Using the STAR Model to Solve 5 Critical Design Challenges* (Jossey-Bass, 2007). This is a good book. I just think it's for our current world, not the future world that I want to live in.

38. Kniberg and Ivarsson, "Scaling Agile @ Spotify." Chapters and guilds were popularized by Henrik Kniberg's writing on Agile at Spotify.

39. "About Code Owners," GitHub, accessed February 2025, https://docs.github.com/en/repositories/managing-your-repositorys-settings-and-features/customizing-your-repository/about-code-owners.

40. Ross Koppel et al., "Role of Computerized Physician Order Entry Systems in Facilitating Medication Errors," *JAMA* 293, no. 10 (2005): 1197–1203, https://doi.org/10.1001/jama.293.10.1197. This isn't exactly the same as the stylized passage here, but it covers exactly the same topic!

41. Eric Schmidt and Jonathan Rosenberg, *How Google Works* (Grand Central, 2014). Contains a particularly evocative example of this general truth.

42. Ed Catmull and Amy Wallace, *Creativity, Inc.: Overcoming the Unseen Forces That Stand in the Way of True Inspiration* (Random House, 2014).

43. Laloux, *Reinventing Organizations*.

44. "Introducing the 2025 Host Advisory Board," Airbnb Newsroom, Airbnb, published January 29, 2025, https://news.airbnb.com/airbnb-introduces-the-2025-host-advisory-board.

45. Phil Jackson and Hugh Delehanty, *Sacred Hoops: Spiritual Lessons of a Hardwood Warrior* (Hyperion, 1995). Jackson has a long section in here about equal pay for teammates. Probably not super resonant today, but interesting!

Direction

1. Eric Ries, *The Lean Startup: How Today's Entrepreneurs Use Continuous Innovation to Create Radically Successful Businesses* (Crown Business, 2011); Clayton M. Christensen, *The Innovator's Dilemma: The Revolutionary Book That Will Change the Way You Do Business* (Harvard Business Review Press, 1997).

2. Henry Mintzberg, *The Rise and Fall of Strategic Planning* (Free Press, 1994).

3. Martin Reeves et al., *Your Strategy Needs a Strategy: How to Choose and Execute the Right Approach* (Harvard Business Review Press, 2015).

4.   Atul Gawande, *The Checklist Manifesto: How to Get Things Right* (Metropolitan Books, 2009).

5.   Peter F. Drucker, "Managing for Business Effectiveness," *Harvard Business Review* (May 1963), https://hbr.org/1963/05/managing-for-business-effectiveness.

6.   Walter Isaacson, *Steve Jobs* (Simon & Schuster, 2011).

7.   David J. Snowden and Mary E. Boone, "A Leader's Framework for Decision Making," *Harvard Business Review* 85, no. 11 (2007), https://hbr.org/2007/11/a-leaders-framework-for-decision-making.

8.   Ries, *The Lean Startup*.

9.   Durward K. Sobek II et al., "Toyota's Principles of Set-Based Concurrent Engineering," *MIT Sloan Management Review* 40, no. 2 (1999), https://sloanreview.mit.edu/article/toyotas-principles-of-setbased-concurrent-engineering.

10.   John Doerr, *Measure What Matters: How Google, Bono, and the Gates Foundation Rock the World with OKRs* (Portfolio, 2018). Doerr recounts learning OKRs from Grove in the 1970s and presenting them to Google's founders in 1999, where the system became core to Google's management model.

11.   Further reading on great decision-making practices: Cass R. Sunstein and Reid Hastie, *Wiser: Getting Beyond Groupthink to Make Groups Smarter* (Harvard Business Review Press, 2014).

12.   Larry Dressler, *Consensus Through Conversation: How to Achieve High-Commitment Decisions* (Berrett-Koehler, 2006).

13.   Laloux, *Reinventing Organizations*.

14.   Dennis W. Bakke, *Joy at Work: A Revolutionary Approach to Fun on the Job* (PVG, 2005).

15.   Hamel, *First, Let's Fire All the Managers*; Bradford Gray et al., "Home Care by Self-Governing Nursing Teams: The Netherlands' Buurtzorg Model," *The Commonwealth Fund*, May 29, 2015, https://www.commonwealthfund.org/publications/case-study/2015/may/home-care-self-governing-nursing-teams-netherlands-buurtzorg-model.

16.   Eric S. Raymond, *The Cathedral & the Bazaar: Musings on Linux and Open Source by an Accidental Revolutionary* (O'Reilly Media, 1999).

17.   The PEP Editors, "PEP 0—Index of Python Enhancement Proposals (PEPs)," *Python Enhancement Proposals*, July 13, 2020, https://peps.python.org/pep-0000. This isn't exactly from the 1990s, but you should nevertheless check out the Index of Python Enhancement Proposals (PEPs) at https://peps.python.org/pep-0000. This is a rare, real-world look at structured, transparent decision-making within a large open-source community, cataloguing every proposal, its rationale, discussion history, and final disposition in one publicly version-controlled document. Thanks to Cullen for sending this one to me!

18.   Mike Arauz, "Unlocking the Benefits of Self-Management Without Going All In on Holacracy," *First Round Review*, March 23, 2016, https://review.firstround.com/unlocking-the-benefits-of-self-management-without-going-all-in-on-holacracy; Joel Gascoigne, "Introducing Open Salaries at Buffer: Our Transparent Formula and All Individual Salaries," Buffer Open, December 19, 2013, https://buffer.com/resources/introducing-open-salaries-at-buffer-including-our-transparent-formula-and-all-individual-salaries; "Transparency," GitLab Handbook, accessed April 30, 2025, https://handbook.gitlab.com/handbook/values/#transparency.; "The Compensation Calculator," GitLab Handbook, accessed April 30, 2025, https://handbook.gitlab.com/handbook/total-rewards/compensation/compensation-calculator.

19.   C. A. E. Goodhart, "Problems of Monetary Management: The U.K. Experience," in *Monetary Theory and Practice* (1984): 91–121, https://link.springer.com/chapter/10.1007/978-1-349-17295-5_4.

20.   Anders Olesen, "Handelsbanken: Consistency at Its Best," *Beyond Budgeting Institute*, September 2013,

https://scrummaster.dk/lib/AgileLeanLibrary/Topics/BeyondBudgetting/Handelsbanken_Consistency _at_its_Best_02.pdf. Details how Handelsbanken abolished detailed budgets in the early 1970s and replaced them with a small set of relative, peer-based profitability targets, embedding trust and branch autonomy.

21. Bjarte Bogsnes, "An Introduction to Beyond Budgeting and Ambition to Action: Business Agility in Practice—The Equinor Model," *Beyond Budgeting Roundtable*, accessed February 2025, https:// agilitysummit.eu/wp-content/uploads/2020/12/Bjarte-Bogsnes-Business-Agility-in-Practice.pdf. Explains how Equinor (formerly Statoil) scrapped annual budgets in 2005 and moved to dynamic, relative targets within its company-wide "Ambition to Action" performance framework.

22. Benedict Evans, "Not Even Wrong: Ways to Dismiss Technology," *Benedict Evans*, May 26, 2017, https:// www.ben-evans.com/benedictevans/2017/5/24/not-even-wrong-ways-to-dismiss-technology.

23. Jeffrey K. Liker and Gary L. Convis, *The Toyota Way to Lean Leadership* (McGraw Hill, 2012).

24. "Key Reviews," The GitLab Handbook, GitLab, accessed February 26, 2025, https://handbook.gitlab .com/handbook/company/key-review. This one is so cool!

25. Mary Parker Follett, *Creative Experience* (Longmans, Green, 1924).

26. Roger Fisher and William Ury, *Getting to Yes: Negotiating Agreement Without Giving In* (Penguin Books, 1981).

27. Harrison Owen, *Open Space Technology: A User's Guide*, 3rd ed. (Berrett-Koehler, 2008).

28. Harrison Owen, "Dancing with Shiva (or Sandy, or Katrina)," TEDxNavesink, September 20, 2013, posted November 11, 2013, by TEDx Talks, YouTube, 14 minutes 20 seconds, https://www.youtube .com/watch?v=APD7oQ3xrSA.

29. "Future Backwards," Cynefin.io, last modified September 9, 2022, https://cynefin.io/wiki/Future _backwards. The wiki is comprehensive.

Practice

1. Karl E. Weick and Kathleen M. Sutcliffe, *Managing the Unexpected: Sustained Performance in a Complex World*, 3rd ed. (John Wiley & Sons, 2015).

2. Read more on alternatives and origins: Lewis Mehl-Madrona and Barbara Mainguy, "Introducing Healing Circles and Talking Circles into Primary Care," *The Permanente Journal* 18, no. 2 (Spring 2014): 4–9, https://doi.org/10.7812/TPP/13-104; Ted Rau, "Sociocracy and Nonviolent Communication (NVC)," Sociocracy for All, April 25, 2022, https://www.sociocracyforall.org/sociocracy -and-nonviolent-communication-nvc; Christina Baldwin and Ann Linnea, *The Circle Way: A Leader in Every Chair* (Berrett-Koehler, 2010).

3. Edward de Bono, *Six Thinking Hats: An Essential Approach to Business Management* (Little, Brown, 1985).

4. David Allen, *Getting Things Done: The Art of Stress-Free Productivity* (Penguin Books, 2001).

5. Joseph A. Allen et al., eds., *The Cambridge Handbook of Meeting Science* (Cambridge University Press, 2015); Kaner, *Facilitator's Guide*.

6. Pivotal Labs became somewhat famous for its pairing approach, as documented in *Wired* in 2013: Cade Metz, "This Company Believes You Should Never Hack Alone," *Wired*, November 12, 2013, https:// www.wired.com/2013/11/pivotal-one.

7. Good reading on pairing from the United Kingdom's Government Digital Service (GDS) here: https:// gds-way.digital.cabinet-office.gov.uk/standards/pair-programming.html.

Learning

1. Mike Arauz, "Unlocking the Benefits of Self-Management Without Going All-In on Holacracy," *First Round Review*, accessed February 2025, https://review.firstround.com/unlocking-the-benefits-of-self-management-without-going-all-in-on-holacracy.

2. Edgar H. Schein, *Organizational Culture and Leadership* (Jossey-Bass, 2010).

3. Esther Derby and Diana Larsen, *Agile Retrospectives: Making Good Teams Great* (Pragmatic Bookshelf, 2006).

4. Charles Duhigg, "What Google Learned from Its Quest to Build the Perfect Team," *The New York Times Magazine*, February 25, 2016, accessed February 2025, https://www.nytimes.com/2016/02/28/magazine/what-google-learned-from-its-quest-to-build-the-perfect-team.html.

5. Jason Jennings, *The Reinventors: How Extraordinary Companies Pursue Radical Continuous Change* (Portfolio, 2012).

6. "Team Health Monitor," Atlassian, accessed February 2025, https://www.atlassian.com/team-playbook/health-monitor. Atlassian has a great guide, if you don't like this one.

7. Cal Newport, *A World Without Email: Reimagining Work in an Age of Communication Overload* (Portfolio, 2021), 11.

8. Matthew Skelton and Manuel Pais, *Team Topologies: Organizing Business and Technology Teams for Fast Flow* (IT Revolution Press, 2019). They argue that teams should be treated as stable, product-like units with clear ownership and interfaces, a framework now widely used in software and product development.

Space

1. Alistair Cockburn, *Agile Software Development: The Cooperative Game* (Addison-Wesley, 2002). Cockburn popularized the idea of "information radiators": key project data in a public, easily glanceable space.

2. The UK's GDS has a guide to good team walls, here: https://www.gov.uk/service-manual/agile-delivery/team-wall.

3. Dominica DeGrandis, *Making Work Visible: Exposing Time Theft to Optimize Work & Flow* (IT Revolution Press, 2017); Taiichi Ohno, *Toyota Production System: Beyond Large-Scale Production* (New Edition, 1988). Ohno's *Toyota Production System* is again a good reference here.

4. Amy C. Edmondson, *The Fearless Organization: Creating Psychological Safety in the Workplace for Learning, Innovation, and Growth* (Wiley, 2018).

5. Franklin Becker and Fritz Steele, *Workplace by Design: Mapping the High-Performance Workscape* (Jossey-Bass, 1995).

6. Ethan Bernstein and Ben Waber, "The Truth About Open Offices," *Harvard Business Review*, November 1, 2019, https://hbr.org/2019/11/the-truth-about-open-offices.

7. Thomas J. Allen and Gunter W. Henn, *The Organization and Architecture of Innovation: Managing the Flow of Technology* (Elsevier, 2007).

Goal Index

About the Author

I've been writing on the internet since flip phones were cool: first about ads, then about the web, and eventually about the messy, marvelous business of organizing people to do great work. That curiosity carried me from a seat at Undercurrent (where we helped brands survive the "post-digital" panic) to co-founding August, a self-managed, employee-owned OD experiment that's still humming a decade later.

After five years of leading transformation practices inside the Interpublic Group—first at R/GA and most recently as chief strategy officer of Black Glass, one of Fast Company's Most Innovative Companies of 2023—I joined Airbnb to build and run an Organizational Design & Development team. My day job has stayed more or less the same: rewiring how creativity-first companies learn, decide, and ship new ideas at scale.

Along the way I've advised Fortune 50 boardrooms, scrappy startups, and everyone in between; delivered keynotes on three continents, depending on how you count continents; and run workshops that people describe as "equal parts revelation and practical how-to." If you catch me on stage, expect plenty of stories, a few frameworks, and zero tolerance for corporate jargon.

Off the clock I can usually be found tinkering with bicycles, perfecting my carnitas, or chasing my cat Ian off the keyboard. I live (and play tennis) in Boerum Hill, Brooklyn, with my wife, Emily.

I do keynotes, podcasts, private speaking gigs, and internal workshops for companies of all sizes and shapes. I'm also still blogging at cpj.fyi and you can find me on most social media platforms:

@clayparkerjones

_____

If you liked this book, and want help bringing some of the core ideas to life, you'll want to talk to a few of my friends. NB: they don't necessarily promote or endorse the book, and maybe even disagree with me in places. But they're great, and you should work with them.

august   BLACK   kindred.
                GLASS

      Plural   THE READY